COMPLICATED

Island Life in the Pacific Northwest

SIMPLICITY

Joy Davis

HERITAGE

VICTORIA · VANCOUVER · CALGARY

Heritage House Publishing Company Ltd.
heritagehouse.ca

Cataloguing information available from Library and Archives Canada

978-1-77203-270-3 (pbk)
978-1-77203-271-0 (epub)

Edited by Sarah Weber
Proofread by Marial Shea
Book design and interior illustrations by Jacqui Thomas
Cover image: detail from painting *Island Getaway* by Greta Guzek

Every effort has been made to trace copyright holders and to obtain their
permission for the use of copyrighted material used in this book.

The interior of this book was produced on 100% post-consumer recycled paper,
processed chlorine free, and printed with vegetable-based inks.

We acknowledge the financial support of the Government of Canada
through the Canada Book Fund (CBF) and the Canada Council for the Arts,
and the Province of British Columbia through the British Columbia Arts Council
and the Book Publishing Tax Credit.

23 22 21 20 19 1 2 3 4 5

Printed in Canada

— Praise for *Complicated Simplicity* —

"In *Complicated Simplicity*, Joy Davis has done for islands what Farley Mowat once did for wolves; she has provided a much deeper understanding and enlightenment of true island life, and the type of hardy, salty souls who choose off-grid islands as homes: where failure is knowledge, simplicity is best, and life is timed not so much by the clock but by the wind, the sun, and the tides. Highly recommended for anyone who has ever lived on an island, or dreamed of doing so."

GRANT LAWRENCE
author of *Adventures in Solitude: What Not to Wear to a Nude Potluck and Other Stories from Desolation Sound*

"Part memoirist and part guide, Joy Davis takes you along for a roller-coaster west-coast boat ride to all my favourite islands with all my favourite islanders as passengers—from Joe Martin on Echachis to the Kellers on Read—in all kinds of weather. If you lose everything else on the crossing, hang on to the book. You'll have everything you need to survive!"

BRIONY PENN
author of *A Year on the Wild Side: A West Coast Naturalist's Almanac*

"Joy Davis provides wannabe islanders with a 'how-to guide for island living,' describing the complex realities of island life on the Pacific coast. Raised on Bath Island, she explores the joys and the hardships that make island life rewarding for some and not for others."

PAT CARNEY
author of *On Island: Life Among the Coast Dwellers* and *Trade Secrets*

"Capturing 'islandness' is as elusive as catching a wave in a jar. But through her love of island places and her joy in island living, Joy Davis provides glimpses into how traits of islandness—ingenuity, living within limits, resilience—help us survive and thrive together on island earth."

DR. LAURIE BRINKLOW
Island Studies, University of Prince Edward Island

"*Complicated Simplicity* captures both the dream and the realities of island life. Interviews with islanders reveal the true skill sets, both emotional and physical, required to overcome challenges and experience the wonder and majesty of life surrounded by water."

SALLY-CHRISTINE RODGERS
author of *Convergence: A Voyage Through French Polynesia*

"It's easy to get it wrong about islands. *Complicated Simplicity*, both the nonfiction endeavour and the phrase, gets it right. Joy Davis digs deeply into the elements that draw people to islands, the challenges they must overcome, and the compromises they must make to enjoy the often-sublime life available there. *Complicated Simplicity* is a journalistic inquiry, executed with integrity and sensitivity, that yields insight, wonder, and even joy."

TOM GROENING
editor of *Island Journal* and *The Working Waterfront*

"Part memoir, part manual for slow(er) living, and part anthropological essay on the culture of small islands in the Pacific Northwest, *Complicated Simplicity* is bound to please armchair travellers, west coast historians, island studies scholars, and small islanders alike. Having read the book from Gabriola Island, Joy Davis's words resounded with familiarity, observational insight, and truthfulness. But be warned: read this book and you'll fall in love with this place."

PHILLIP VANNINI
author of *Ferry Tales* and *Off the Grid*

"Joy Davis is an old-growth islander who values practical advice and good stories. She brings both to this funny, smart, poignant guide, along with a caution that the experience of island living is something you carry with you the rest of your life."

DONNA LIVINGSTONE
president and CEO of the Glenbow Museum

For Mom and Dad,
and all the others who have loved
the islands of the Pacific Northwest
over millennia.

CONTENTS

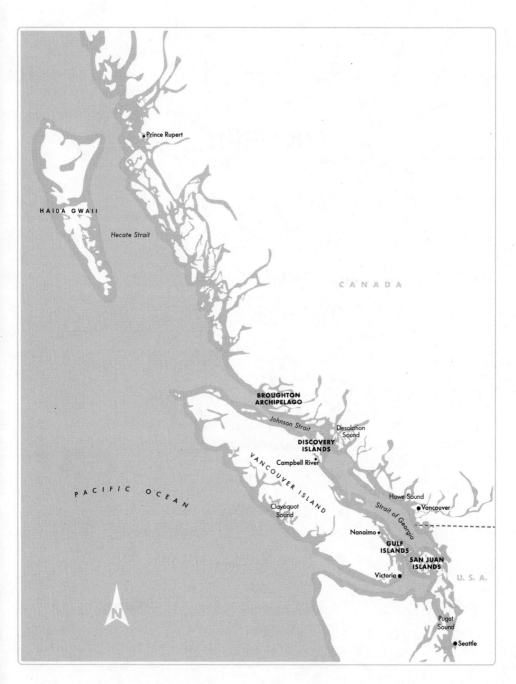

Prince Rupert

HAIDA GWAII

Hecate Strait

CANADA

BROUGHTON
ARCHIPELAGO

Johnson Strait

Desolation
Sound

DISCOVERY
ISLANDS

Campbell River

VANCOUVER ISLAND

PACIFIC OCEAN

Clayoquot
Sound

Howe Sound

Strait of Georgia

Vancouver

Nanaimo

GULF
ISLANDS

SAN JUAN
ISLANDS

Victoria

U. S. A.

Puget
Sound

Seattle

N

PROLOGUE

I **WAS TEN WHEN** a small island changed my family's world. The log of our sailboat *Whereaway* captures Mom's thoughts the day we first went ashore on Bath Island.

Sunday, July 8, 1962—In Pirates Cove. Up around 0800 and had breakfast and usual clean up. Left at 1000 to go through Gabriola Pass at slack. Decided to go over and have a look at Bath and Saturnina Islands that Doc Nicholl has for sale. When we wrote, he said they were $15,000 each. Fun to look anyway!

Anchored in nice bay off Bath Island, open to the south, and fell in love as soon as we set foot ashore! Don found Doc Nicholl who just happened to be on the Island and he was soon learning all about it. The rest kept on exploring and the next thing we knew, Don informed us that we should buy it. We went all around it and were delighted with what we found. No anchorage unfortunately but Silva Bay is close enough. Looked at Saturnina too, but still like Bath. Mr. Nicholl said one island has water, but he would not tell us which.

Children had a fine swim off south end. I went back to *Whereaway* to fix lunch which we took to "our" island and had a picnic. Did some more looking and made up our minds to buy it. The price has dropped to $11,500! We sailed over [to Doc's house on Breakwater Island] and told Doc our decision and he informed us we had picked the right one, the one with the water!! PS. Saw a school of blackfish.

One week later, Mom, Dad, Clair, and I made the four-hour passage from Vancouver to Silva Bay on the south end of Gabriola Island to explore our new island. Mom noted,

> Up at seven, had breakfast and off to Bath Island by 0900. Well equipped this trip with long jeans and gumboots to ward off the prickles. Took another tour of the Island and liked it better than ever! Settled down to business and swamped a trail through the centre. The Island seems to have a valley down the middle, the ground is moist and the vegetation is dense—a thoroughly lovely place. Started to look for water and after one false start, found it! The Skipper dug down three feet through the darkest, richest loam imaginable and the water began to flow. Decided to call it a day at this point and use the natural facilities—so we both had a bath! Back to the ship and returned highly jubilant to Silva Bay. Lit the barbeque and enjoyed our steak dinner. Off to bed for a well-earned sleep.

In those first weeks and months my parents, Joyce and Donald Smith, envisioned Bath Island as a recreational property, a respite from busy family and business lives in Vancouver. But by March of 1963, they had sold the West Vancouver house as well as their precious MGB. They built an eight-by-sixteen-foot barge to transport building materials. And Clair and I started correspondence school. Dad left his job in the headquarters of a prominent logging company and we all moved aboard *Whereaway* as a temporary home while we embarked on our island adventure. At the end of that first busy summer an A-frame house, looking out across a broad sandstone beach toward the distant lights of Vancouver, became the Smith home for the following twenty-two years. "Islandness" shaped our identities, defined our approach to life.

Worn tangles of driftwood, the coarseness of sun-soaked sandstone on bare feet, and the tangy smells of salt, seaweed, and creosote always evoke island memories. Winding trails through dense fir, salal, and arbutus were so familiar I could walk them with my eyes closed. Adjacent islands, the distant outlines of Lasqueti, Texada, and Bowen, and the arc of coastal mountains from Garibaldi to Mount

Baker defined my day-to-day world. As days went by, wind and cloud transformed the Strait of Georgia from leaden grey to translucent blue to ultramarine and back. I became adept at reading the weather. Otters, mink, seals, orcas, countless birds, and a cheeky raven kept us company. Local log salvagers, storekeepers, and other islanders became friends. A parade of familiar coastal cruisers, sailboats, tugs with tows, and fishboats passed through my childhood landscape, only occasionally going aground on nearby reefs. And constant tasks—from helping with house construction to collecting firewood, grooming trails, caring for chickens, and jigging cod for dinner—gave me skills that puzzled mainland friends. They thought it odd that I kept a spark plug in my pocket, but then they didn't know how useful it might be if the boat engine was reluctant to start.

All these years later, that island holds a central place in my heart and identity, and fuels my fascination with other people who find islands compelling places to make their lives. This book focuses on the perspectives and experiences of people who live on Pacific Northwest islands, particularly those not served by ferries. Why? Because life on islands off the ferry grid involves independence, complexity, and self-sufficiency. Ingenuity, creativity, passion, and hard work lie at the heart of making satisfying lives in these special places.

(I)

THE DRAW OF ISLANDS

A**LONG THE BEAUTIFUL** coast of the Pacific Northwest and on oceans and lakes around the world, you'll find intrepid people who choose the self-sufficient way of life uniquely linked with islands—although many of these islanders point out that their life-styles aren't simple and are rarely idyllic. For each, the experience differs. Their lives are defined by their interests and abilities as much as by the islands they choose. And those who opt for islands that are not served by car ferries find their experiences further complicated by the need, some say the joy, of crossing "enisling" waters.

This book interweaves the voices of numerous islanders to explore what draws people to islands and to consider what it takes to make successful lives off the ferry grid. You will meet them along the way as they talk about their goals, joys, perspectives, and insights, and tell remarkable, sometimes improbable stories that go with this dis-tinctive way of life. Some of these people speak through memoirs that capture both practical and philosophical perspectives. Others have shared their experiences with me through interviews. It was a particular pleasure to visit with almost twenty permanent and sea-sonal islanders who live in the San Juan Islands and along the coast of British Columbia and to learn about their varied motivations, resources, talents, and interests. All have been generous in sharing their experiences on island and quick to laugh at the things that have challenged them along the way. And their compelling love of special island places shines through, sometimes tempered by cautionary tales. Their stories overlap and intertwine to give you a palpable sense of life on an island. If you glimpse yourself in these stories, perhaps you're also an islander—or an islander at heart.

The ways we look at islands

THERE'S AN APPEAL to islands that intrigues people, compels them to spend time in these special places. It's hard to capture in words, though many people have tried. But complex emotions are clearly at play. Understanding their powerful draw is a starting point in making sense of why and how people make meaningful lives on island.

What is an island? Most of us envision a fragment of land completely surrounded by water. Still, this question stimulates confusing debates. When does an island become a continent, for example? What is the difference between a rock, an islet, and an island? Is an island connected to other land by a bridge still a true island? And how do numerous metaphors colour our understanding of islands?

Size is the primary measure of island status. Although water surrounds all land on this ocean-laden planet, sheer magnitude distinguishes the Americas, Africa, Australia, Antarctica, and Eurasia as continents rather than islands. Geologists offer more detail. They explain that continents are contiguous land masses that sit above sea level on the earth's lithosphere, or outer layer. The lithosphere straddles the earth's tectonic plates and also provides a base for numerous islands on continental margins. Powerful volcanic, tectonic, and glacial forces have had a hand in shaping these relatively accessible coastal islands. And far offshore, oceanic islands rise from the deep. Like icebergs, only the tips of these mountains are visible. Islands of all shapes, sizes, and origins cover 7 percent of the world's surface. They are home to more than 600 million people, or 10 percent of the world's population.[1]

It's the small islands, pinpoints on charts, that capture people's imagination. As D.H. Lawrence writes, "An island, if it is big enough, is no better than a continent. It has to be really quite small, before it FEELS LIKE an island."[2] But smallness presents its own definitional challenges. The 1982 United Nations Convention on the Law of the Sea specifies that an island must be above water at high tide.[3] And Scots expect that full islands, as opposed to diminutive islets, rocks, and crags, will support at least one sheep.[4] More systematic measures propose that the surface area of the smallest "island" must be more than ten hectares. There are 86,732 islands worldwide that meet this criterion. As well there are 370,000 islets of between one and ten hectares,[5] along with an estimated seven billion "nano-islets" that are smaller than one hectare. By this measure, my family's three-hectare island, and many others along the coast, would qualify only as islets, although it seems likely that they could support more than one sheep. Regardless of islands' formal size, bays and beaches complicate their measurement and add interest.

Size and geology define coastal islands. But our perceptions are also coloured by the many ways that the idea of an island crops up in language and culture. In the second part of its definition of *island*, the online Oxford Living Dictionary suggests that the term describes a thing or location regarded as resembling an island, especially in being isolated, detached, or surrounded in some way.[6] Oases, ecosystems, gated communities, urban ghettos, traffic separators, monasteries, and even kitchen counters are islands by virtue of their separate or insular nature. Strange as it might seem, so are lakes "enisled" by surrounding land. The words *islanding* or *islanded* are used to describe isolating processes.

With so much flexibility in definition, island metaphors are commonplace, often contradictory. Both water-defined islands and others evoke notions of social and psychological self-sufficiency, separation, individuality, freedom, prison, romance, escape, or privilege. Perhaps the most persistent metaphor is "individual as island," with associated inferences of independence, distinctiveness, isolation. John Fowles explains that "it is the boundedness of the small island, encompassable in a glance, walkable in one day that relates it to the human body closer than any other geographical conformation of land."[7] Paul Simon's lonely lyrics in "I Am a Rock" call to mind separation and self-sufficiency. But John Donne offers us a different view. He says, "No man is an *Iland*, intire of it selfe; every man is a peece of the *Continent*, a part of the *maine*." And nineteenth-century psychologist William James finds a middle stance in the individual-as-island debate. He suggests that we are like islands in the ocean, separate on the surface but comingled in the deep.

Over millennia, real and metaphorical islands have been seen as generative places linked with creation stories and imbued with spiritual significance. Iroquois and Ojibwa peoples, for example, recall how Sky Woman took refuge on the back of Great Turtle, carrying soil that transformed into the world as we know it today. Turtle Island, a name for North America, is an enduring metaphor of First Nations living in harmony with others. Farther west, Tsimshian people tell how Great Boy, on a journey across the sea, dropped rocks that became islands in places that he wanted to rest.

Islands, with their aura of being "away," are also perceived as sites for testing our personal boundaries, preferences, and self-sufficiency. How often have you been asked which foods or companions you would choose if marooned on a desert island? Remote, uninhabited islands are settings for popular reality television series, including *Survivor* and *Castaways*. And despite their silliness, perpetual reruns of *Gilligan's Island* also attest to our fascination with ways we'd cope if stranded.

The notions of separation, paradise, exile, or individuality are so embedded in island metaphors that they shape perceptions among people who have never set foot on islands. As a result, islanders everywhere deal with romanticized, often improbable stereotypes. As one wryly points out, "Remote islands, exotic islands, are remote and exotic only when you are not an inhabitant of one."[8]

Islands of the imagination

OUR ENDURING FASCINATION with islands as places of voluntary—or involuntary—separation, independence, and reinvention has inspired fertile imaginations over the ages. The lost island of Atlantis has long preoccupied mythmakers. Avalon is central to Arthurian legend. William Shakespeare situated *The Tempest* (1611) on a desert island where characters dreamed of freedom and explored unrealized potential. And a century later, as Europeans turned their exploratory gaze to new worlds, Daniel Dafoe wrote the quintessential castaway story, *Robinson Crusoe* (1719). This fictionalized account of Alexander Selkirk's real-life sojourn on a remote Pacific island has intrigued us for centuries and inspired a genre of writing known as Robinsonade.[9] Johann David Wyss's *Swiss Family Robinson* (1812) and Robert Louis Stevenson's *Treasure Island* (1883) draw on our fascination with exile. Island settings continue to serve as evocative literary devices.

Fascination with islands starts early. Many of us grew up with island characters who captivated our imagination, inspired a sense of adventure, and shaped our world views. In J.M. Barrie's *Peter Pan* (1904), Peter was captain on the Island of Lost Boys. Max, in Maurice Sendak's *Where the Wild Things Are* (1963), encountered island monsters. The children in the many print and film versions of *Swiss Family Robinson* romped on tropical beaches and lived in a romantic treehouse. The protagonist in Astrid Lindgren's *Pippi Longstocking* (1948) visited Kurrekurredutt Isle. These characters carried us with them as they explored boundaries and tested their abilities. And the resilient children in Enid Blyton's *The Secret Island* (1938) and *Island of Adventure* (1944) offered us exotic places, intrigue, danger, although these tales now seem jingoistic and sadly racist.

And even the smallest child has been enticed and cautioned by metaphors of island freedom. In Ella Wheeler Wilcox's swashbuckling poem "The Island of Endless Play" (1892), children learn of a magical place that abounds with the pleasures of swimming, flying kites, and playing marbles, an island where they can do as they please. But they also learn that too much time in this delightful place will eventually consign them to Stupid Land because they haven't done their lessons. "Boys that don't study or work," says the narrator, "must sail one day down the Ignorant Sea."[10]

Islands shift from places of delight to settings of personal assessment in literature for young adults. I remember deconstructing, in high school English classes, the ghastly island-induced dilemmas of stranded British schoolboys in William Golding's *Lord of the Flies* (1954). Walter Farley's *Black Stallion* (1941) offered a more inspiring tale, as a boy and a horse rely on each other on a deserted island. Ingenuity and growth are also themes in *Island of the Blue Dolphins*, Scott O'Dell's 1960s novel. Contemporary teen literature offers numerous tales of youth finding their identity, testing skills, discovering romance, and appreciating nature in island settings. Characters benefit from these experiences and almost always return to the mainland wiser and better adjusted.

There are many islands in adult literature, popular fiction, movies, songs, and other creative media. Think of the hideaways of megalomaniacs and places of romance, escape, adventure, exile, or self-reflection. Islands are important sites for adventure, exploration, and celebration of individuality. A search for *island* on Amazon.ca will result in well over 100,000 titles. Histories, thrillers, travel guides, love stories, science fiction, memoirs, and board and video games all portray islands as catalysts for adventure and self-discovery. Escape from day-to-day norms and social constraints is a common theme. Some play up the boundedness of islands as sites for horror, paranormal, and futuristic tales. H.G. Wells's *The Island of Dr. Moreau* (1896) is an enduring early example. And the various movies in the *Jurassic Park* series, the first of which was based on Michael Crichton's 1990 novel, offer a frightening vision of island-based experimentation. Stories of survival, retreat, and reinvention are commonly located on "sea-estranged" islands, to use P.D. James's evocative term from *The Lighthouse* (2005). So are mysteries. These can involve simmering passions with lethal results. *And Then There Were None* (1939) is Agatha Christie's convoluted tale of mysterious deaths during an island house party. It is the world's bestselling mystery novel of all time. Many more contemporary crime, romance, fantasy, and science fiction novels provide us with virtual escapes to real and imagined islands around the world.

You can probably identify popular movies and television series that are shaped by and contained within real and imagined islands. Many are based on novels. The various movie versions of *Blue Lagoon*, the first of which appeared in 1923 and the most recent in 1991, the 2000 movie *Cast Away*, and the television series *Lost*, which ran from 2004 to 2010, all reinforce the mystique of islands. The 2012 movie adaptation of Yann Martel's novel *Life of Pi* (2001) includes a strange multisensory island interlude. In each, the setting invokes tension. Castaways survive, even thrive, in isolation while yearning to return to a prior life. Self-discovery is a persistent theme.

Banishment to dreaded island prisons also captures our imagination and reminds us of the sad wealth of real-life examples that have inspired literary works. More than 500,000 inmates died on Devil's Island, the penal colony off French Guiana where Henri Charrière's memoir *Papillon* (1969) is based. St. Helena, one of the remotest places on earth, was Napoleon's storied punishment after defeat at Waterloo. And such feared prisons as those on Robben Island off Cape Town and Alcatraz near San Francisco represent exile and lost hope. Islands are understood as lonely isolated places of quarantine as well. On Ellis Island, in Upper New York Bay, thousands of immigrants were held and then turned away from the United States due to illness, a criminal record, or perceived insanity. And when you visit beautiful D'Arcy Island within sight of the Saanich Peninsula on Vancouver Island, you'll find nineteenth-century building foundations and neglected apple trees. These recall harrowing tales of people with leprosy who were forced to stay there, cut off from family and medical care, until the end of their lives. Marilyn Bowering's novel *To All Appearances a Lady* (1989) provides a haunting account of their abandonment and grief.

Other stories focus on tensions triggered by isolation. M.L. Stedman, for example, explores the devastating results of seclusion for light-keepers in *The Light Between Oceans* (2016). At the same time the book highlights how islands free us to reimagine our realities, to create new truths.

And many memoirs focus on life on real islands. Some are practical accounts of day-to-day activities. The intriguing ones also explore islanders' joys and fears as they come to appreciate paradise found and, in a few cases, paradise lost. These accounts of the charms and hard realities of island living are of particular interest if you want an island life, since they offer a wealth of practical advice. A few also showcase the eccentricities of fellow islanders. Take these amusing vignettes with a grain of salt. In my experience, stereotypes of indolent dropouts, shiftless contractors, or enduring hippies don't honour the complexity of skills, character, and circumstances normally revealed as you get to know islanders.

Studying islands

ISLANDS HAVE A powerful presence in our world, so it's hardly surprising that people, whether they have set foot on them or not, hold diverse views on their roles and meanings. This fascination has inspired a global academic focus on "island studies," also known as "nissology." Biologists and geologists study islands' physical processes. And social scientists focus on their distinctive psychological, geographical, cultural, and economic characteristics. Many scholars value islands as bounded laboratories for studying natural and social change.[11] Most researchers are "islophiles," fascinated to study their disciplines in remote and insular settings. Although diverse philosophical and methodological perspectives make it hard to pin this field down, the very range of interests that come together is one of the strengths of island studies.[12]

All this research helps us understand the notion of islandness. This concept offers a way to think about how the nature of islands shapes people's lives. An island's location, size, resources, culture, history, and environment, along with its proximity to mainland services, all contribute to the quality of a resident's islandness, as does the individual's sense of identity and connection. For example, if you live on Vancouver Island, your day-to-day life probably feels very different from that of friends on Haida Gwaii or on a private island in the San Juans. You are all islanders. But the nature of your islandness differs. You need different skills, have different relationships, and probably value different things. With so much diversity in islands and islanders, most scholars resist efforts to generalize islanders' characteristics or perpetuate stereotypes. And as islandness is seen as a state of mind, it "can be as simple or as complex as we wish it to be."[13]

Even though scholars debate how to make sense of varied island experiences, most suggest that insularity is a defining feature. Surrounding waters set the margins for life on islands and shape experience, particularly if the island is isolated, hard to reach. Does separation make island life simpler, less sophisticated? Are remote islanders out of tune with world events? With islanders' increasing ability to cross enisling waters, both physically and electronically, the notion of insularity, with its somewhat negative connotations, is called into question. Although stereotypes imply that islanders are out of step with the mainstream and culturally disconnected, most move comfortably in non-island settings "precisely because they have an island to anchor their journey."[14] One way or another, island studies offers us thoughtful insights on people's powerful engagement with islands.

The appeal of islands

JUST AS ISLANDS are remarkably varied, so are the reasons why we seek them out. Motivations are complex and intertwined but seem to divide roughly into two sorts of impulses. On one hand, many people turn to islands out of a desire to *escape from* a mainland lifestyle, often with only a simplistic understanding of the realities of island life. On the other, many are motivated by a desire to *go to* meaningful island places.

Escapism involves seeking relief or distraction from unpleasant realities. And those who turn to islands for such experiences are drawn by idealized expectations of beauty, pleasure, intimacy, perhaps fantasy. Happiness is derived from *getting away* from something as much as it is from *going to* a pleasurable place. How often have you been tempted by ads for island holidays, as well as for longer-term island ownership, that sell the notion of fleeing the pressures, pollution, and worries of an urban lifestyle? This is the clichéd sun, sea, and sand marketing theme for many tropical resorts and travel experiences. Cruise companies even create artificial islands where you can be a castaway for a day. Island travel promotions are all about escaping troubles, relaxing, being less inhibited. Humidity, heat, insects, local tensions, and the complex challenges of an isolated lifestyle are never mentioned. The gap between dream and reality is evident to cynics. "You could call it...nostalgia for a place that never was, and really never can be. Tourism of course is the great dream factory of the 20th and will continue to be in the 21st century. And we're sold places that never were. Never can be."[15]

Holidays on warm-water islands have been described as dream vacations for decades. But trips to cold-water islands are gaining in popularity. Fishing, hiking, and watching storms, glaciers, birds, whales, and other sea life, appeal to people seeking new horizons and experiences. "Cold water island locations tend to have harsh, pristine and fragile natural environments, characterized by wide open spaces. They become contexts for an exceptional and expensive form of vigorous, outdoor adventure or cultural tourism, and direct encounters with nature."[16] Resorts and tours on Fogo Island in Newfoundland, the Hebrides (combined with Scotch distilleries), and the west coast of Vancouver Island, for example, all offer rugged, bracing escapes. The emphasis is on the differences between urban and rural, tame and wild.

Every year, over 700 million tourist journeys occur worldwide. Because many of these involve island destinations, a massive vacation economy shapes ways that mainlanders perceive and value islands. The appeal is not so much the character of the island as the brief interlude that it offers: a liberating break from reality. The assumption is that you will return to the mainland, perhaps with a new sense of self, to deal with the demands of life.

For some people who are seeking escape, a holiday is not enough. They want a complete break from busy, stressful, and unfulfilling lives. "Today's lust for islands is unmatched in scope and avidity. It is fueled by a yearning for seclusion from modernity. Islands are fantasized as antitheses of the all-engrossing gargantuan mainstream—small, quiet, untroubled, remote from the busy, crowded, turbulent everyday scene."[17] This desire for a simpler life drives many prospective islanders to escape to an alternative, albeit vaguely understood, lifestyle. In the 1950s, for example, Margaret McIntyre and her partner were pondering the futility of their Vancouver lives. They set out to find an island, on the basis of "the horrible state of the world and the equally horrible state of [their] finances."[18] The property they found at Billings Bay on the west side of Nelson Island had immediate appeal. But their decision to move on island was grounded in a desire to get away, rather than in an urge to go to a known place and lifestyle. McIntyre's engaging memoir *Place of Quiet Waters* illustrates the many challenges that result from a naive romantic impulse.

A search for sanctuary, for seclusion, might also guide you to an island. In a world where most frontiers have been explored, the notion of living in a remote, hard-to-access place is compelling. Making a home on one of BC's Discovery Islands, for example, "is like living in a castle and the water around us is the moat, cutting off the outside world, keeping us safe and insulated from many of the world's evils."[19] Privacy, peace, and the absence of strangers are valued. A Saturna Islander repeats this theme of refuge. "The water wraps you around and seals you off and everything else is foreign territory."[20]

Islands can also be spaces for reflection, for coping with sadness. As an east coaster reflects, "At the risk of sounding fey, there is a healing energy to be found in the Cranberry Isles. The internal noise of life can be muffled by a walk through the quiet woods. At the beach, the resonance of waves breaking against rocks or rolling smaller stones on the shore provides a recognizable rhythm of life. The sound opens the soul to peace."[21]

Utopian dreams of a new life, away from external contamination, are almost always island based in literature and reality. This is because the bounded and discrete nature of islands allows for control and exclusion. Hippie communes scattered along the southern BC coast in the 1960s and '70s tried to create new social orders, as did the earlier Finnish experimental community of Sointula (or "place of harmony") on Malcolm Island. BC's most dramatic so-called utopian initiative was Brother XII's Aquarian Foundation. It established settlements on De Courcy and Valdes Islands in the late 1920s. Many wealthy and socially prominent people left lives and families in search of a haven from the end of the world, predicted for January 1, 1934. Sadly, actual living conditions there had little resemblance to Utopia. Residents of adjacent islands told me about desperate late-night visits from disillusioned disciples of Brother XII who were seeking ways to escape their island escape.

The notion of escape can take other forms. Grant Lawrence, broadcaster and seasonal Desolation Sound resident, writes about "a certain type of individual" who came to the Sound seeking "the land beyond the map—a place of hope, refuge, hiding, and escape."[22] In fiction, islands serve as sites of concealment, bad behaviour, and criminal activity. They also play such roles in real life. As another island observer notes, "There is...a certain element of a rough hermit philosophy...While a lot of people come to the BC coast to slow down and live a peaceful life, some others come here because they want to find a place to hide. The local underground economy—the cultivation of marijuana in particular—is a clear testament to the protection from the outside world that islands afford."[23]

Along the coast, islanders whisper of drug dealings, grow-ops, domestic violence, smuggling, and other criminal activities. The district RCMP website indicates that "by land, sea and air, we proudly work with various partner agencies to keep Vancouver Island and its surrounding islands safe places to live, work and visit." It also notes that its marine assets "assist our officers in policing the picturesque and rugged coastal waters." And its Comox-based helicopter "assists in reaching the more remote land and mountainous areas across the island."[24] Despite these efforts, scrutinizing islands is difficult. It is well known, for example, that word of approaching law enforcement officers circulates long before their ferry docks. But with such technologies as Google Earth and drones, islands don't contain secrets as effectively as they used to.

If seeking escape from mainland realities isn't your primary motivation, it is more likely that you are drawn to islands out of a powerful attraction to a special place. You may be under the influence of "islomania," an obsessional enthusiasm for islands. This does not specify the nature of islands or the experience of being there. It suggests only that your attraction is guided by desire. The ways islomania is enacted are personal. Island scholar Pete Hay suggests that a "deeply visceral lived experience" underpins people's motivation to go to islands. "Islands—*real* islands, real geographical entities—attract affection, loyalty, identification. And what do you get when you take a bounded geographical entity and add an investment of human attachment, loyalty and meaning? You get the phenomenon known as 'place.' Islands are places—special places, paradigmatic places, topographies of meaning in which the qualities that construct place are dramatically distilled."[25]

It is tempting to understand "sense of place" as simply an attraction to an appealing physical setting. But it's deeper than that. Again and again I heard that an islander's unique sense of place emerges from an evolving interaction between the characteristics of the island and the ways it is understood and used. Over time, an island's significance emerges and deepens. Yvonne Maximchuk, who settled with her young family in Echo Bay on Gilford Island, writes about her personal sense of place.

I'm in love with the coast life now and I find I cannot tear myself away. My attunement to the sea and the environment, the combination of purification, exaltation and liberation I feel here, have become as essential as oxygen. I love the sweet breath of the westerly wind and the stone taste of the cold, clean drinkable water running down to the shore. I love the small flower-carpeted islets, the mutable silver light on the water and the holiness of the moss-draped spruce forest. I sit in the old tin skiff . . . and expand my listening for miles, hearing the kingfisher chatter before it dives for a fish or the faint, far-off whoosh of a humpback's blow. I even love the feeling like I have taken on more than I can handle . . . All my senses are more alive here and I can't give that up. The confinement and protective desensitization of city life seems intolerable: my stomach heaves when I think about it.[26]

Sense of place is normally understood as a positive feeling of connection. There are instances, however, in which a negative sense emerges if things do not go well. Elizabeth Arthur and her husband experienced tensions during a long winter on their remote island in Stuart Lake near Fort St. James. "There is silence in the house today. We talk little, and that is too much. The wind blows again, and the snow falls. I sit and walk and stand. I pick up wood and burn it. Nothing has happened. Nothing is wrong. But just getting through the day is like fighting my way through dense brush, thin branches whipping my face. I feel a growing rage which slowly chokes and consumes."[27]

Heritage, for some people, creates profound meaning and attachment in island settings. Indigenous peoples have deep roots on coastal islands. Their sense of place is intimately entwined with their ties with ancestors, traditional ways of knowing and doing, spiritual beliefs and practices, and a commitment to stewardship. As the Union of British Columbia Indian Chiefs states in its argument for an indigenous view of certainty in treaty negotiations,

> For Indigenous Peoples, our Aboriginal Title and connection to the Land is certain, it is in the bones of our grandmothers buried in the earth, and in the blood which beats in our hearts: Our Sacred connection to the Land is certain.
>
> Our relationship with the Land, our Title, rests over every square inch of our traditional territories: Every rock, mountain top, stream, valley and tidal swell. This is certain.[28]

Non-indigenous islanders also describe their lifelong affinity for islands. Children who have grown up on islands, as well as people who have worked on the coast over a lifetime, express a powerful sense of connection to land and water. Misty Lawson was born and raised on a remote island at the mouth of Clayoquot Sound and has since moved to yet another beautiful small island. She feels like the "luckiest person in the world" to have such profound ties with these islands and the lifestyle that goes with them. Misty and her brother "played on the island's beaches and in its old growth forest, nurturing a keen sense of [their] surroundings and gaining intimate knowledge of the marine and land-based wildlife that thrives around Tofino."[29] And Donna Livingstone, who grew up on Lasqueti Island before spending forty years in major urban centres, told me that

it's not that the island draws me back, it's that it never leaves me. Every June, wherever I am in the world, and it's raining, I think, "This will be good for the salmonberries." I go to sleep at night retracing the walk home from school to Scottie Bay (I'm usually asleep by Fort's corner). Growing up on a remote island in a tight community means you have a life-long role in the island play. Sometimes you're the star, but more often you're the bit player whose contribution can be made without even being there. You run into someone on the Nanaimo ferry or on a bus in Edmonton and find an island connection, and the play is extended with a story. But you always have something to contribute.

She emphasizes that island roots run deep and wide. "People still talk about island people even when they are long gone. I reached out to a fisherman in Cowichan Bay who bought the *Lasqueti Fisher* and converted it, to point out that I was one of the island daughters who christened it over fifty years ago. It meant something to us both to enrich the story that way. It means I am still an island girl."

Farther away and well over a century ago, Celia Thaxter reflected on the powerful appeal of her home on the Isles of Shoals off New Hampshire. "Nobody hears of people dying of homesickness for New York...but to wild and lonely spots like these isles humanity clings with an intense and abiding affection. No other place is able to furnish the inhabitants of the Shoals with sufficient air for their capacious lungs; there is never scope enough elsewhere...they must have sea-room."[30]

Other prospective islanders crave the dynamic convergence of land, water, and air that gives islands their special character. Living within cycles of nature, responding to the interplay of foreshore, shoreline, and upland elements, and savouring changing weather and seasons are key to an evolving sense of place. Rob Wood felt an immediate tie to Maurelle Island when he and his friends pulled into a small bay after an exhilarating passage through Surge Narrows in the early 1970s. "It's quite likely that I was already sold. Other than the occasional little beach shack there had been no sign of civilization for miles. As soon as the boat was tied up to the makeshift bundle of logs that served as a dock, the silence, beauty and peaceful serenity were a marvel... My imagination was working overtime on the fantasy of building a home and settling down in such a beautiful and stimulating place."[31] Rob and his wife, Laurie, settled on Maurelle as part of a co-operative community, dedicated to living in tune with their natural environment.

The Orth family had a similar sense of connection when they moved to a remote Alaskan island in the Stikine River estuary to live more closely with nature. Even after their careful search for an island that would meet their needs for independence and self-sufficiency, Joy Orth reflects that "I do not delude myself into thinking we will ever know this island. It has many parts; morning parts and evening parts and parts that stay always in twilight. We have still not explored it all, nor ever will. It is 3.3 acres large and several millennia wide."[32]

Another islander notes that he deliberately sought a remote island experience in the Broughton group. But his immersion in a natural world yielded unexpected rewards. "I had found a truly wild place and I was now alone to prove myself. The richness of the actual wilderness far surpassed my wildest dreams."[33] The island as a treasured natural place is a persistent theme in islanders' memoirs and comments.

Getting in touch with your inner self is both a motivation for—and an outcome of—engaging with an island. Richard Nelson, for example, comments that his purpose in exploring a beloved north coast island "is to understand myself in relationship to a natural community of which I am, in some indefinable way, a part. I've come seeking a better sense of how I fit into this place, not only as a visitor and watcher, but as a participant... The island is not just a place to pleasure my senses—it is my home, my ecological niche, my life broadly defined."[34] While Nelson never lived on island, the frequent visits he describes in his book, *The Island Within* (1991), were important to his sense of well-being.

You may also be drawn to islands off the ferry grid to fulfill dreams of autonomy, perhaps dominance. To be lord of all you survey, make your mark, and create an exclusionary domain have considerable appeal. For some people, "to island is to control."[35] I suspect that this was one of the reasons that my father traded a career in head office for island living. After years of working in remote coastal communities and leading small logging operations, he found the structure and formality of Vancouver life restrictive. The daily commute across the Lions Gate Bridge was tedious, and he was exasperated with the limitations of office work. Bath Island offered a return to an unrestricted and much more independent lifestyle.

A life of simple and healthy pleasures without the competing distractions of mainland living might also be a reason to go to an island. For David and Jeanne Conover, who moved to Wallace Island in 1947, their new life on this long and narrow island off the east coast of Salt Spring Island was both difficult and transformational. "Before we had only been half alive. Now lean from hard work and bronzed by the sun, we felt wonderfully limber and strong...We had spring to our steps, a feeling of well-being."[36] They became more attuned to the rhythms, sounds, and smells of the island, more self-sufficient in the absence of city amenities. "Simplicity had stolen into our lives."[37] And farther north on Read Island, David Cox writes that "living off the grid is a form of therapy, a way to mental health. I had no idea that it would turn out that way but I think it has. Of course it has the positive influence of nature, whales, ravens and fresh air but it also insulates me from so much that is wrong with this world...The ratio of good to evil is just so much better."[38] Other islanders see the island as an opportunity for challenge and change, an undertaking that stretches them emotionally, physically, intellectually.

You may find that a sense of island time, intertwined with a sense of place, is enticing. Notions of slowing down, determining your own schedule, moving in tune with seasonal, daylight, and tidal rhythms are integral to perceptions of island life. On Gabriola, Phillip Vannini observes that "the feel of island time is everywhere."[39] He points to a relaxed pace of life, laissez-faire attitudes, casual interactions with fellow islanders, engagement with nature, and an appreciation of peace and quiet. These are evidence that time on island is distinctive. Vannini also notes that island time is often described in such comparative terms as "slower" or "less hurried." Islanders do this subconsciously to emphasize the contrast with less desirable off-island temporal zones—generally the cities they are so pleased to have left behind.

Opportunities for adventure, play, and tests of personal skills and ingenuity on island are also appealing. The attraction is not so much escapism as a desire to lead a more self-sufficient and inventive life in a congenial environment. June Burn, who moved with her family to a small "gumdrop" of an island in the San Juans, described her time there in the 1930s as "first hand living." She and her husband made a commitment to "retire first" and spend time on their island before taking on a conventional urban life. They wanted to "taste life at first hand, dig for our own food, scratch about just anyhow for what we needed, going at it the hard way, letting our children see into the primitive mechanics of living." The "fun, happiness, joy, splendid hardship, fine adventures"[40] that Burn describes have inspired others to see island living as a possibility.

Natural, simple, meaningful: these words repeatedly describe idyllic island lives. Yet few islanders equate living on an island with a relaxing idyll. Developing and caring for island properties, along with the complexities of provisioning and socializing across surrounding waters, poses perpetual challenges. But the pleasures of this unusual lifestyle are deeply appreciated. A Nova Scotia islander writes,

> While others scrimp and save all year long, then cram children, pets and beach balls into the station wagon for a frantic two-week vacation... we're free—12 months a year—to take a zesty plunge into the surf or drop a line into crystal-clear waters any time we want to. And all only a few feet from our front door. When we get tired of that, there's all those miles and miles of spruce-rimmed shoreline and secluded beaches "out there" constantly tempting us to explore them. And when *that* gets boring, we

can just hop into . . . our two-place kayak—hoist the little boat's sails and go "yachting" around the bay for hours at a time.[41]

Interesting neighbours may also attract you to islands. Certainly on islands served by ferries a move involves participation in a distinctive community. On islands without ferries, however, the scale, scope, and role of community varies. Some have no community, although neighbours on adjacent islands or in nearby mainland towns offer a social network and helping hands. Other islands have been subdivided in a way that allows multiple residents to co-exist quite separately. Still others feature communal approaches to moorage, water, power, and other systems. This creates an interdependent community. Your interest in social interactions affects how you may feel about such arrangements.

And finally, pride and pleasure in owning a special and exclusive place—in common with the likes of the Emir of Qatar, Johnny Depp, or Malcolm Forbes—might pique your interest. "For many people, the mere idea of an island—the tangible embodiment of wealth, status, safety, sovereignty, privacy and freedom—compels and captures the imagination."[42] Islands that are owned and developed as settings for the social side of business, for example, are scattered along the BC coast. In some cases, they have airstrips or helipads, golf courses, small sport-fishing fleets, and deluxe accommodations. These encourage privileged conversations away from prying eyes.

Categorizing the motivations that make island living attractive is, of course, an inexact process. The impulses that draw people to this unusual lifestyle tend to be interconnected and evolving. And all the motivations discussed above assume a voluntary interest in spending time on islands, although this too can vary with circumstances. Adam Nicolson lives on the Shiant Isles in the Hebrides. He writes about his mixed relationship with the stark and complex islands in *Sea Room: An Island Life* (2002), noting that centuries of occupation create a human landscape laden with happiness, cruelty, drama, and isolation. Nicolson describes them as heavenly, but also acknowledges that they can be "malevolent as Hell" when devastating poverty, accidents, attempted murder, and witchcraft threaten islanders' well being. He sees the barriers between islanders and their world as "tissue-thin."[43]

Nicolson is, for the most part, entranced with his complicated islands. There are many situations, however, in which people's island experiences may be involuntary, dark, or devoid of a sense of privilege or wonder. Local work, relationships, and family expectations, or some need to take refuge, can all make island life necessary if not appealing. A desire to escape the very qualities that attract others may be in play when an island becomes an obligation rather than a choice.

John Fowles sums up the compelling draw of islands. "True islands always play the sirens' (and the bookmakers') trick: they lure by challenging, by daring. Somewhere on them one will become Crusoe again, one will discover something: the iron-bound chest, the jackpot, the outside chance."[44] With so many interconnected reasons for choosing a distinctive lifestyle, islanders are a fascinating group. They tell remarkable stories about how they came to be there and what they have done since to make island lives fulfilling.

Identifying as an islander

REGARDLESS OF WHAT draws people to islands, they begin to identify as islanders as they spend meaningful time in these distinctive places. The details—and degree—of that identity are bound to differ according to the person, place, and experience. And the label "islander" seems to be both externally and internally bestowed. At what point do you become an islander? How dominant and lasting is this identity?

Becoming a true islander typically requires involvement with and acceptance into an island community, at least according to island studies scholars. The politics of inclusion are a reality on larger, more developed islands where deeply rooted customs, attitudes, and social dynamics shape the continuity of life. To be welcomed as a community member, you are expected to conform with local behaviours, use the specialized lingo, perform island rituals, and internalize commonly held values. This helps perpetuate tightly knit and interdependent lifestyles on island. Inevitably, the tension between community engagement and the desire for independence becomes a paradox of island living. Islanders are "both highly communal and highly tolerant of obstinate individuality."[45]

Because every island is unique, the identity (islandness) of residents also varies. You will find a different lifestyle on fashionable and accessible Salt Spring Island, for example, than on off-the-grid Lasqueti that describes itself as "halfway between Dogpatch and Shangri-la."[46] Acceptance processes also diverge. It may take years for full inclusion in centuries-old Atlantic island communities. However, the relatively short settler histories of West Coast islands, their economic and residential fluctuations, and the fluidity of lifestyles make acceptance easier. Communities on the West Coast are likely to welcome you when you start to act like you belong, although experienced islanders caution that newcomers should show humility and willingness to learn while they work into the islander identity. And some distinctions are enduring. "Full-time, year-round islanders often look down upon many of the seasonals and the weekenders for not being a true part of the community, for treating our island as a second bedroom, for not contributing to causes. There are times when the tension is strong."[47] Relative proximity and ease of access also influence identity within archipelagic islands. "There can be a pecking order of islandness: the farther away you are from the main island, the more credibility you have as an islander."[48]

Many mainlanders have a romanticized vision of island life. They also tend to typecast islanders. This could be because mainlanders find people who choose to live offshore unusual, eccentric, puzzling. The following oft-quoted list of qualities may not apply to all islanders all the time, but it aggregates the qualities that tend to set them apart:[49]

- *Independence*, which small boats and social circles demand if a personality is to survive

- *Loyalty*, the ultimate mutual care and generosity, even between ostensible enemies

- A strong sense of *honour*, easily betrayed

- Polydextrous and multifaceted competence, or what islanders call *handiness*

- A belligerent sense of competition, interlaced with vigilant *cooperation*

- Traditional *frugality* with bursts of spectacular exception

- Earthy *common sense*

- Opinionated *machismo* in both male and female mode

- Live-and-let-live tolerance of *eccentricity*

- Fragile *discretion* within a welter of gossip

- Highly individualized blends of *spirituality* and *superstition*

- A complex *oral tradition*, with long memories fuelled by a mix of responsible record keeping and nostalgia

- Canny *literacy* and *intelligence*

Externally endowed recognition and acceptance are important to a sense of islandness when you join an island community. At the same time, it is likely that you are developing your own personal sense of identity, particularly if you live in a more solitary setting. The island and the lifestyle become intrinsic to who you are. "A small island is knowable. You can get your arms around it. An island is not something apart from you, but is something you can be a part of. You can live your life with certainty knowing where your edges are."[50] And as Jo Kenny, a long-time Gabriola resident, reflects at the age of 102, "Some places you own. Other places own you."

Becoming an islander and making a success of island living also draw on a range of other identities. Boater, mechanic, fisher, carpenter, problem solver, ecologist, philosopher—these special-izations, and many more, help shape the innate sense that you are "of" an island. With so many complex elements, a personal sense of islandness evolves in a gradual and fluid way as islands work their transformative magic.

And as I can confirm, islandness becomes part of who you are, regardless of whether you are on island or not. Even though I left Bath

Island years ago to take up additional identities as an adult, wife, mother, heritage professional, and educator, my time on the island and my powerful connection to that place continue to be a profound part of who I am. It helps that I can sail the coast and visit islands regularly, but it goes deeper than that. A visceral feeling of home when I step ashore on a sandstone beach, an enduring sense of independence combined with the delight of sharing the place with friends, and the instinct that problems should be solved quickly through some form of practical action are all, in my mind, a legacy of growing up on a small island.

Shared experiences

THESE REFLECTIONS ON the draw of islands and ways they shape identity set the stage for the following chapters on finding your perfect island, crossing surrounding waters, making a home, adapting to island time, maintaining relationships, coping with challenges, and reflecting on the fit of an island lifestyle. My interest in self-reliant islanders who live off the ferry grid is clearly grounded in my own experience but also recognizes that the added task of crossing surrounding waters changes, complicates, and enhances island life.

Complicated Simplicity alludes to, but is not about, island societies, politics, economies, or ecosystems. A flourishing island-studies discipline looks at islands from such perspectives. This book is about islanders—real people—and their lived experiences. When I first considered writing about life on islands in the Pacific Northwest, I knew a few people who chose to live off the ferry grid. While they share boundless enthusiasm for this distinctive lifestyle, I was intrigued by the diversity of their islands, experiences, and perspectives. It struck me that much could be learned from their approaches to making successful lives on island. And when I began to plan interviews with these islanders I was delighted that many friends and colleagues knew other islanders along this coast. Through them I met many of the fascinating people whose stories are such an important part of *Complicated Simplicity*. All these islanders' voices are authentic, passionate, humorous, and frank. Some prefer to go by only their first name, and others prefer that the name of their island not be mentioned. All were welcoming and happy to share their experiences. The following brief introduction to the islanders you've already encountered in this chapter and to others you'll meet in upcoming chapters provides you with a bit of background.

A number of the islanders I spoke with make their homes above sandstone beaches, among the iconic arbutus and Garry oaks that characterize the southern islands of the Georgia Basin. This is the landscape I know best. Kathy and Chic have two very different island properties in the lovely San Juan Islands, which are just below the Canada–US border at the south end of the Georgia Basin. One of their properties is on the outside edge of a busy harbour with relatively easy access by plane or by ferry and car. It's a comfortable retreat on an island shared with a number of other permanent and seasonal residents, but a bit too "suburban" to be perfect, at least from Chic and Kathy's perspective. Their other property, nicknamed Snowberry Island in their stories, is approximately fifteen kilometres away in a cluster of more remote small islands. This is the private island that challenges them, gives them tremendous pleasure, and tests their ingenuity as they build a house on a high bluff with sweeping views.

Not far away on Sidney Island, one of the southernmost Canadian Gulf Islands, Geri and Frank Van Gyn have immersed themselves in off-the-grid living on an island shared with a number of other residents and a national park. While they make frequent trips between Sidney Island and nearby Victoria by boat or plane to balance professional and family activities, their beautiful house, looking west across Haro Strait toward Mount Douglas, is definitely home. Building it, Frank says, along with a guest house, workshop, corral, enclosed gardens, ponds, and various chicken coops, has been an adventure, a labour of love, and a remarkable learning experience.

Valdes Island, just south of Gabriola Island and not far from Bath Island, has always been home to Linda Harrison. Her parents first settled in a small house on Gabriola Pass in the 1930s. Growing up, Linda and I rode the school bus together every day. As an adult, Linda trained as a nurse, but love for Valdes took her back, and for many years she and her husband lived in a small house farther down the east coast of the island, overlooking the Strait of Georgia. While they now have a home on nearby Gabriola, she still visits her Valdes cabin whenever she can. It was fascinating to talk with Linda about our parallel experiences growing up on neighbouring islands in the 1960s.

And I am always happy to visit with Roger Boshier, who purchased Bath Island from my parents in 1986. He had spent several summers visiting and caretaking on the island before approaching Dad about buying it when my parents started considering a move. As a professor of adult education at the University of British Columbia, Roger took on a challenging life of balancing work with island living. Retired now, he continues with research that takes him around the world, but he always returns to his island home. I am delighted that he loves Bath Island as much as we did.

The youngest islanders I spoke with were Emily Barnewall and Tom Barchyn, who chose Protection Island, near Nanaimo, as an ideal location to raise a family. This Gulf Island is close to the amenities of the city but a long way away in terms of their sense of independence and connection with nature. Among other things, they travel to and from the island by kayak, savour surrounding beaches and forest trails with growing children, value the support of a highly collaborative island community, and are very focused on living lightly on the land.

Jan and Sy live on a more remote island, tucked alongside Nelson Island south of Powell River. The landscape on the east side of the Georgia Basin at the mouth of Jervis Inlet is rugged, with granite outcroppings and thick forest cover. Jan and Sy had been working in the entertainment world in Las Vegas in the 1980s when friends phoned to ask if they wanted to share an uninhabited island that they had first visited the previous summer. They jumped at the opportunity, packed up their two small daughters, and completely changed their lives. I spent a lovely day with them, looking out across their beautiful garden toward the protected bay near their house, and heard about the many adventures and pleasures involved in making their lives on island. They would not want to be anywhere else.

The Discovery Islands at the northern end of the Georgia Basin feel quite different from more populous and accessible islands to the south. Located between Quadra Island and towering mountains on the mainland, the landscape is precipitous, forest cover is dense, beaches are toeholds on granite shorelines, and strong currents challenge boaters. In this setting, both independence and participation in scattered island communities are important aspects of living on islands off the ferry grid.

My afternoon with Laurie and Rob Wood in their lovely home on Maurelle Island in the Discovery group was fascinating. They shared wonderful, often funny stories about homesteading as part of a co-op, raising "free-range" kids, navigating the treacherous waters of Surge Narrows, and celebrating a lovely place that captured their hearts the moment they stepped ashore. Rob is the author of two books that talk about both island living and his love of coastal mountains: *Towards the Unknown Mountains* (1991) and *At Home in Nature: A Life of Unknown Mountains and Deep Wilderness* (2017).

Around the same time that Laurie and Rob were settling on Maurelle, Judith Wright was leaving Ontario to seek "a life that felt real to me." By that she meant a life more closely connected with nature, where daily actions yielded tangible rewards rather than a wage and a hazy dream of deferred happiness through money. Judith found it on Rendezvous Island, where she and her husband purchased a previously logged acreage that was big enough to garden, raise animals, and settle in. As she says, "The island gave us a sense of separation from the main society, like a moat, so that we didn't have someone telling us how and when and why to do things. We could be real human animals instead of tortured social constructs. The beauty alone is enough to keep a person here." I thoroughly enjoyed meeting and talking with Judith, who clearly loves the island life she has carved out for herself and her family.

Ralph and Lannie Keller moved to Read Island in the heart of the Discovery group in the 1970s. They have raised a family in a glorious—at times challenging—setting and have introduced many people to the beauties of the area by providing guided kayak and alpine adventure tours through their company, Coast Mountain Expeditions.

On another of the Discovery Islands, David and Suromitra have devoted summer after summer to building a beautiful home. It perches atop a bluff, looking south toward Cortes Island and east to the mainland's coastal mountains. Because much of their time is devoted to busy careers in distant cities, their sojourns on island are brief but intense. But both stress that the island is central to their lives and to their sense of well-being.

Island life on the exposed west coast of Vancouver Island has particular challenges imposed by the dynamic intersection of ocean and weather. I spent a morning with Joe Martin, renowned Tla-o-qui-aht master carver, talking about navigating local waters to reach Echachis Island off Tofino, the challenges of building above a surf-washed beach, and the deep spiritual connections that generations of his people have forged with this island. He describes his time on Echachis as a special gift.

And Misty Lawson told me that her profound connections with islands and the lifestyle that goes with them help define who she is. Misty was born on her parents' island at the mouth of Clayoquot Sound and grew up surrounded by nature on the verge of the Pacific Ocean. She and her family now live on a small and, as she says, "relatively easy" island in Tofino harbour.

It was enriching to sit with all these people and learn about how they came to be islanders, the challenges they faced, and the many pleasures they experienced. All see their island worlds in unique ways. At the same time, many share similar perspectives on the practical dynamics of life on island. Distilling their thoughts and stories on myriad themes has been a pleasure, although I am aware that I have left out many details in the interests of creating a cohesive book. And, of course, there are many, many intrepid islanders I didn't talk with and many wonderful stories I didn't hear. It would have taken much longer than the two summers that I set aside to gather stories for this book to connect with all the islanders who make their lives on the islands scattered throughout the Pacific Northwest.

WHILE ISLANDERS' EXPERIENCES are central to *Complicated Simplicity*, I was also delighted to find a wealth of experience and perspectives in memoirs of island living. Such records are a treasure trove that took me to places and times I couldn't otherwise access and revealed a depth of introspection that doesn't tend to emerge in enjoyable and relaxed summertime interviews on island decks and docks. Here is a bit of background on the authors who have written about islands and whose insights and experiences are shared throughout *Complicated Simplicity*.

In 1873 Celia Thaxter, a favourite author at the time in the United States, published *Among the Isles of Shoals*, which describes her remote island home in the Gulf of Maine. Her poetic descriptions of land, sea, and weather and her sensitive observations of the people who make their lives offshore are a testament to the notion that some things don't change a great deal over the centuries.

Another noted author who loves islands is John Fowles. His oft-quoted essay and photos in *Islands* (1978) take you on a journey to the stark and beautiful Isles of Scilly off Cornwall. And the Hebrides provide a backdrop for Adam Nicolson's book *Sea Room: An Island Life* (2002). Nicolson explores the geography of his stark islands, the legacy of centuries of occupation, and the troubled notions of ownership that go with receiving his islands as a birthday present. The words of Thaxter, Fowles, and Nicolson affirm that islanders, regardless of location, share many experiences and perspectives.

Closer to home, June Burn and her husband chose to move to a small island near San Juan Island in the 1930s. Her book *Living High* (1941) is a lively account of the adventure of making a home on island, coping with boats, earning a living, and rejoicing in the surroundings.

David Conover's memoir *Once Upon an Island: The Adventures of a Young Couple Who Did Buy Their Dream Island* (1967) is a classic for island lovers in the Pacific Northwest. This engaging book describes the decision that Conover and his wife, Jeanne, made to buy Wallace Island in the Gulf Islands in 1947, and their steep learning curve the first year on island with no experience and little money.

Margaret McIntyre's *Place of Quiet Waters* (1966) was a wonderful source of island stories. From the time that Margaret and her partner Jerry (wearing skirts and heels) stepped ashore on Nelson Island in the late 1950s to their adventures in building, boating, and befriending other islanders, they gained thoughtful insights on life on an island well away from the stresses of city life, though they also recognized that island life has its own stresses.

Elizabeth Arthur and her husband, Bob Gathercole, chose to homestead on a 1.2-hectare island in Stuart Lake in the 1970s. They were seeking a refuge from busy urban lives and were determined to build a lasting home. Her graceful memoir *Island Sojourn* (1980) offers an honest account of the challenges they faced, the lessons learned, and the difficulties that they worked through. Arthur went on to explore other islands, literal and metaphorical, in another memoir and five novels, including her epic *Antarctic Navigation* (2005), in which an American woman recreates Robert Falcon Scott's British Antarctic Expedition of 1910–12.

In the 1970s Joy Orth and her family went in search of an island where they could live a more self-sufficient life. Her book *Island: Our Alaskan Dream and Reality* (1987) is a powerful memoir of their lives on a remote island in the Stikine River estuary. In addition to offering a wealth of advice on island living, it captures their deeply satisfying and occasionally terrifying experiences.

Inside Passage (1991) provides an entertaining account of the time that Michael Modzelewski, naturalist and media personality, spent on a small island in the midst of Blackfish Sound off northern Vancouver Island. His descriptions of adventures on island and in boats and of the intriguing people that he encountered are engaging and insightful. He comments that "after seducing you with beauty" the island "would shake you with fear."

While Richard Nelson did not live on—or even name—the large northern island that captured his heart, his book *The Island Within* (1991) is a wonderful read. In addition to sharing lyrical descriptions of the island in all seasons, he explores the ways in which it profoundly shaped his sense of place and self.

In her fascinating book, *The Inlet: Memoir of a Modern Pioneer* (2001), Helen Piddington describes vignettes of her life with her family in Loughborough Inlet. Her life on this remote and mountainous fiord north of the Discovery Islands is in most ways similar to that of island dwellers who are off the ferry grid.

Drawn to Sea: Paintbrush to Chainsaw—Carving Out a Life on BC's Rugged Raincoast (2013) is a description of the pitfalls and transformative pleasures that artist Yvonne Maximchuk experienced when she moved with her two children to Echo Bay on remote Gilford Island in the Broughton Archipelago. Her evocative words, lessons learned, and personal insights offer valuable perspectives on island living. Her voice is also heard in *Tide Rips and Back Eddies: Bill Proctor's Tales of Blackfish Sound* (2015). This is the story of coastal logger, fisher, and trapper Bill Proctor, who tells tales of his life in the area around Echo Bay.

Moving to remote Read Island in the Discovery group from a "cul-de-sac existence" in Vancouver inspired David Cox's insightful, often funny memoirs *Our Life Off the Grid: An Urban Couple Goes Feral* (2015) and *Choosing Off the Grid* (2017), as well as his blog posts and YouTube clips. In addition to recognizing the many pleasures of island life, Cox offers practical advice (and cautions) for people considering life on islands not served by ferries.

And Caroline Woodward has served on a number of British Columbia lighthouses. Her book *Light Years: Memoir of a Modern Lighthouse Keeper* (2015) provides an engaging look at the challenging and multifaceted lives of the people who work around the clock to ensure that lights protect mariners along the coast.

These are the voices that share their experiences and bring insight to the pages of *Complicated Simplicity*. And as all these voices attest, there are many ways of understanding islands and their compelling roles in culture, society, and people's lives. As Richard Nelson notes, "Even with all the study and reflection that surrounds islands, their meanings are not fully revealed. The mystery and complexity

of an island...that it defies all but the faintest comprehension—
even in a lifetime of intense, thoughtful experience—is a fact worth
celebrating."[51]

(2)

THE PERFECT ISLAND

I treasure the notion that acquiring Bath Island was a wonderfully spontaneous decision. We went ashore, fell in love, and made a commitment. I still recall the exuberant sail back to Vancouver. Mom and Dad marvelled at the island's beauty, character, and proximity to Gabriola and Vancouver. And as the trip went by, I expect they were increasingly bemused about how it would fit within busy lives. As a ten-year-old, I was entranced by the notion of homesteading, accessorized with bonnet and apron. There was no looking back.

Serendipitous? Perhaps. But years of exploring the coast and a desire for a piece of recreational property had, no doubt, shaped Mom and Dad's appreciation of the special nature of the island and its fit with their personalities, values, and interests. They knew that the island suited their needs, even if they didn't know the degree to which it would shape their lives. Years later, Roger Boshier, who bought Bath Island from Mom and Dad in 1986, commented that he thought it was "very beautiful and unique, being the closest Gulf Island, other than Bowen Island, to Vancouver."

FOR MOST PEOPLE, fulfilling an island dream involves myriad and protracted debates, choices, and decisions. The brochure of an island realty company cautions that "finding your perfect island is a process that may take a significant amount of time, and may actually become an obsession. There's even a term for it—'islomania'—and it is understandably easy to catch."[1] Islomania is not classified by Western science as a disease. Lawrence Durrell, however, describes "islomanes" as having a rare affliction of spirit. "There are people who find islands somehow irresistible. The mere knowledge that they are in a little world surrounded by sea fills them with an indescribable intoxication."[2]

Searching for an island

THERE ARE TWO reasons why island searches may be time-consuming and complex. One is the rarity of properties on small islands off the ferry grid, at least compared with properties on the mainland or larger islands with ferry service. This is not for want of islands in the Pacific Northwest. The coast of BC stretches 965 kilometres as the crow flies. Indentations extend it to over 27,000 kilometres. Sailor and travel writer Jonathan Raban comments that he has "never seen charts on which land and sea were so intricately tangled, in a looping scribble of blue and beige."[3] We are fortunate in our array of Pacific Northwest islands. They are one of the world's richest island treasuries. There are estimated to be 40,000 islands along this convoluted coastline.[4] This seems to offer considerable choice. But many are remote, inappropriate for residency, or under land-use designations that exclude private ownership.

Indigenous peoples have made year-round and seasonal homes on the most favoured islands for well over 10,000 years. Today many First Nations communities and individuals continue the traditions of their ancestors. Most live on islands now designated as reserve lands (IR on charts) that were set aside under Canada's Indian Act, beginning in the 1870s. These bounded places do not begin to reflect the intimate and complex relationships that Indigenous people have had with their much broader traditional territories along the coast. Not surprisingly, many Indigenous islanders are islomanes with deep roots. They are passionate about the ways that islands and surrounding waters frame their worlds, shape their heritage, define their lives. "Stories, dances, songs, art, and cultural teachings are ways of remembering, of understanding this world," maintains Joe Martin, whose Tla-o-qui-aht ancestors have treasured Echachis Island at the mouth of Clayoquot Sound for millennia. With few exceptions, individuals do not own islands and other lands under First Nations tenure. Instead bands manage them as part of a communal land base. This tenure system, combined with strong and complex family and community ties, draws many First Nations together in village settings on islands along the coast.

Even as reserve lands were being designated in the mid- to late-nineteenth century, long stretches of British Columbia's "magnificently eventful"[5] coastline were also being set aside as provincial Crown land, in keeping with Western approaches to land use and ownership. Many stretches of the coast are managed as timber supply areas; others are set aside for recreation. And areas such as Barkley Sound and the Great Bear Rainforest have more recently been given additional protection through park and protected area status. These public lands provide a haven for squatters who, while hard to track, follow a long tradition of "adverse possession" in philosophical resistance to Western notions of land title. Avoiding the costs and complications of ownership may be another motive. British Columbia law no longer recognizes squatters' rights to land title after twenty years of uninterrupted occupancy on Crown land, nor does it have any provision for pre-emption. An amendment to the Lands Act in 1970 eliminated these long-standing methods of acquiring islands.[6]

If you're looking for island property, your best bet may be to look where immigrants settled, starting in the nineteenth century. Islands near upcoast communities are often in private hands. And islands in Clayoquot Sound, the Georgia Basin, and archipelagos stretching north through Desolation Sound, the Discovery Islands, the Broughtons, and the US San Juans offer the greatest opportunities for private ownership. Early homesteaders pre-empted much of this land in quarter sections and made basic improvements—houses, clearings—to meet government requirements. Many of these properties have been further subdivided for recreational and year-round residences, since many farming and resource-based communities along the coast became economically unviable in the final decades of the twentieth century.

Another source of BC island property is privately held forest land that is being divested by logging companies. Such properties may be for sale because generations of trees have been harvested or because the owner finds the land of greater value for subdivision. It is likely that you will find second-growth timber and remnants of camps, roads, cut-blocks, log dumps, and booming grounds on these properties. The possibility of using existing woodlots to generate income might add to their appeal.

Not surprisingly, island properties for sale, even in remoter coastal areas, are not numerous and can be expensive, though not nearly as expensive as waterfront properties in and around urban settings. Websites offer appealing images and descriptions. A handful of realtors specialize in such properties in the Pacific Northwest and beyond, and play helpful roles in arranging access and providing advice. Other island properties change hands through word of mouth as families face the reality that they cannot sustain their island lifestyle or as children dispose of acreages, homes, or summer cabins. If you lack personal connections, finding and inspecting available properties involves keeping an ear to the ground. It helps to have a good sense of your motivations so that you can act quickly if the perfect island presents itself.

Affordability is an obvious concern. For my parents, $11,500 was a stretch in 1962 and had to be covered by a mortgage. This purchase price was roughly equivalent to their annual income. Since that time, there has been an exponential increase in values, largely because islands are a finite resource in an increasingly affluent global marketplace. A similar island today would be valued at well over $1 million, certainly more than most islanders' annual income. No matter how you look at it, purchasing an island is a major undertaking. But given the specialized nature of islands, as Misty Lawson points out, it is more likely to be an investment in yourself, in your soul, than in your financial portfolio. One way or another, pricing islands is subjective. Assessed values rarely reflect market values, comparisons among unique islands are challenging, and the nature of amenities varies. At the same time, the market for island properties is relatively small and selective. A Connecticut realtor comments that island properties are less expensive than mainland waterfront "because they appeal to only a select and adventurous few willing to put up with what most people consider as inconveniences." He speaks from experience when he says that "everybody immediately falls in love with the idea...Then they start thinking about problems such as bringing fuel out in an inflatable tank or taking their own garbage back to shore. Islands are very special but they're not for everyone."[7]

Look carefully at ads. Realtors often highlight alluring lifestyles rather than the island itself. This responds to buyers' attraction to the "idea" of the island. Seclusion, relaxation, socializing, swimming, fishing, sailing, cool breezes, and spectacular sunsets feature as prominently in ads as physical characteristics. Descriptions like "rustic," "potential," and "ready for the creation of your dream home" suggest that work might be involved. But this aspect of island living is framed only in positive terms. Who could resist, for example, this realtor's ad: "If...you think your own private island would benefit your health and...you have the odd £11M to spare, consider this. Ginger Island is completely unspoiled, meaning that it has no buildings, services or, indeed, any sort of port. If you are an experienced sailor, or able to dredge your own channel, the heart-shaped island offers complete seclusion and fabulous potential."

And, not surprisingly, considerable turnover in island ownership occurs when imagination is overtaken by reality. You must also anticipate a range of hidden costs, including the need to own and operate a commuter boat, to maintain both island and mainland moorings, and to keep a car somewhere. Arranging financing and insurances can also be challenging, since security services and fire protection might not be readily available.

The other major reason an island search may be protracted is the highly personal process of finding the perfect island, the island that matches your dreams. Let's assume that you're in the market for an island. How will you know it when you see it? Will it be big or little?

Remote or accessible? You will deal with countless questions relating to location, community, access, cost, and character. And just as there is no universal islander, there is no single vision of island perfection to guide your search. It is clear from talking to many islanders that every islomane brings preferences, limitations, and desires to this quest, and these play important roles in island match-making. It may be that, despite the apparent spontaneity of their decision to purchase Bath Island, my parents knew, deep down, that the island was perfectly suited to their emotional and practical needs.

So how would you approach a search? Being clear on why an island lifestyle appeals to you is an important first step. Escape? Prestige? Connection to nature? Challenge? Simplicity? Knowing what your ideal experience should look like creates a filter for evaluating an island's characteristics.

Surrounding waters

THE NATURE OF encircling waters seems like a logical starting point in identifying the perfect island. In many ways, enisling waters are *the* common and defining feature of most island experiences. Water is the dynamic counterpoint to the solidity of the island, constantly in motion, constantly challenging you to adapt and respond. It profoundly influences everything from the shape and nature of the island to its degree of separation. It creates context, sets the endlessly level horizon, and changes daily. For many people, water lies at the emotional heart of an island's attraction. In her account of life on Quadra, Hilary Stewart reflects that she remains puzzled why islands are so special. "Perhaps it is the element of the sea enclosing a defined space. Islands (small, of course, as they should be) allow for easy access to the sea—the sights, the sounds, the scents, and the rich life that abounds on, under and at the edge."[8]

Psychologists tell us that the innate appeal of bodies of water is linked with our evolutionary trajectory, our first experiences in the womb, and water's life-giving role. Beyond this visceral connection, the aesthetic, therapeutic, emotional, economic, and recreational dynamics of water contribute to people's profound sense of attraction. Like our bodies, our planet is 70 percent water. Eighty percent of the world's population lives, works, and plays in proximity to oceans, seas, lakes, or rivers. And for centuries physicians have recognized water's healing potential. As many researchers note, coastal areas, beaches, and inland waterways provide three major benefits: lower stress levels, increased physical activity, and social connections.

Neuroscientists tell us that deep-seated and inscrutable emotions are at play. Wallace Nichols conducts research on the psychological, chemical, and structural processes that underlie our subjective responses to bodies of water. He comments that beyond its physiological value, the most profound benefits of water are emotional. People everywhere love being in proximity to water and go to great effort and expense to be on or around it for recreation, adventure, relaxation, and socializing. Even as he reflects on the compelling draw of water, Nichols notes that measuring the nature or extent of this very human response is difficult.[9] But he reports that people who make their lives near water—in urban, rural, and island settings—indicate a high sense of life satisfaction. Strong connections to nature, a sense of (potential) freedom, fascination with the ever-changing dynamics of the marine environment, and appreciation of its restorative, aesthetic, and inspirational values also contribute to the powerful cognitive and emotional lure of coastal and marine environments. Melville captures that sense in *Moby Dick*. "There is magic in it...as every one knows, meditation and water are wedded forever."[10]

It follows that this intrinsic desire for proximity to water is particularly pronounced among current and prospective islanders. By choosing a sea-bounded landscape, particularly a remote one not served by ferries, you connect in profound practical and emotional ways to the seascape and intertidal zones that define your island and that offer constantly changing moods, rhythms, and experiences. Michael Modzelewski, who learned a great deal about himself during a sojourn on a remote island in Blackfish Sound, writes about the role of water in the island experience. "On the islands, the surrounding sea enters your subconscious, creating a rippling mirror that reflects reality...The world around constantly flows in many levels, swirling deep fathoms into you, loosening holdfasts and safeguards, stirring up sediment, provoking protean change."[11] Almost all the islanders I spoke with are drawn to the water for its range of pleasures and for the way it defines island life. David, who travels by plane, car, ferry, and then private boat to a remote upcoast island in the Discovery group, reflects, "We realize that so much of this place is the journey— it wouldn't be the same if you could get here in five minutes from Vancouver. We call this the 'back of beyond.' It's accessible, but it's remote and that journey across water makes it that way." Islanders everywhere are challenged and stimulated by the skill and vigilance needed to negotiate potentially dangerous marine environments.

Whether you feel drawn to water or not, it's important to think deeply about how surrounding waters might shape your day-to-day experiences, positive and negative. Water temperature, for a start, influences the nature of your island. Equatorial islands are famous for balmy waters that nurture coral reefs and create tropical ecosystems, complete with coconuts, sharks, and typhoons. By contrast, arctic islands are rarely free of a mantle of ice that has its own ecological and logistical implications.

Along the temperate coast of British Columbia, nearshore surface temperatures are cool. For the most part, they range from seven degrees Celsius in winter to around thirteen degrees Celsius in high summer[12] on all parts of the coast. These waters are rich in shellfish and other forms of sea life, but you don't want to swim without a wetsuit or a survival suit. How important is waterplay in your island experience? Few people swim in the thirteen-degree water of Haro Strait near the San Juan Islands. But the farther north you go in the Georgia Basin on Vancouver Island's east coast, the more you encounter warm water in protected, shallow, or stratified areas.

Sea state (most often understood as wave height) is an even more important factor. Its restless energy affects every aspect of access, boat operation, and personal safety. Coastal topography, air temperature, and pressure systems all determine wind. Wind, in turn, influences sea state, in conjunction with fetch, tides, currents, ocean swells, and wave patterns. These complex dynamics vary regionally, even locally. The *British Columbia Regional Marine Weather Guide*[13] combined with the *National Marine Weather Guide*[14] offer a surprisingly fascinating analysis of weather and sea state patterns along the coast. Although sea conditions may appear chaotic, it's reassuring to read that "changes in the winds and weather off the coast of British Columbia are parts of patterns that can be recognized."[15]

These patterns have a major impact on island life. On Bath Island, for example, waves created by prevailing winter southeasterlies have a long fetch up Georgia Strait from the San Juans, sixty kilometres south. A rising gale in the middle of the night, signalled by rippling shingles on the east side of the A-frame, promises crashing swells by morning. And while Bath Island's dock is somewhat protected at this point of wind, the twenty-minute trip to Silva Bay is sure to be lumpy and often cold and wet. We knew how to plan our passage relative to the wind and waves to minimize discomfort. But the need for caution was always there, especially if high tides stirred up logs and deadheads. Conversely, high summer northwesterlies bring sunshine and usually blow for three days. These fierce winds funnel straight down the channel toward the dock, making departures and landings rough if current is against wind. Although adjacent islands offer a bit of protection from swells building in the strait, passages to Silva Bay are often bouncy, with lots of spray. These trips never seemed particularly dire in warm sunshine. But when northwesterlies kicked up in the winter, fuelled by williwaws crossing glaciers at the head of upcoast inlets, trips were cold, sometimes difficult.

Even if you find the constantly changing marine milieu one of the great appeals of your perfect island, being attentive to potential dangers is prudent. Passages that may appear benign in the dog days of summer when you are most likely to fall in love with your island may become perilous in winter storms. Wind against current, cornering effects around headlands, confused seas off cliffs and in shallowing areas, gusty outflow winds from mainland fiords, and "great and perplexing"[16] tidal patterns, rapids, and whirlpools all affect how and when passages to the island are best negotiated. They also test your boating skills. Winds of fifty knots or more are periodically encountered in the Strait of Georgia. They bring ferry and other marine traffic to a halt. Michael Modzelewski observes the changeable character of local conditions farther north in the Broughton Archipelago. "The Inside Passage is thought by outsiders to be gentle ocean, calm corridors of water between island buffers. The reality is that the Passage contains some of the most dangerous water in the world. Those corridors can act as wind funnels, and many islands jumble tides and stack up steep waves."[17]

The approach to Tofino can be tricky as ocean waves and strong tides converge. Locals know how patterns vary, depending on the shapes of islands, locations of reefs, and wind. And conditions can change quickly. Joe Martin, who travels these waters in an open boat, emphasizes that it is vital to move in tune with tide, current, and wind. "Inside of a few minutes it can be very, very nasty." Being aware, recognizing developing weather systems, plotting courses below buffering islands, and being flexible about comings and goings are all part of island living.

Weather patterns that affect sea state also determine your perfect island's microclimate. Hours of annual sunshine and rainfall, seasonal temperatures, and the prevalence of fog all influence the livability of an island. They shape everything from gardening to house design to mood. Living in the Mediterranean climate of the San Juan and Gulf Islands with eighty-nine centimetres of annual rainfall feels quite different from living along the west coast of Vancouver Island or BC's central and northern coasts. In the latter places, rainfall is three to four times greater. And coping with late-summer blankets of fog on days when travel can't be delayed can be frustrating. Nevertheless, these are favoured shores. Long ago the *British Columbia Pilot* (1888) observed that "taken as a whole, the climate, differing widely as it does in places, is salubrious and invigorating. No miasmatic infection from ague-breeding marshes taints the atmosphere whatever locality may be selected for a residence...The climate will be found healthful, invigorating, and calculated to inspire activity, comparing more than favourably with the same latitude on the Atlantic slope."[18]

Island landscapes

TOPOGRAPHY, DEFINED AS "the arrangement of the natural and artificial physical features of an area," is another key consideration, since "geography makes every island to varying degrees its own world."[19] The peaks of hills and mountains that rise from the seabed to form islands take a variety of shapes, depending on location and geographic dynamics. British Columbia's coast, in most locations, is a dramatic intersection of mountains and ocean. Powerful tectonic and volcanic forces have raised the Pacific, Kitimat, and Boundary Ranges to towering heights, divided by precipitous fiords. In Princess Louisa Inlet and Desolation Sound, for example, a vessel can sit alongside a sheer cliff with over seven hundred metres of sea under its keel. This gives an odd sense of being suspended on a watery membrane above mysterious depths. The only footholds are small river estuaries, often exposed to unpredictable outflow winds. Most shorelines, however, have gentler profiles, with shallowing foreshores that offer a wealth of intertidal life. These also create navigational hazards that deserve respect.

With few exceptions, the topography along the continental shelf in the Pacific Northwest is archipelagic: mazes of islands, delineated by intersecting channels that hide the connecting seabed. We talk of the San Juan, Gulf, Discovery, or Broughton Islands, for example. These geographic webs, combined with wind, weather, and many other factors, establish ecological character. Your perfect island may have dense forests overhanging steep granite shorelines if it lies to the north, or sculpted sandstone bluffs and beaches fringed with arbutus and Garry oak if it is tucked alongside Vancouver Island's eastern shore. For the most part, these terrains are underlaid by intrusive igneous rock, offset in places by folded and faulted metamorphic and sedimentary materials that have oozed up.

Plants and wildlife are rich and varied on coastal islands. Naturalist Alison Watt spent four months studying puffins at one of BC's most remote bird sanctuaries. She comments that "like thousands of islands scattered over these waters, where the hem of the continent unravels, Triangle [Island] is a lifeboat far from shore, carrying creatures whose histories are woven into both land and sea."[20] Depending on location, climate, and proximity to other landforms, the perfect island may feature a remarkable cycle of life. Wolves, bears, deer, elk, and raccoons feed on the voles, mice, rats, shellfish, and other creatures found along the shoreline. Otters and mink are common, moving comfortably in both marine and terrestrial environments. Mosquitos, horseflies, wasps, and other nuisances provide food for diverse birds, ranging from sparrows and robins to eagles and vultures. And, of course, ever-present gulls feed on almost anything that comes their way. Migratory birds mark the passage of seasons. Spruce, hemlock, cedar, fir, and yew shelter animals in their shadowed depths. They share islands with deciduous oak, dogwood, and maple. Arbutus ranges from the San Juans to Desolation Sound, punctuating dark shorelines with its contorted red limbs. And salal, sword ferns, ocean spray, flowering currant, blackberry, huckleberry, and Oregon grape form dense understoreys that resist penetration.

The interplay of conditions and species on islands is dynamic, always seeking equilibrium. Island biogeographers tell us that the number and richness of species is a function of the distance of these isolated ecosystems from other landforms. The farther an island is from a source of immigrant species to replace resident species that are becoming extinct, the greater the challenge in achieving balance. The characteristics of the island, including size, habitat, human activity, and ocean currents, also influence island biogeography.[21] The Galapagos Islands provide a wonderful environment for the study of the ways new gene pools arise through a process of natural selection in truly insular settings.

Not surprisingly, immigrant and invasive plants and animals create havoc in sensitive ecosystems with few defensive systems. English ivy, holly, broom, and daphne choke out indigenous vegetation on many islands, even as drying climate conditions thin the understorey and starve water-loving native plants. And deer, both native black-tailed and introduced fallow deer, are overwhelming established ecosystems in the absence of their traditional predators. At the same time, displaced predators have an increasing presence on more remote islands, seeking food along the shores and upland areas. For example, grizzlies have been seen swimming to islands adjacent to Vancouver Island and wolves are commonly encountered on the west and central coasts. And people are the most invasive species of all. They change the balance of their perfect islands' fragile ecosystems as they cut trees, build roads and breakwaters, construct buildings, dispose of waste, introduce exotic plants, include dogs and cats in their households, and overharvest native plants and animals. Thoughtful ecological stewardship is critical to maintaining the very qualities that attract people to islands in the first place. Misty Lawson, whose family has lived on one of the rugged islands at the mouth of Clayoquot Sound for decades, emphasizes the importance of respect for the animals whose territory they share. "You learn so much from the experience of being around wildlife. Just watch a deer—it is so attuned to its environment, to other animals. You need to get to know wild animals instead of being impatient with them, instead of seeing them as a problem. In seeking to displace them, we're valuing the wrong things. Integrating a love for the natural world is vital to life."

Water is a perennial concern for islanders. Most of BC's islands receive ample seasonal rainfall as moisture-laden winds from the Pacific hit coastal mountains. But ensuring a reliable and consistent source of fresh water is critical to island living. "Water, water everywhere, nor any drop to drink" has particular relevance for islanders on rocky sites. An island's topography helps determine its capacity to capture and hold fresh water, as my parents knew from the minute they set foot on Bath and Saturnina Islands. Despite the islands' proximity to each other (they are also known as the Twin Islands), they are different. Saturnina is an uplifted, elongated rocky wedge with cliffs on its west and north sides and a steeply sloping sandstone beach to the south and east. It has one of the most beautiful double-sided shingle beaches in the Gulf Islands. A skim of soil supports trees and underbrush, but there is no sign of the conditions that would support a well. Bath Island, just a hundred metres to the east, is vaguely triangular in shape, with a central valley that features rich soil. It captures and holds sufficient water for a year-round—but limited—supply of brackish water. This was a huge asset in many aspects of island life, although it was still necessary to capture or transport palatable drinking water. Some islands have lakes or aquifers that provide excellent water. Others have nothing and require catchment, desalination, or transportation systems.

While water is vital to island living, it is possible to have too much. The rain that often accompanies extended clouds and wind contributes to island fever. As well it complicates gardening by rotting crops on the vine, acidifying soils, and leaching nutrients. Boggy land on or adjacent to your property can also cause problems. On one of the prettiest Gulf Islands, for example, a long shallow pond meanders along its middle. Fringed by bulrushes, the pond is attractive from a distance. But no mention is made in real estate ads of the stagnant odour, swarms of summer mosquitos, or rumbling noise of frogs at dusk.

Like fresh water, arable soil is a precious commodity, particularly if you want to create either vegetable gardens or landscape features. Most undeveloped islands are dense with trees, along with an understorey of brush that must be cleared—and held back—to create building and garden sites. And where open meadows on south sides of islands promise easy access, you may find they offer shallow and dry growing conditions. Potential for landscaping or gardening is a personal preference but may be worth considering in the pursuit of perfection.

Shape and orientation also help define your perfect island. Long and narrow? Round? Large enough to grow hay, keep horses, build an airstrip or a workshop? Small enough that surrounding waters are visible at every turn? From a functional perspective, the perfect island should allow you to pursue your interests, feel engaged throughout the seasons, and enjoy extended stays. If the stereotypical desert island with its single palm tree had more diversity, I suspect stranded sailors would be less anxious to leave. From an aesthetic perspective, expansive views that showcase the interplay of island and marine environments seem desirable, particularly if they are linked with a sunny, protected, and well-placed building site. At the end of a long working day, the view from a deck serves as an important reminder of your reasons for being on an island. It follows that evaluating potential views is an important part of the search for a perfect island. Will you be looking at a pulp mill? A clear-cut? A ferry landing that operates until late in the evening? Do the sun and moon rise and set at desirable angles? And does high-bank waterfront afford a spectacular perch for overseeing surrounding waters, or does it inhibit easy access to more intimate beaches?

The confluence of land and water

ISLANDS, OF COURSE, are more than their upland features. Most also include fascinating beaches. These serve as "ecotones," or transition zones, where upland and marine ecosystems intersect to create unique and dynamic environments. "There are large islands whose shores have little impact on their interiors, but, for most islands, where the shore to interior ratio is greater, the ecotone is a largely underexplored dimension of island life."[22] Shorelines are where much of the action is. While upland areas are subject to gradual seasonal changes, the liminal space between land and water is in constant flux. Tides rise and fall, offshore rocks and weather shape wave action, and various animals, driftwood, and detritus appear and disappear. Richard Nelson is the author of a lyrical memoir of a year visiting a north coast island. He describes the endlessly fascinating contents of a tide pool.

> Each pool is filled with an array of living things, a little independent universe of movement and color—thickets of slippery kelp and seaweeds, coralline algae, and surf grass; incrustations of scarlet and amber sponge; fleets of purple shore crabs and tiny hermit crabs wearing periwinkle shells; clusters of bottom-hugging sculpins and other darting intertidal fish; patches of barnacles and mussels, scatters of limpets, dog winkles, chitons, and purple urchins; and rare glimpses of brilliant, decorated nudibranchs. Red, yellow, and orange starfish cling to the walls of every pond and crevice. One sand-bottomed pool has a scatter of sunflower starfish.[23]

Ecotones are also vulnerable spaces. Changing environmental conditions, declining water quality, and pollution have worrying impacts. "The intertidal zone is one of the largest and richest of habitats. But it is also, unlike woodlands or savannahs, uniquely distended, stretched, and squeezed, and it is exceptionally fragile and vulnerable to human thoughtlessness."[24] As one of the most productive areas in the world's oceans, the coastal margin of the Pacific Northwest is attracting considerable concern. The Hakai Institute, for example, works with First Nations and local universities to support in-depth research and public education in such areas as archaeology, earth sciences, ecology, microbiology, cultural and natural resource management, and oceanography, placing scholars and students in field settings along both the Georgia Basin and the central coast. Monitoring change, minimizing impact, mitigating threats, and advocating for coastal stewardship are all parts of island living.

The scope and nature of beaches and bluffs that encircle an island also contribute to its appeal. Many hard granite islands north of Powell River have lovely rocky outcroppings that overlook sweeping vistas. But some provide only a bit of sand or shingle for a soft landing spot at middle or low tide. Other islands have sweeping sandy strands that rival the tropics in their appeal. Savary, Thormanby, Sidney, and James Islands in the Georgia Basin, for example, are almost entirely composed of glacial till. And farther north in the provincial marine protected area known as the Hakai Lúxvbálís Conservancy, stunning pockets of golden sand are tucked among granite outcroppings. A shingle beach, another legacy of glaciation, is my favourite type to explore. Wave action stirs these rocky stretches daily, hiding and revealing pebbles worn smooth by millennia of tidal movement.

The "tafoni" sandstone cliffs and beaches of the Southern Gulf Islands are iconic, known for their distinctive weathering patterns, sculptural erosions, and fascinating honeycomb forms, large and small.[25] Malaspina Galleries at the north end of Gabriola, the imposing bluffs along the west side of Valdes, and the sculpted formations at East Point on Saturna are among the most dramatic legacies of constant erosion. All sandstone beaches, however, provide fascinating sinuous patterns in warm, soft, honey-coloured rock. Bath Island, legally 3.2 hectares, expands to almost double that size twice daily. Receding tides reveal sloping sandstone benches and planes, pools, and sandy patches covered with seaweeds and a wealth of small animals. Pocket bays on the north and south edges narrow to tiny, boulder-strewn indentations. And abrupt drop-offs along the north side of the island show where the hill that became the island was side-swiped by glaciers thousands of years ago. This typical pattern of broad sweeping beaches on the southern edges and bluffs to the north affects how and where you can locate docks and position homes on these islands.

With beaches go driftwood, seaweeds, occasional messages in bottles, and other flotsam and jetsam tossed up by the sea. Such places offer endless opportunities for solitary or social beach combing and play. They also contribute in practical ways to island living if wood-fuelled stoves and fireplaces serve as sources of heat. And beaches and intertidal zones provide delicacies. Oysters, clams, mussels, crabs, and seaweeds are there for the taking, as long as the waters are clean and harvesting is sustainable.

Lovely beaches are important on a perfect island. But the most valuable feature at the intersection of water and land is a protected and accessible bay. Ideally it will be navigable at all tides, with room for a secure dock to accommodate one or more sizable commuter vessels. This bay could also offer good holding ground and room to swing at anchor or on a buoy in multiple points of wind. A pleasing beach for swimming and relaxation is nice but probably not necessary. Without secure moorage, life on an island is, at best, tenuous. If a perfect bay isn't available, an effective breakwater (and the necessary funding and permissions for building it) could be a backup strategy.

Stewardship

IF LOCATION AND topography have worked together to create your perfect island, it is probable that other people have also found it attractive. As noted, islands lie within the traditional territories of many different First Nations along the coast and continue to play deeply meaningful roles in their lives. For millennia, coastal First Nations have made these islands their permanent and seasonal homes, harvested the whales, fish, shellfish, plants, and animals needed for day-to-day and feast occasions, travelled widely to visit and trade, and celebrated life and death in sacred locations. It is estimated that prior to the arrival of Europeans in the Pacific Northwest, over fifty thousand Indigenous people lived along the coast.[26]

Many islands bear evidence of long-term use. White shell middens indicate ancient village sites. Piles of whale bones mark the locations of seasonal camps. Petroglyphs, fish weirs, clam farms, culturally modified trees, the remains of dwellings, stone tools, and carved house posts signal past occupancy and use. Burial sites, in particular, are sacred places with "deeply held and strict customary laws, inherited rights, beliefs and cultural practices associated with the care of the dead and their resting places."[27] It goes without saying that all these significant places and cultural resources deserve respect. Developments, including building construction and dock, breakwater, and cable installations, may be subject to both archaeological investigation and permissions from the local First Nation, as specified in BC's Heritage Conservation Act. And jurisdiction over unceded territory and marine resources is the subject of ongoing treaty negotiations in many areas. Conducting island development in a manner that is sensitive to the heritage and current concerns of local First Nations requires time for consultation, resources to cover associated costs, and an appreciation of the depth of history and meaning that these places hold.

In the past two hundred years, coastal islands have also been sites of immigrant exploration, settlement, work, and recreation. The displacement of Indigenous place names with names assigned by settlers speaks of the scope of recent occupation, use, and control. Many islands bear evidence of the forest, mining, whaling, and fishing industries that attracted settlers from Europe, Asia, and elsewhere to this coast. In some cases, early homesteads have evolved into viable farms and appealing residential properties. In others, overgrown roads, derelict equipment, remains of abandoned cabins, and rusted stoves and bedsprings are quiet reminders of abandoned dreams. Roses clambering through brush, old lilacs, unpruned apple trees, feral sheep, and lonely pilings also speak of efforts to make homes. These leave memories on the land but also suggest that if other people have chosen these sites, they may be well suited to new roles.

Contemporary land uses, both near or on an island property, must also be considered in the search for your perfect island. On subdivided islands, legal rights-of-way may allow people to walk through otherwise perfect building sites en route to a beach or viewpoint. Or locals may have long-standing habits of helping themselves to blackberries or apples. Less developed islands might be popular with locals for hunting or camping—or partying. Offshore activities, including oyster and fish farming and booming grounds, can also have an impact on island living.

Islanders have a strong sense of stewardship over all they survey. But they must remember that ownership extends only to the high-tide mark. Below that, the island foreshore is normally under the jurisdiction of the provincial government. The landowner has the right to unimpeded access to and from deep water at any point along the boundary of their island property for the purposes of navigation. Private docks, however, normally require authorization and cannot impede public or neighbours' access to the foreshore. Owners also have the right to reinforce natural boundaries that are subject to erosion. The public can access public lands below the high-tide mark for their enjoyment and have the right to land boats on, or embark from, a foreshore area in cases of emergency. The public also has rights of navigating, anchoring, mooring, and fishing in adjacent waters. But when islanders arrange foreshore leases (as opposed to permits or licences), they can limit public use of the beach or waterways.[28]

Despite legal definitions of tenure, islanders' concern about public uses often goes well below the high-water mark. Most keep an eagle eye on campers and partiers who light fires, as these have the frightening potential to ignite surrounding driftwood and move upland. Waste disposal, noise, personal and commercial overharvesting of shellfish, and the disappearance of dinghies, kayaks, and paddleboards also worry islanders. And if you are seeking year-round privacy and quiet in your perfect location, it may be wise to avoid popular anchorages that attract hundreds, perhaps thousands, of boaters during high summer. The intrusive sound of generators can ruin an otherwise perfect evening for boaters and islanders alike.

Other considerations

IN THINKING ABOUT your perfect island, keep in mind that the maze of islands in the Pacific Northwest spreads along a 27,000-kilometre coastline. Some, like Eagle Island nestled alongside West Vancouver, are intimately connected to an urban environment. But most islands are more remote, even isolated, from towns and other settlements. Proximity to desired services is therefore another key consideration in your quest for the perfect island, and one that is highly subjective, depending on your social, medical, economic, and logistical concerns. For example, Emily and Tom, who live on Protection Island near Nanaimo, pursue professional careers in town while also living a life of deliberate simplicity on island. And Roger emphasizes the importance of mainland access and proximity to the services you value. He says that "the perfect island is one where you could live your entire life, not just holidays and weekends. You could live in such a way that life was just as productive as if you were living not on the island."

The distance to convenient access and supply points will influence the cost and complexities involved in getting to your island, along with the ways that you keep it supplied, welcome friends, sustain an appealing lifestyle, and deal with emergencies. And even if your island is not directly served by a ferry, you may find that you have to take one or more expensive and time-consuming ferry trips from the nearest town before your final passage by private boat or water taxi. Being twice, even three times removed from supply centres, by virtue of the number of ferry and boat trips involved, can present logistical challenges.

The perfect island also conforms with your social preferences. Do you enjoy your own company, or would you prefer to be part of a community of like-minded islanders? My parents were happy with the relative isolation and self-sufficiency inherent in owning a private island, although they turned to nearby marinas and towns for various supplies from time to time. They were slowly welcomed to the Gabriola Island community as they worked, shopped, and exchanged stories over the years. But I don't think they took the nature of that community into consideration in their decision to move to Bath Island. Nor did they ask local people to lend a hand with the many tasks involved in settling and living on an island. Instead they relied on their own resourcefulness, their daughters, and occasional help from sailing friends. Sailors were also their social circle, so my parents enjoyed visits and barbecues on beaches and boats in the summer but saw little of these friends in the winter months.

If you live on an island with others, however, settling in generally involves entry into a community and befriending a group of "personalities" with varied social and political values. On some subdivided islands, interactions are primarily social—or at least cordial—as each owner makes his or her own way, lends a hand as needed, and shares a common love for the place. In other cases, particularly on larger islands, owners work collectively to create and maintain shared wharves, roads, airstrips, firefighting protocols and equipment, island management strategies, and such improvements as power, water, and waste systems. They might also collaborate in arranging for barged supplies or organizing work bees. The social dynamics and administrative complexities of such communities are not unlike those of strata councils. As shared assets, projects, and expenses evolve, the degree of order and accountability may trouble people seeking an independent lifestyle. In such situations, you might encounter tensions between those who live on island year-round and those who are seasonal or occasional occupants.

Local governments also play a role in shaping community and monitoring the regulatory aspects of your life on island. For example, over 220 islands and islets in BC's Georgia Basin are within the jurisdiction of the Islands Trust, formed in 1974. Its board and staff preserve and protect the islands' unique amenities and environment. To do this, they work with local trust committees and staff of adjacent regional districts to oversee land-use planning and development, administer building codes, monitor ecological well-being, enforce land-use bylaws, and determine the nature of services provided. Residents require permission to install docks, ramps, stairs, and boathouses along shorelines. Building design and siting, tree cutting, and ramps and stairways for beach access require authorization and inspection. This is complicated by the challenges of arranging officials' visits. On one hand, regulatory systems protect the very qualities of island life many seek. On the other, they fly in the face of islanders' desire to escape external controls.

If you are seeking a less regulated environment, you could look farther north to find an island where fewer controls are in place. But no places (aside from those occupied by squatters) are immune from government oversight. Archaeological and environmental impact, permits for fish farms and shellfish harvesting, compliance with building codes, occupancy permits, and health and safety regulations on land and at sea may be less easily scrutinized in remote areas, but they still impose clear expectations on island life.

And finally, you should consider the costs of an ideal island lifestyle. Does the perfect property have an existing dock, house, and outbuildings, and are they appealing and in good shape? If new construction is required, you need to acquire the many tools, materials, and supplies needed for building on island and transport them to the island. What are the annual taxes? And have you thought about acquiring and operating boats, island vehicles, and other equipment, as well as making provision for mainland mooring and parking? A caretaker may be required for maintenance or security purposes. I heard again and again that island living is not an inexpensive alternative to city living. There are many expenses, both expected and unexpected, that demand resources. And your ability to earn a living might be an issue. Practical islanders will consider whether capital and operating costs are less than those encountered for a mainland household. They might also enquire whether a reasonable return on island investments seems likely, should the need to sell arise. This is the point at which the value of island living—as opposed to the cost—must also come into play. Connections with nature, escape from urban pressures, and the numerous satisfactions of making a home on an island presumably outweigh financial considerations.

As the perfect island weaves its way into the hearts of islanders, some express a profound shift in their sense of tenure and stewardship. The owner of the Shiant Islands in the Hebrides feels that he does not have the right to exclude others from these special places."[29] Closer to home in the San Juan Islands, Chic sees himself as a guardian of the two San Juan Island properties that he and his wife, Kathy, own and care for. "It's so much better for an island to be owned and managed by somebody with a sense of stewardship." A slightly different take on ownership is offered by a Thetis Island resident who says, "Over the years I have come to understand that I don't own this acreage...it owns me and I am happily enslaved."[30]

Fulfilling an island dream is complicated by many factors. But islanders tell me that as they develop a personal sense of the qualities they value, the search narrows, the choices become more straightforward. The hard work of pondering motivations and finding the perfect island may discourage some people. For those who persevere, the act of acquiring and making a life on an island is a deeply satisfying experience. And as Roger Boshier says, it doesn't matter how deliberate you are in choosing an island: the notion is always a bit crazy. Moving to an island, particularly one off the ferry grid, is a profoundly personal, unusual, perhaps irrational impulse.

(3)

SEA ROOM

It is ironic that the boat that brought us to the island was not the boat that met our island needs. *Whereaway*, a much-loved thirty-seven-foot, double-ended sloop designed by Bill Garden, was the perfect vessel for exploring the coast. Seaworthy, comfortable, and eventually rigged with one of the first aluminum masts on the coast, this boat allowed us to travel the waters from Haida Gwaii to Vancouver. Once Bath Island came into our lives, however, *Whereaway* transformed from a pampered pleasure vessel to a workhorse. We lived aboard for six months and used it to make regular trips to Vancouver and Nanaimo for supplies. Its seventy-horsepower Cummins diesel (the kind of engine my dad loved) came into its own as the boat towed an eight-by-sixteen-foot barge to and from Vancouver or Nanaimo repeatedly for the summer it took to construct the house.

Once we moved to the island, *Whereaway* sat at Page's Marina in Silva Bay. The boat rarely left the dock for pleasure trips as Mom and Dad's fascination with island life replaced their compulsion to cruise. Teak was neglected, brass unpolished, and plans for upcoast explorations abandoned. In the mid-1960s the boat became an odd-looking troller. Dad installed poles, gurdies, and a stern cockpit for two memorable years of commercial fishing near Prince Rupert (more about that later). And for a number of years *Whereaway* made weekly commutes to Vancouver so that Dad could return to work in the forest industry. During this period the boat served as a tidy home in Coal Harbour, although Dad complained that his clothes smelled of diesel. *Whereaway* was no longer the centre of family activity. The boat took a back seat to the island, particularly as other more suitable boats came into our lives.

The first was *Tubby*, a carvel design eleven-foot open dinghy powered by a Seagull, "the best outboard motor for the world." It was a pretty little boat and had enough freeboard for even bouncy crossings to Silva Bay. The following year, it became backup to *Molly*, a clinker-built vessel that, at 14 feet, seemed much more grand. This boat got its name from the musical *The Unsinkable Molly Brown*. A windshield protected the steering wheel and forward bench. A five-horsepower Briggs & Stratton engine sat amidships, and seating and cargo space lay behind. Never fast, almost always steady, *Molly* made countless twenty-five-minute trips from the island to Silva Bay in all kinds of weather, with all kinds of loads.

Molly plays a major role in my memories of island life. Clair and I soon learned to operate the boat quite happily, choosing various routes to Silva Bay according to tide and wind. It was our commuter boat, supply vessel, and link to a bit of independence. We would head off to school at 7 AM—in the dark at midwinter—and make the passage to Silva Bay, where we caught the school bus to the ferry that delivered us to Nanaimo. We always missed the first fifteen minutes of junior and senior high. At the end of the day, the ferry and school bus would deliver us back to Silva Bay around 5 PM. We'd coax the engine to start, cast off, and head home. On dark winter afternoons, when we came around the point of Tugboat Island, we'd see a pinpoint of light on the dock, cast by a coal-oil lantern that my mother had set out. It was years later that Mom confided that the only thing that worried her about island living was watching her young daughters heading out in the morning. Long before cell phones, she never knew if we reached Silva Bay until we returned to the island in the early evening.

AS CELIA THAXTER said more than a century ago, islanders "must have sea-room."[1] The island experience is as intimately connected with the surrounding—and separating—waters as it is with the island itself. And choosing an island without ferry service adds a fascinating layer of complication to what is already a distinctive lifestyle. Patterns of coming and going are unique to each islander, shaped by wind, tide, distance, and need. Well-founded boats are crucial, as are seamanship and maintenance skills. You sleep better if you know that your moorage is secure. Provisioning by boat involves both planning and a strong back. Airplanes and water taxis take on appealing new roles. And the pleasures—and occasional fears—of being on the water reinforce, even define, the island experience.

Passage making

IN MANY WAYS, the island experience starts at the mainland dock, where the physical and mental transition begins. Loading the boat—or plane—is a reminder that islands are separate, away. What is missing? Have you planned properly? Casting off is a liberating moment that leaves the mainland behind, entering the between space that sets the island apart. It also signals a change of pace, a disconnection from mainland living, and a step toward a slower island sense of time. Islanders everywhere comment on the pleasure of marine passages. Rob Wood on Maurelle says, "Up here, every time we go out on the water, heading to the island or taking the kids to school, every time we go out on the water, it's like, 'Ahhhhhhh.' The act of being on the water, exposing yourself to its ambience, the vibrations, the things that are going on around you and, at the same, releasing stress … you get a natural high, you become conscious, you open your mind."

Passages offer time for thinking, planning, anticipating, or simply enjoying the movement of the boat, the feel of the water. But when sea conditions are difficult, passages demand complete attention. Every wave has to be anticipated, and decisions on approach are taken in the moment, with one eye on what lies beyond. Regardless of conditions, scanning for logs, crab traps, and other boats is a constant ritual, as is monitoring position. Most islanders have an intimate knowledge of the chart and are comfortable with wayfinding until fog, rain, snow, or darkness sweep in and a sense of disorientation draws attention to the compass or GPS.

Passage making also heightens awareness of tide and current. Islanders constantly monitor the state of the tide, observing the force of the current, profiles of rocks, the flow of seaweed, the position of boats at anchor, the snaking bands of foam and detritus, and the look of the beach. They know when to avoid shallow patches, where to take advantage of invisible rivers of current, when shortcuts are safe, and where to cast out a fishing line if time allows. And smart islanders don't fight tides; they use them as aids. They keep tidal patterns and current flows in mind when determining geometries of docks, ramps, and mooring buoys. And they plan their comings and goings, deliveries, work, and play in tune with tides' inevitable thirteen-hour cycles.

Roger Boshier describes three stages in passage making between Bath Island and Vancouver: the beginning, middle, and end. The beginning involves decision making. Is everything aboard? Is the boat in proper running order? Is it safe to go? Are the rituals of "getting away" complete? He reminds himself to check fuel, secure everything, ensure that radio and navigation gear are working, and provide safety orientation to passengers. And he is cautious about sea state. "In bad weather the typical strategy is to 'put the nose' into the strait to take a look. After a few miles bucking big seas or peering into fog or snow, there comes a point where it is almost as far to turn back as plunge forward." The middle is time for commitment, contemplation. "Commuting by boat can be like attending a symphony concert. There is time to think, make lists and consider priorities. Compared to being stuck in freeway traffic or jammed in a bus, there is nothing like the rhythm of a boat." And the end brings a sense of completion. "Arriving at the destination means firm ground, coffee and escape from boat noise." Nonetheless, "arriving in the city involves complications...[and], just as there are 'getting away' rituals, a proper shut down will better ensure the boat is ready when next needed."[2]

As Roger notes, returns are as significant as departures. Getting back to the island, tying up, unloading, and making your way to the house complete the journey. Geri Van Gyn, who lives on Sidney Island, agrees. She describes coming into the dock on a winter afternoon, just as dark falls, as "glorious." It is the moment she truly leaves the mainland behind.

The ideal boat

BOAT AND ENGINE technologies have changed a lot since Mom and Dad created their Bath Island fleet. Rubberized synthetic fabrics, fibreglass, and aluminum have replaced labour-intensive wood in the construction of hulls. And much more powerful outboard and inboard engines have cut travel time and increased safety in remarkable ways. Given the many choices, it is fascinating to talk with islanders about how their tastes, needs, budget, and circumstances affect the boats that they use, and to keep in mind the observation that "no matter what size boat you're in, in the hands of Mother Nature, all boats are small."[3]

Simplicity, for some people, is key. For example, Emily Barnewall and Tom Barchyn almost always travel to and from Protection Island in their kayaks, preferring them to the small commercial passenger ferry most island residents use. It does not take long to cross Nanaimo harbour and, as Tom says, there is no need to struggle with an engine that is reluctant to start. They laugh when they describe the complexities of carrying construction materials or a bicycle in Tom's double kayak. And their kayak was a comfortable and private way to cross to Nanaimo the morning that Emily went into labour with their first child. "The last thing I wanted to do was go on the ferry and have the tourists and others fussing over me...So we got down to the kayak and, after a contraction, I got in and we paddled into town. It was really nice—the waves rocked me. I had two contractions going over, then we got in the car and went to the hospital." Life is a bit more complicated now with two children, but they continue to use kayaks as their primary form of transportation.

Simple vessels also appeal to Judith Wright on Rendezvous Island and reflect her philosophy of paring island life down to the basics. For four decades she and her family have been negotiating tidal currents in and around Surge Narrows, first in the sailboat from which they spotted Rendezvous, and then in a small aluminum speedboat. Now she would like to buy a really nice rowing boat. "I'd never have to do any more monkey wrenching." She goes on to say she could choose her time to cross over to Quadra Island or rely on water taxis in tricky weather or with heavy loads. "It would be a whole different pace. It would be slower. And a rowboat could have enough sleeping accommodation that if I did get stuck somewhere, I'd be comfortable. That would be a fun way to be out on the water. And I wouldn't need to be constantly paying for parts and gas and repairs and upgrades and on and on...it just goes on and on, all the layouts a machine demands."

Island boats tend to be workhorses, built for the multiple challenges that go with lives of complicated simplicity. For example, Gilford Islander Yvonne Maximchuk indicates that she needs a boat that she can "beach and climb in and out of easily. I want it to be powerful enough to tow home a firewood log and fast enough to make a fine-weather run to Port McNeill in an hour and change."[4] Her version of the ideal boat is a sixteen-foot fibreglass speedboat with a fifty-horsepower outboard and a windscreen that offers some protection from wind and rain.

In the wild waters between Tofino and Echachis Island, Joe Martin uses a seaworthy fibreglass Panga from Mexico, driven by a powerful outboard. This open boat, with its upswept bow, flotation bulges along the gunwales, and planing hull, offers the stability, protection, and speed he needs to transit Templar Channel and tuck into the rocky bay on the east side of Echachis. Perpetual swells make for tricky passages, precarious landings.

Aluminum boats, ranging from basic car-toppers to elegant thirty-foot commuters, are the most commonly used vessels among the islanders that I spoke with. A shallow-draft, twenty-three-foot aluminum boat with two fifty-horsepower outboards allowed Misty

Lawson and her parents to make the difficult crossing between Tofino and their remote island and, like Joe, to come ashore on a rocky beach. Their boat sat on a mooring buoy in the bay when not in use. And Linda Harrison, who has spent all her life on Valdes Island, relies on a tough open aluminum skiff with a well-used outboard to make her way through the tidal currents of Gabriola Pass, down the east side of Valdes, and to the protected beach inside the reef outside her house. She is adept at running its bow up onto the shingle beach, unloading groceries, fuel, and other household supplies, and then towing the skiff to an offshore buoy, using a Sport Yak for shore access. When big southeasterlies make the run uncomfortable, she crosses to the sheltered north end of Valdes where an old logging road offers overland access to the house. Rugged, practical, open, and seaworthy, Linda's aluminum boat has served her well since her husband built it in the 1980s.

A very similar boat serves Laurie and Rob on Maurelle Island, where even more challenging tidal rapids also demand power and astute seamanship. A planing hull allows them to skim the surface of tidal races that sometimes achieve sixteen knots. But that wasn't always the case. When they first moved to Maurelle in the '70s, the more common displacement hulls and smaller engines on their "low-budget" boats meant that every trip to and from the island had to be planned to coincide with slack water. Social lives, off-island work, supply runs, kids' schooling, and access to help were all regulated by the powerful ebb and flow of water through the aptly named Surge Narrows. And even now at times it is necessary to find another way home. "If we're coming back from town and get through the rapids and the final section is too bad in a big blow, we nip around to the south end of the island, we beach the skiff, and we have a half-hour walk to get to the house."

Several islanders opt for more skookum aluminum boats, with powerful engines and with cabins that afford year-round shelter, a galley, sleeping space, and a much greater cruising range. Frank and Geri use a twenty-seven-foot Lifetimer almost daily in all weathers to make the eight-kilometre trip to and from nearby Sidney. It has carried everything from slate, cedar trees, lumber, and windows to chickens, peacocks, and hay. Several lifts of concrete had it so low in the water one day that they were a bit concerned about getting to the island. Another day they towed four water tanks rather than going to the trouble of booking a barge. I'd love to have seen their slow progress. Frank tells a funny story about a precarious experience towing a forty-foot mast that he had acquired to support wind vanes and a generator. He secured one end to the boat and the other to an inflatable dinghy, and headed out. The inflatable began to take on water, and they had an eventful passage keeping the far end afloat. Their workboat, like Mom and Dad's, replaced a much-loved sailboat. But they still find time for occasional excursions along the coast and take considerable pleasure in making the passage from Sidney Island to meet us at Silva Bay in less than an hour, while we take up to ten hours in our sailboat. And the similar twenty-five-foot Eaglecraft that David and Suromitra now use to access their island property is, in many ways, the epitome of an island commuter. It is seaworthy, powerful, and fun. They make trips in almost any weather and can explore local fiords and islands for days on end. And as they acquired it after the bulk of their construction work was done, it has none of the scrapes and dents typical of island boats.

Aluminum has been the material of choice for Roger as well. Like many islanders, he first visited Bath Island on a sailboat. He turned to a vessel better suited to the practicalities of island life once he moved there in 1987. His twenty-six-foot welded aluminum boat from Trinity Marine, powered by an inboard 250-horsepower diesel engine, plays diverse roles. Because Roger commuted to Vancouver to teach at the University of British Columbia for many years, it has made the forty-kilometre trip to a marina in the North Arm of the Fraser River countless times, often crossing in big seas and encountering tricky tidal conditions where the fast-flowing Fraser empties into the Strait of Georgia. And on return trips to the island it has carried everything from water tanks to internationally renowned scholars. Roger recalls his boating experiences.

I never missed a class. But even though it's a fairly robust boat, I was kind of new to powerboating. And I had to be a fairly quick learner about stern drives—they're really the worst kind of propulsion system in these wood-infested waters, and I'm still struggling after thirty years. Logs. The other day, I had a leg blow up, heading home about half-way across from Vancouver—it happened about eleven in the morning. I got towed back up the river at great bloody expense. Got a haul-out straightaway from my Musqueam buddies. Drove home. Got a spare leg and was back at the marina within an hour. Had the old leg off, the new one on, and still arrived at the island before dark, which is pretty impressive for an old professor.

This powerful boat has also enabled Roger to assist many vessels in distress over the years.

Finding the ideal boat can take time, laments Joy Orth. Her family had to cross challenging river waters to and from their island. She says,

The idea that you can get by with a cheap boat as you might a cheap car, especially if you have to depend on it for transportation under conditions that are less than ideal, is just not so. We've had a lot of bad experiences on the water since coming here. Many of them are caused by inexperience and ignorance, some by just plain bad luck, but whichever, they were painful—and dangerous. If we had bought a tough aluminum-hull boat when we first came here, we would have been money ahead and certainly ahead in our enjoyment of the water around us . . . Our experiences with water have certainly not been all bad. A day of exploring the channels and sloughs around us can be one of pure joy . . . nothing is finer than to pile into a boat with your lunch and a fishing pole.[5]

Chic and Kathy looked around for several years before buying a boat to access their two islands. As Chic notes, choosing a boat "is a big decision. If you have the wrong boat, it dictates your life." Rather than going with aluminum, they chose an attractive twenty-four-foot Sea Sport fibreglass boat with a cuddy cabin for year-round use.

If we just used it in the summer, an aluminum boat would be a good idea because aluminum hulls are very durable. You can bang into stuff and they don't break. But if you're going to go somewhere overnight in the winter, it's like sleeping in a refrigerator. Aluminum conducts the heat right out, and you have to work really hard to insulate the boat or heat it in order to stay on it. In our fibreglass boat we can snuggle up at a dock anywhere in the middle of winter in subfreezing temperatures, just crack a window to get ventilation, and sleep under a down comforter. We have a galley to make coffee and food.

Chic goes on to say, "I'm very attached to my boat. It's big enough and small enough, and powerful enough and comfortable enough for the way we use it. It's a big part of our life up here."

Some alternatives for passage making

WHILE A BOAT is essential to Chic and Kathy's island lives, it was their Cessna 180 float plane that first prompted them to seek an island getaway. A comfortable flight radius from Seattle along with the capability to safely land and secure the plane defined their search. The first island property they purchased has many attractive qualities. But its immediate appeal was an existing dock that allowed them to approach and tie up with few hazards to wings and floats. Their plane continues to allow them quick access to the island and to other spots along the coast, although they have switched to wheels in order to commute from Seattle to a local airport.

Frank and Geri also keep a Cessna 182 on Sidney Island and use it to make quick trips to the Victoria airport almost as often as they use their boat. And it has allowed them to explore Canada and beyond from their back door. I love the notion that they can step outside their door, load the plane, and head for Newfoundland. The airstrip on Sidney Island is also attracting other pilots to the island, creating a community of islanders with common interests and far-flung connections.

Most islanders don't own planes, but many charter these coastal workhorses, particularly when pressures of time make commutes by boat impractical. As a kid, I was thrilled to go along with Dad when he used float planes to inspect upcoast log booms for an export enterprise he was involved with. And annual visits from his buddy who owned a Seabee were always a highlight. Negotiating this odd-looking flying boat at our dock took some skill to avoid clipping the ramp with its wings. Roger, who is now on Bath Island, is glad to have a much longer dock in the channel as it makes float-plane service much easier to arrange. Float planes are also a great comfort when there is an emergency. When Mom experienced severe internal pain in the middle of a February night in 1970, I called Dad in Vancouver by radio telephone, and he arrived by float plane at first light. A quick injection of some form of painkiller allowed Mom to climb aboard, and off they went to the hospital. Her problem was quickly resolved.

Many islanders rely on water taxis to deliver everything from guests to refrigerators or to completely replace a commuter boat. A return trip to and from a distant island must be organized in advance and may cost hundreds of dollars if other passengers are not sharing the cost. But the reality is that owning and operating a boat can be much, much more expensive. The initial purchase price is one thing— boats and their engines can range from almost nothing to hundreds of thousands of dollars. Less obvious are recurrent operating costs: fuel, insurance, moorage on the mainland side, regular maintenance, and occasional engine replacement. And tows if engines fail. Less tangible costs of boat ownership include worrying about the security of island moorage, along with concerns about piloting a boat in tricky conditions. It's not hard to understand why water taxi service is a good alternative to a commuter boat until you think about the desire most islanders have to come and go at their pleasure and to make seamanship part of their island experience.

Seamanship

HAVING A BOAT well suited to the waters around an island is important. But knowing how, and when, to operate it is critical. As Joe says, "Any boat is only as good as its captain. Seamanship is key." He grew up on the waters around Tofino and learned to hear and read the wind and water over time. He says,

> My father was a fisherman and he never listened to the forecast. He would open the window, have his coffee, and listen to the waves on the beach—you can tell what the weather will be like, just listening to the crash of the waves, not even seeing them. It took me a while—finally I learned it. When I was living on the island, people would play loud music, and I'd ask them to turn it down. I'd say, "I have to listen, I have to be aware of this stuff." I grew up doing this—it was a part of my teaching from my dad and my grandfather.

Joe is particularly attentive to rapidly changing weather conditions and talks about how important it is to know local conditions and move in tune with tide and wind. These dictate when you can come and go. Things get dangerous when you choose your time incorrectly. He reflects that often people from away don't understand or respect how sea conditions can change within a short time span. In the waters off Tofino, as well as in many other places along the coast, steep swells form quickly when tide turns against wind.

David Conover, a newcomer to boating when he moved with his wife to Wallace Island, tells several hair-raising stories of being caught in changing conditions. Lack of experience, lack of local knowledge, and lack of forethought brought him close to disaster. "The straightest line between two points is never the shortest, rarely the quickest, and seldom the safest. In an open boat, you become a quick learner or a lost pupil. For the sea is the only school that never gives you a chance to fail a grade."[6]

Negotiating tidal rapids in Surge Narrows also requires attention to their powerful dynamics. "We go through the rapids all the time without worrying because we've learned to see the patterns—you can read them with your eyes but you can also feel them. You engage and commit yourself and become part of it," says Rob Wood. He reflects on longer passages through the Discovery Islands. "The primary thing is being attuned to the situation. I listen to weather forecasts, but I don't make plans according to weather forecasts—I'm all in favour of going into the situation. If you're in harbour, the weather is bad, and you want to make a passage, don't make the decision tied up at the dock. Go out of the harbour, see what it's like. If you don't like it, come back and wait. Then you're poised, waiting for the situation to change. You can go back out."

Judith on nearby Rendezvous Island also relies on local knowledge and judgement.

I know when I can go and when I can't go, depending on the boat I've got and how the clouds are moving. The Bute winds can be really bad as they howl out of the inlet, pulling up water spouts, and it's so cold that things like the steering system will freeze up. Or you have to scrape the ice off your eyeglasses so you can keep on seeing. Or the freezing spray hits the boat and coats any kind of superstructure, like trolling poles or a mast, so your boat gets top-heavy really fast and can turn turtle—so you don't go out, sometimes for days or weeks.

She laughs and goes on say, "The southeasters are not so bad among the islands, and I can travel these channels in a big blow most any time. But the last stretch to Heriot Bay or to Whaletown can get really snotty—it's the whole Strait of Georgia piling up as the water shallows. The waves get steep and it's slow going, uncomfortable, and just not nice. There's a point where it's simply not worth going out." Jan, who lives with her husband, Sy, on a small island at the mouth of Jervis Inlet, describes a winter passage that was trickier than expected. "It was blowing and when I went across, the snow was thick. The compass wasn't working, and I didn't know if we were headed for Texada—you know how you have to watch your wake if you're not sure if you're going straight. It was really an interesting crossing."

Being attuned to the elements is not unique to islanders on the West Coast. A couple living on an island off Nova Scotia express the same sense of watchfulness that Joe, Rob, and Jan discuss.

When you live as isolated and as close to the elements as we currently do, you quickly learn to become very self-reliant. You always have your ears tuned to marine weather forecasts on the radio. And your eyes just naturally develop the habit of constantly scanning the horizon for down-home atmospheric clues that you can use...things like "mackerel sky, not 24 hours dry" or "red in the east, not fit for man nor beast." Then too when a blow does come, it's not enough to simply *know* about it as soon as possible. You must also have the physical strength, skills and equipment you'll need to "batten down all hatches"—protect your livestock, garden, cabin and other possessions—before and during the storm...we always wear divers' wet suits during cold weather (life vests, of course, are a must at all times), just in case we're capsized into the frigid water.[7]

Asking for local information about sea conditions is also helpful. Roger on Bath Island says, "I sometimes see that it can be thirty knots at Entrance but only five knots at Sandheads. I'll call up the light-keeper—I've got his phone number—or I can use VHF and call on 82Alpha, which is only one channel up from the Coast Guard channel, and ask, 'Hey, what's the story of the thirty knots?' I used to have a VHF at my house in Vancouver, and I'd call the ferries in the middle of the strait and ask for a weather report at Thrasher Rock. They don't mind." Caroline Woodward, who serves as lightkeeper on Lennard Island, often provides local mariners with information on sea conditions along the tempestuous and rocky stretch of coast off Tofino.

Not many islanders describe truly devastating moments on the water, although Rob comments that fellow Discovery Islanders have all "experienced harrowing adventures, with many lessons learned the hard way about riding the fine balance between sheer joy and sheer terror."[8] Others tell ironic or funny stories involving breakdowns, groundings, fog, or the need to rescue passing boaters. And most are attentive to seamanship skills. Michael Modzelewski knew that he might need to act instinctively in navigating the waters of Blackfish Sound. "I practiced tying clove hitches and bowlines until I could do them automatically, without thought...I began memorizing the local nautical charts and the outboard motor manual."[9]

What struck me in the conversations I had with islanders was the way they take on-the-water difficulties in stride. When things go sideways, practical intelligence and coping skills kick in. Problems are assessed, safety needs prioritized, anchors deployed, pumps activated, navigational backups consulted, mechanical knowledge and spare parts put to use. And each time, lessons are learned. Few islanders make the same mistake twice.

Having boating skills is important for safety but also for independence. This can be an issue for island couples when one tends to assume the role of "captain" and oversees mechanical matters. My mom, for example, was an able deckhand but never brought *Whereaway* in or out of the dock. And Judith comments that in the early days, few women on nearby islands in the Discovery group operated boats.

> Most of the time they were content, but they had to ask their husbands if they could go to book club or pop down the channel for coffee with a friend on the next island, even though it was only going to be an hour-long visit. He'd have to come along and hope there would be other men around, or another distraction, while his wife was in visiting. If the menfolk went away for work in logging camps or the oil patch, women were stuck in these little coves and inlets, all by themselves. They couldn't get out unless they begged a ride from a neighbour.

She adds,

> After a while it got to be too much—they realized they had to drive the boat. But the husband would say, "You can't, you don't know how." So we got together the Ladies' Skiff Club. I'd generally start off in my boat because I was the farthest out, and I'd pick up Marney in her boat, and the two boats would go in convoy and pick up the next boat, and the next boat, and the next boat. We felt supported in our little fleet and, at our various destinations, we'd do a lesson for the day: docking (always docking), or changing a spark plug, checking for water in the gas tank, going through the rapids, things like that. After five or six sessions all these women had built up their confidence enough that they could say

to hubby, "See you later, I'm taking the boat." As an added bonus, they got to explore beyond their normal travel paths. That was a worthwhile activity, and now it's a rare woman around here who won't drive a boat.

Boating at night brings a whole new set of challenges. Your circle of awareness is compressed by darkness. An extra level of caution slows things down, challenges your memory of familiar seascapes, and demands vigilance. Eyes adjust and readjust as they encounter lights from instruments, running lights, and navigation aids. Logs and drift lines laced with seaweed appear suddenly. It's hard to read the trajectories of other boats. And your sense of distance and proximity becomes less confident. When rain or snow further limit visibility and comfort, all you can do is hunker down and focus on getting to safe haven.

But I know from all my evening passages returning from school or a weekend job in the local marina that nighttime also brings pleasures. There is a surprising amount of light to transform the seascape. Stars form a familiar map from horizon to horizon, sparkling in the absence of city light. The moon casts a glow reminiscent of soft daylight. Not only does the night sky assist in navigation, it creates a special nocturnal space that rarely fails to inspire wonder and a sense of privilege in people on the water at night.

Another extraordinary source of light, best seen on a dark night, is marine bioluminescence. The scientific explanation that phytoplankton convert chemical energy to light energy when disturbed does not begin to capture the magic experienced when the waters around your boat glow and sparkle. I grew up entranced as fish darted away from the hull, as crests of waves glowed and disappeared, and as the prop created a shimmering sweep of light astern on night passages. And I would love to have shared Joe Martin's remarkable experience, late one dark night, when he was making his way from Tofino to Echachis. He was moving slowly when he noticed a glittering spout off to one side. A grey whale surfaced, then gracefully dove beneath his boat, wrapped in streaming light—one of those memories that he sees as a special gift of island living.

Other observers share the magic of boating at night, although Judith laughs when she talks about the importance of caution.

I had an experience with the neighbours' kids, six and eight years old, who lived over on White Rock Pass. I had talked their mom, Marney, into letting them come home with my two kids. It was dark, and Marney was nervous as her kids had never been out in a boat at night before. I said, "It's not really a big issue—I do this in the dark all the time." I was using the oyster boat, which is a big, flat-bottomed kind of skiff. The kids were thrilled by our sparkling wake and the darting fish trails in the biolumi-nescence, and we were going along just fine. There's a different way of seeing on the water at night, when another sense kicks in, but it takes full concentration. You might not see an object ahead, but you'll notice a shift in the shadows and patterns on the water. All of a sudden I saw a huge log awash, dead ahead, and only had time to pull back on the throttle and slow right down so that when I hit it, the boat was almost stopped. Unfortunately, it was flat topped, and the boat had just enough momentum to slide up so that we were sitting right on top. I tried to back off with the motor, but the log was so wide I couldn't budge. My son, Ian, and I ended up climbing out of the boat on each side, amidships, stand-ing on the log to sink it a little with our weight, and trying to wiggle the boat off. Took us ages—about twenty minutes. And Marney was waiting for our call. When we finally got off, I hightailed it to Rendezvous and said, "Ian, I'm not even going to tie up. As soon as we touch the dock, you jump out, run up to the quad, get to the house, and call Marney on the VHF. Tell her we're home, but don't tell her what happened." The kids were just having a whale of a time while we were doing our gymnastics on the log. They had the bailers out, tossing shining arcs of water into the darkness—they'd never seen bioluminescence before because they'd never been out on the boat at night.

And there are days and nights when you just shouldn't be on the water, when seas are too steep, too confused, too powerful to control even a large and well-founded boat. The Van Gyns have turned back halfway across Sidney Harbour, where strong currents can counter wind-driven waves to create ugly conditions within sight of Tsehum Harbour. If we were on Bath Island on such days, we would stay there, generally pleased to be missing school. But storms also required us to monitor the landing area to ensure that boats were safe and logs weren't battering the dock or getting wedged beneath the pier at high tide. If we had already gone off to school when a big blow came up, Mom would call the school by radio telephone to advise us to stay with friends for the night. This was always a treat. Only now do I reflect on her resilience, alone on the island in a howling gale (Dad was working in Vancouver during the week in those days).

One of the treats that I had when talking with Roger was his account of Dad's advice to him about operating boats. I can hear my father's voice in the list that Roger includes in his article "Wet and Boisterous: The Lumpy Romance of Commuting by Boat":

- Think laterally.

- Do not assume the worst. It might be something small.

- Assume the worst. It is bound to be a "major" problem.

- Water inside the boat must not be ignored. Find the source and fix it.

- New or unusual engine sounds usually mean trouble.

- If you have doubts about dock lines, get out of bed and check them.

- Change the oil often.

- The best place for a boat is on land.

- Three or six months of "trouble-free" boating means a problem is imminent.

- Deal with boat problems immediately . . . new noises must be diagnosed and repaired without delay.

As Dad indicated to Roger, an important part of seafaring is boat care, maintenance, and monkey wrenching. These become constant chores of island life. There's always something that needs attention, whether it's as simple as bailing out an open boat after a rainstorm or checking fuel and oil levels. And every boat has idiosyncrasies that the owner indulges. We knew exactly how to adjust the cable steering system on *Molly* when it stretched to the point the steering wheel would spin, and we rarely went anywhere without a spare spark plug, as this was the first thing we'd change when the Briggs & Stratton was reluctant to start.

Periodic engine maintenance is a prudent way to avoid inconvenient and embarrassing breakdowns, and annual attention to the bottom of a boat must be planned to coincide with either a low tide suitable for careening or the availability of a sling or marine railway at a shipyard. Of course, the perfect island would have a tidal grid that makes it easy to beach the boat to repair, scrape, and paint the bottom and rudder, and inspect propulsion systems as needed. More likely a day or so is involved in hauling at a local (or distant) shipyard. One way or another, these are jobs that can't be neglected.

Safe havens

BATH ISLAND IS not quite perfect. It lacks a sheltered and deep bay that affords around-the-clock protection. The absence of secure moorage was the primary thing that kept us awake at night. Many times as the years went by, a rising wind had us up checking boats. On one memorable windy night I sat on the dock for hours watching the capsized hull of my sailing dinghy strain against a mooring buoy. I'm not sure what I'd have done if it had broken free, but there was no way I could go back to bed knowing it might be gone in the morning. On other windy nights that coincided with very high tides, we took turns pushing away logs that threatened to get under the pier and damage its infrastructure. A pike pole in the hands of a thirteen-year-old is invaluable when debris threatens the dock.

I expect that one of the things to affect Dad's sleep that first winter after buying the island was the location and design of a dock somewhere along the relatively sheltered west side of the island, away from the Strait of Georgia. Some degree of protection from wind and waves was his first priority, with accessibility and depth being close behind.

He couldn't have it all, however. The spot that was most protected and accessible from the upland part of the island was halfway along a somewhat protected channel separating Bath from Saturnina. It was deep enough for small boat access, but too shallow for *Whereaway* on anything below a tide a metre or so high. But even today Roger, who took the Island over when Mom and Dad moved on, says, "Yeah, I think your father made absolutely the right decision."

Once Dad settled on a spot for the dock, he came up with an ingenious design for secure moorage, drawing on years of practical engineering experience working in the woods and along the coast. At the heart of the area we came to call the "landing," we built a broad wooden pier above the high-tide mark, made from salvaged timbers and planks. It was almost two and a half metres wide and nine metres long, set on short creosoted pilings cemented into a sandstone ledge that was just covered at high tide. At one end of this pier a mast with a movable boom was erected, made from peeled logs. A wire cable ran from the hand winch to a block at the top of the mast, and then out to the end of the boom. The cable threaded through a double-purchase block and tackle system that allowed us to hand winch boats out of the channel and swing them onto the pier.

On the outside edge of the pier, a nine-metre ramp was installed on heavy-duty hinges. The far end of the ramp rested on the eight-by-sixteen-foot barge that Mom and Dad had built during the first winter after buying the island. A large pin at the end of the ramp was inserted into a metal socket embedded in the middle of the barge deck. Rather than rolling along the dock as the tide rises and falls as most ramps do, the ramp acted as a stiff-arm and pivot point, holding the dock away from the rocky beach. Cables parallel to the ramp kept the barge cum dock square to the pier, while heavy chains, running off each corner at forty-five-degree angles and secured to sandstone boulders, compensated for the pressure of wind and current, keeping it in place through some remarkable blows.

That mast and boom arrangement proved to be invaluable over the years. While *Molly* was generally tied at the dock, a growing collection of other small boats could be stored on the pier for maintenance and security. We became adept at securing, lifting, and swinging boats onto the hard on a regular basis. Heavy cargo, including a garden tractor, was winched off the decks of various vessels. And the ramp itself could be lifted and pivoted onto the pier for the annual barge refit.

That was always a memorable occasion. Heavy lines were tied to the railing on the outside edge of the barge and then looped underneath to act as a sling. The ends were knotted on the heavy-duty hook at the end of the cable that came off the boom. Strenuous winching followed until the inside edge of the barge was raised to vertical. Then the barge slowly and grandly flipped over to reveal its barnacled bottom. A day of scraping, along with repairs and a fresh coat of bottom paint, prepared it for another year. And then the whole process was reversed, the ramp resecured, the cables and chains checked and reattached. That system lasted Mom and Dad the full twenty years they lived on the island and still strikes me as an elegant solution to the perennial problem of securing a collection of small boats.

Even the best system, however, is vulnerable to wind and tide. There were many times when the combination of current and wind-blown waves made things very choppy at the dock. I lost the tip of my thumb in one landing attempt in such conditions. Another time, *Whereaway* was secured to the dock during the Easter weekend when an unusual westerly came up out of nowhere. Dad was so concerned about the force of the wind pushing the sailboat against the dock and ramp that he and Mom cast off and took shelter in Degnen Bay (a local hurricane hole). Guests were stranded on the island until the wind dropped the following day.

The challenges of mooring on Bath Island continue to be a major preoccupation for Roger. His larger boat and his reliance on float planes for occasional commuting required a longer dock. Roger, who is well-known for his resourcefulness, located two nine-metre wooden docks as Expo 86 was closing down. After towing them across the strait, he sought advice about securing them from locals and quickly encountered a predictable variety of opinions.

I went around asking other people with docks and fisherman and nautical people, "How should I mount this dock?" And the contrasts were black and white. Many had firm opinions and said, "The other guy is full of it," describing various disasters that would happen if I followed others' advice. "My way will work. You must do it my way." The choices were basically pilings, anchors, or stiff-arms where something rigid holds the dock offshore, with St. Andrew's cross–type chains to keep it all in place. It gives with wind and tide. Your father's view was that with pilings, you fight nature. First of all they cost you a lot, second the piling won't go in very far in this channel, and third, one day you'll come down and find your dock leaning on an angle with the hoops stuck, left high on the piling as the tide drops. They will not work here. So I went with stiff-arms for about the first ten years.

Since the channel is relatively shallow and muddy, it offers secure holding ground for the big anchors and heavy ground chains that hold Roger's current dock. The sheer weight of the chains keeps them more or less in position, even at low tide. The weak links in the system, not surprisingly, are the chain links. Roger tells a cautionary tale about the value of maintenance. He found the dock skewed and aground, with one end dragging a broken portion of chain. Corrosion over a seven-year period had led to this inevitable outcome. He was faced with the major task of acquiring and transporting new chain, locating the anchors, and swapping new for old. Roger waited for the below-datum tides of midsummer when the channel shallowed to around a metre deep, put on an old wetsuit, located the anchors, and marked them with buoys. The hard labour of lifting these, all by himself, and securing the new chain in a blustery northwesterly wind and choppy waves was done from the stern of his boat. And he used the occasion to reposition the anchors and inspect all the various parts. As he says, it was an unexpected way to spend a few sleepless nights and a lot of time and money.

When Dad's old plywood ramp needed replacing, Roger commissioned a wider and sturdier aluminum ramp from a Vancouver fabricator. A premade structure of this size is a luxury in island life, and getting it to the island was tricky. He arranged for a helicopter to neatly set it on the dock, ready for installation. I would love to have seen that ramp dropped into place. Sadly it came to a mysterious end in a big windstorm a year or so later. When Roger returned to the island after travelling, the ramp was gone. He wasn't able to snag it by dragging the channel and still wonders how something so substantial could disappear. Another was delivered and is still there.

Corrosion is also the bane of dock owners who rely on stiff-arms. The dock on Snowberry Island, for example, is secured by steel I-beams that hold it off the cliff face in a narrow but deep indent in the thirty-seven-metre sandstone embankments that wrap round this eight-hectare oval island. Chic knew that they were overdue for replacement but hadn't been able to find a time for his dock guy to come over to do the work. He and Kathy arrived one day to find a detached stiff-arm standing vertically in the water and the dock askew. "I was circling, thinking, 'What the hell is going on here?' It was the oddest thing—the stiff-arm is thirty feet long, and it's thirty feet deep in the cove. The shore end must have separated first, dropped to the bottom, and then broken loose from the dock. Somehow the dock swung out and the stiff-arm became a post holding up the ramp." Inspection and maintenance of these arms has become a regular priority since that time. The small cove is too deep for pilings, and mooring chains rot away too quickly in salt water to be a viable alternative.

Strategies for secure moorage are as varied as the islands they serve and as complex as circumstances, resources, and inclination allow. Property owners on Sidney Island, for example, share a communal pier and dock, along with a launching ramp with a useful crane and winch. There are protocols for use and maintenance. As the bay is exposed to the north, however, most residents have stories to tell about difficult landings and damaged vessels. It took several years of collective planning, fundraising, and consultation with local authorities and First Nations, but the island now has an impressive breakwater that affords a comforting degree of protection. Residents shared the considerable construction costs, but few would argue that creating more secure moorage wasn't worth all the time and effort.

Another carefully planned dock is tucked away on Jan and Sy's small island across from Nelson Island. Protected at all points of wind, deep and rock free, it comes close to being a perfect moorage for both families that live on this island. The dock is a product of inventiveness and past experience. The initial dock, made of cedar logs, was assembled with the help of rudimentary tools. Jan describes their efforts.

We carried the logs using two pairs of old jeans. We tied a knot at the end of each leg to give us something to hold on to. And the crotch served as the sling. Four people can move fairly hefty logs this way. Sy and our neighbour, Bob, moved to the far edge of the dock, balancing on the outer log, while Sue and I supported the inside end. It wasn't the first cross-member, so there was some stability. Both guys were sharing the weight of the log when Bob saw something he needed to do and let go. Sy, still exerting lots of effort, went backwards in slow motion into the chuck. He got a "10" for style as he waved and smiled as he went in.

The dock did the trick for a while, but cedar logs eventually degrade in the marine environment. "They lasted a number of years, but the bugs got in eventually. And they were heavy—maybe a little too heavy, as we'd get some slop over top." Their current dock is carefully engineered.

We really thought about it. We built it up in our field. Put it together, then took it apart and dragged it down to the water. You want to keep the wood out of the water—that's really important. You want to make sure that whatever you have for flotation is sealed off at the top so the otters can't build their nests or drag in every bit of smelly fish they possibly can. We wrapped big Styrofoam blocks in heavy plastic and boxed them in so there's no way the otters can get on top. We used plywood and screening, whatever suited the area. And it's high so we can bring a big vessel alongside.

The dock includes a slip and canopy to shelter an open boat, and stiff-arms connected to concrete pillars on the beach hold it offshore.

The skookum aluminum ramp is wide enough for a golf cart. As Sy says, "You learn as you go along."

At the other end of the spectrum, moorage at exposed Echachis Island is simply a buoy attached to an engine block, located in a bay on the east side of the island. Even though it is somewhat sheltered from prevailing winds, the area's renowned surf wraps around the island and surges into the bay. As Joe comments, "The ocean isn't going to let you have a dock here very long." There aren't docks on nearby islands for the same reason. "Anchoring off, with a rope to shore, is all you can do," he adds. This system has worked well over the years, although it requires nimbleness in the transition to the beach. Joe uses a float system to keep tension on the anchor line of the mooring buoy. This prevents it from tangling with the anchor block as the tide rises and falls. He also uses heavy lines to increase security. But like other systems, it is subject to failure when high winds and underwater conditions create trouble. Joe tells the story of seeing his boat go aground one day when the wind was blowing so hard his house was shaking. The boat's mooring line had become caught underwater on the mussel-laden anchor rode between the float and the block. The sharp shells had severed the line, and "the boat went ashore with a sickening crunch...My neighbour, Steve Lawson, came over with his two daughters to help me...The boat was smashing on the rocks. I grabbed a 240-foot line and tied it to the bow. The Lawson girls went across to the other side of the bay and pulled every time the waves lifted the boat, while Steve and I pushed it. We got it off and made a temporary patch until I could take it to Tofino for repair." Misty smiles when she recalls this incident. "We just suited up in our boots and raingear and rushed to help get his boat off the beach. Joe had to get the boat to Tofino in a big blow as he had nowhere to moor it."

The Lawsons also had their share of challenges keeping their boat on a mooring buoy at their nearby island. When a combination of rain and rough seas swamped their skiff one blustery winter day, Misty's father put on a wetsuit and swam to the half-submerged boat to bail it out. There was no way they could safely launch a canoe to paddle out to the heaving boat.

Designing workable island moorage is, for most, an absorbing challenge involving both ingenuity and local knowledge. Finding moorage on the mainland side, however, is generally described as frustrating and expensive. As one islander I spoke with laments, "There are few places to tie commuter boats. Even short runs into bays inside the Gulf Islands can trigger less than congenial interactions with marina owners trying to eke out a living from businesses in decline." On one hand the islander may be seeking only occasional but reliable access to a dock for a few hours or a few days; on the other, the marina, not surprisingly, favours regular customers. Should a slip be permanently reserved? And at what cost? And keeping a car at the marina requires a separate negotiation. One islander pays over four thousand dollars a year for mainland moorage and parking to ensure he can get to work, while another ties in at a government dock and parks an old car on a mainland street. He'd rather risk theft or fines than pay a monthly parking fee for a vehicle that is rarely used.

Seafaring

FEW PEOPLE LIVING on islands without ferry service are so self-sufficient that they can stay on island for extended periods. Most islanders spend time on the water most days. Whether they are coming, going, working, or playing, the demands and pleasures of passages are an integral part of their lives. Travelling by sea has a fluidity that is part of its appeal. You choose your moment, your course, your speed, as mood, need, and sea conditions allow. There is time to enjoy the passage, time to explore, time to savour the intersection of water, land, and sky. While there are rules and protocols for navigation, you do not have to negotiate lockstep city traffic grids. And negotiating sea room brings challenging conditions that test skills, stimulate senses, and complicate travel.

While the freedom and challenge of commuting by boat helps define island life, some islanders have the added complication of crossing an adjacent island served by ferries as a stepping-stone to the mainland. Our family, for example, spent a great deal of time driving the length of Gabriola and riding the ferry to get to shops and schools in Nanaimo. When your boat trip has to be coordinated with a ferry trip, the fluidity of travel is reduced: ferry schedules and lineups impose a rhythmic structure to the commute that cannot be ignored. But at the same time, the highly social act of riding ferries draws you into the life and rituals of the adjacent island and links you to a community that may provide important supports over time.

One way or another, life on islands not directly served by ferries is dominated—and for many people, enhanced—by the process of seafaring and passage making. Seascapes, boats, tides, moorings, and seamanship are integral parts of the experience. According to an East Coast islander, "You have to enjoy it. If you didn't enjoy it you wouldn't do it. This is one of the great things about living on an island."[10]

(4)

SETTLING IN

Once Mom and Dad decided to move to Bath Island late in the fall of 1962, they had several months to think through next steps. Leaving the comforts of West Vancouver to create a home on a small, unoccupied island must have had them weighing options and making lists through the long winter months. By Easter they had severed work, school, and housing ties, built a barge for moving materials, and were fully focused on the complex task of house building.

Their initial building site was a treed bluff facing north toward Lasqueti and Texada, next to a pocket bay where the barge could come aground. The site was convenient, practical, and pretty. We hauled a great variety of building materials from the shore up to this spot. But even as we were getting organized, Mom and Dad were having second thoughts on siting. The house would have its back to the sun and focus only on a part of the spectacular views available from all around the island. The site needed clearing and wasn't adjacent to a water source. A new grassy location, looking southeast toward Vancouver, became even more attractive. And Clair and I spent hours once again lugging materials across the island. Not efficient but certainly a good decision in the end. Good siting is a big part of a positive island experience.

A-frame houses were at the height of their popularity in the early 1960s, a period when postwar affluence allowed the construction of many vacation homes across the continent. This simple design offered an appealing way to quickly construct a livable house with a modern aesthetic. Mom and Dad purchased plans and compiled meticulous lists of all the tools, materials, and supplies needed to build a house. Getting building materials to the island was a major undertaking. Lumber yards in Vancouver and Nanaimo delivered to government wharves pallets of dimensional lumber and plywood, along with boxes of nails, cement, bricks, chimney flues, shingles, plumbing supplies, and tools. These awkward piles were loaded onto the barge. What didn't fit was laid along *Whereaway*'s decks or placed in the cockpit. I'm sure the odd sight of a heavily laden sailboat hauling a barge attracted attention as *Whereaway* headed out into the strait.

Dad kept a careful eye on wind conditions and, after a slow trip to Bath Island, the barge was beached on a falling tide. As the barge dried, we scurried to carry the varied materials above the high-water mark. Lengths of additional lumber on *Whereaway*'s deck were cast overboard so that Clair and I could corral them with the dinghy and push them ashore. There was no dock at this point, so *Whereaway* lay at anchor while we did the heavy work of unloading and hefting things to the building site. There was always a sense of urgency, as wind and tide never stand still.

The first step in house construction was laying foundations. Creosoted beach logs were cut into posts and cemented to sandstone slabs. These supported a framework of joists, which were sheathed with plywood to form the main floor. This served as the platform for constructing the two-storey trusses that gave the house its distinctive shape. It had no sidewalls, just a steeply pitched roof on both long sides. You need only look at the shape of a capital A to see the basic framework.

Occasionally friends and relatives came by to lend a hand, but Dad, my petite mother, and two girls under the age of twelve did the bulk of the construction. We all worked hard that summer. Mom and Dad positioned lumber, measured, measured again, cut (often with a chainsaw in the absence of other power tools), and then braced and bolted, and took care of countless other details. Clair and I must have played important roles hauling and holding things, and tidying up the detritus of a building site. Dad rigged a high-lead system in adjacent trees, and by late June twelve A's created a skeleton for the house.

Once the frame was complete, the next step was closing it in. Endless lengths of shiplap created the roofing surface. Tarpaper and hundreds of asphalt shingles went on top, installed from a precarious scaffold system that stretched across the long roof and up to its ridgeline. At almost nine metres off the ground, hanging those final shingles must have been dizzying and strenuous work. I wish I could ask Dad now how he planned the process, and what stressed, scared, and pleased him. Those shingles kept the house dry for five decades and have only recently been replaced.

End walls were framed to close in the house. Windows and wide French doors on the south side captured views from the living room and upstairs bedroom. Dutch doors and smaller windows provided light, access, and air to the kitchen and the upstairs bedroom on the north side. Because internal stairs would take valuable space, an exterior ladder-style staircase provided access to upstairs bedrooms. Going to bed involved a cold dash in the winter. But a convenient hatch in the ceiling of a closet off the kitchen allowed all manner of things to be passed up and down.

At the heart of the house, a double-flue chimney vented both the living room fireplace and the wood stove in the kitchen. Because it extended several feet beyond the ridgeline, that chimney was a major project. A silver dollar at its base brought luck to the house. Large grey concrete bricks enclosed two courses of clay flue liners. At the top, tapered "vortex" chimney pots drew smoke upward. I still remember how raw our hands were from handling those bricks, mixing concrete, and lifting it all up with a pulley. In the fireplace, a Heatilator venting system warmed and circulated air in the living room. And eventually Mom found time to craft a raised hearth and face from carefully chosen pieces of tafoni, the sculpted sandstone that makes Bath island so distinctive.

We laid cork-patterned linoleum-tile floors throughout the house and hung soft grey walnut panelling. Propane lights bathed all rooms with their softly hissing, slightly smelly glow. Kitchen and bathroom cabinets were topped with orange Arborite. And a Finlay wood stove occupied the heart of the kitchen. Copper coils carried fresh water through the stove's firebox and into a hot-water tank. The bathroom featured the harvest gold fixtures so popular in the sixties and a toilet was plumbed, although the septic field came a bit later. The outhouse just down a path from the house was used a lot in those years, and then served as a backup when water levels were low. The step to that outhouse still bears the imprint of my sister's small hands and the date 1963.

And as that first summer turned to fall, two barge loads of household goods were towed from Vancouver. Familiar carpets, beds, sofas, armchairs, paintings, a sideboard, a desk, and the dining room set transformed the house into home. Electric lamps were positioned throughout, although it took a year or more for a generator system to power them, and then only sporadically. It always seemed strange when electric lights changed the feel of the rooms. Precious electricity was normally reserved for the radio telephone and for the tiny television that allowed us to be among the millions who watched the Beatles perform on the *Ed Sullivan Show* and American astronauts take the first steps on the moon. We became accustomed to groping for matches and carefully lighting the mantles of propane lights. But we used them only when truly necessary, since propane bottles were heavy to carry from Silva Bay.

Over the years additions and renovations extended the A-frame and made it more comfortable. But it was always a simple house, with functional areas centred on the warmth of the wood stove and fireplace. Indoor spaces embraced sweeping views, as did a wide front deck that ended just a few feet above the high-tide line. The house was more gracious and comfortable than the plain accommodations that Mom and Dad had lived in at logging camps along the coast, and was much better suited to them than the large West Vancouver house they had so happily left behind.

BUILDING ON AN island has a compelling appeal. You're staking a claim, creating a haven in a special place. What you choose to build is an expression of who you are. At the same time, the building process should be a thoughtful one that honours the island and balances environmental, heritage, and aesthetic sensibilities with functional needs. And it involves radically rethinking lifestyle as you move off the ferry grid, off the energy grid, and away from mainland amenities. Even as you establish a presence on the island, the act of building creates roots. This is an important step in becoming an islander.

In her engaging description of moving to an island in the estuary of the Stikine River, Joy Orth observes that "when you first move into remote country, your concerns are shelter, water and warmth."[1] Practical, yes, but dreams, values, tastes, and creativity also come into play. The authors of the *Private Islands Buyer's Guide* describe the demands of building an island home.

> This little piece of land will become more yours than anything in your life and it will be easy to see only its potential for paradise. However, island development is often a complex undertaking that will require a clear understanding of local laws and regulations, a substantial investment, and a willingness to take risks on unfamiliar technologies and see the advantages of "green living." Most of all, it will take energy and passion. It may easily become an obsession and dominate your life. But while you may have fallen in love with your new island, it's important to stay sharp and not let your fantasies cloud your vision.[2]

When you cruise through the many Pacific Northwest islands not served by ferries, you glimpse hundreds of intriguing houses. They are perched on bluffs, tucked into surrounding forests, and settled among arbutus above the high-tide line. Some are modest, others grand. Most fit, some don't. All could tell stories about how owners moved from fantasy to reality in selecting the site, choosing the design, and building in a place that lacks easy access to materials, power, water, and tradespeople. Their stories are also likely to include uncertainty, frustration, problem solving, and physical aches and injuries, as well as immense pleasure and satisfaction in creating a home. Everywhere I went I was welcomed into comfortable, functional, often beautiful homes ranging from rudimentary cabins to architectural master-pieces. I was reminded of Witold Rybczynski's observation in *The Most Beautiful House in the World* that the art of building flows from the art of living.[3] All were unique. They reflected—and shaped—the lives of the people who crafted them.

First steps

SINCE A HOUSE and all the roads, trails, gardens, outbuildings, and systems that surround it permanently alter the island, there is much to be said for approaching things slowly and thoughtfully. Getting to know the island, responding to its rhythms, communing with its special places, and considering how you want to live are all-important first steps. They help affirm that you want to take on the complicated simplicity of an island life. Suromitra and other islanders observe that skipping this step may cause problems. "There are people who live in these islands who came from completely urban settings and thought, 'I'll just slap something together.' We've seen how sad they were and how taken aback with the cost. Also just how difficult it can be—carrying a washing machine up a cliff, for example. So you really have to have a feel for it and want it, so that there's no chore about it."

Creating a rudimentary place to stay and to store things while pondering options becomes a first priority. Many islanders point to what is now a garage, workshop, or guest house with nostalgia. These simple buildings offered opportunities to gather tools, hone construction skills, set up water and sewage systems, and get a taste of island life before committing to a larger housing project. Kathy and Chic on Snowberry Island, for example, waited several years before starting their main house. They camped while exploring and clearing trails, and then built a combined cottage and workshop. Chic describes their first building project.

> It's a charming little cabin and the truth is it could be everything you need here. It's sixteen by twenty feet. Half is devoted to a shop and tools, and the other half is living space. We've got a tiny loft for sleeping and a little galley on the side with a sink and propane stove. And we carry potable water and collect rainwater, but we haven't started purification. The cabin has been an experiment in how to do stuff in this location, off the grid, on an island. It has been a great preparation for building the house. We learned a lot about systems and how we want to do things.

Their story is remarkably similar to the first island experiences that Geri and Frank, David and Suromitra, Laurie and Rob, and Jan and Sy describe. Exploring, thinking, and experimenting are all part of settling in. Several islanders comment that constructing a first simple building gave them confidence that they could tackle a house. As Sy reflects, "We wanted to do it ourselves, but we realized it might be just a dream—so we thought we should make sure that we were capable." They found that it was "very satisfying to actually get something level and square in the end." But building that first workshop also convinced them that hiring someone to frame their house was the smarter, faster, and safer way to go. Other people came up with ways of expanding the first cabin to meet longer-term needs. And one person, looking across to a luxurious home that took several years of hard work, reflected back on the simplicity of living in what is now a lovely guest house. "If I'd put in a better kitchen, we could have just stayed here."

Another high priority is an adjacent outhouse of simple shed construction, with the requisite hand-dug hole. "If you're going to do something up here, the first thing you need is a biffy," recalls one islander who prefabbed an outhouse in his garage in the city. "Brought it out here on a rental boat from Campbell River. That was our first structure." Outhouses are normally placed far enough away to afford privacy but close enough that nighttime walks aren't too daunting. A view is nice. And they must be maintained to ensure that odours and spiders aren't off-putting. Composting systems are increasingly a preference, and art and flowers enhance the appeal of such buildings.

Choosing a site

LOOKING BACK AT building experiences, islanders reflect that choosing a building site (or lot), particularly on islands with multiple possibilities, raises complicated, at times conflicting aesthetic, personal, and practical questions. These deserve a lot of thought:

- Are panoramic views preferable to proximity to the dock? Or the beach?

- Is the building site sheltered from prevailing winds, and will the sun brighten the house in the morning or the afternoon? Or at all?

- Are water, arable soil, and a potential septic field close by? Is the site well drained or swampy and mosquito ridden? And could climate change alter site ecology?

- What characteristics of the island should be enjoyed and protected? Are there archaeological sites or natural resources that must be respected?

- Will trees need to be cut, stumps pulled, rocks blasted, and roads built to prepare the site? Are these measures overly intrusive?

- How can building materials be delivered and stored?

- What are the safety issues?

And perhaps most important: do I want the same things as my spouse or partner?

Every island offers different possibilities, challenges, and ways to address these questions. And because islands change as the year goes by, seasonal dynamics deserve consideration. A site that appeals to you at the height of summer may feel too exposed when winter storms sweep in. And dappled overhead sunlight on the north side of an island may disappear entirely when the sun is low and days are short in December and January. Years ago an elderly fisherman who had lived on Musclow Islet near Sidney advised me not to live on the north side of an island. He said it would make me unhappy. I wish I had asked which side he had settled on, although I can guess.

When Mom and Dad chose a site that had a spectacular view and easy beach access, I'm sure they weighed all other options. Every day we woke up to a changing seascape and were entertained by the constant stream of vessels in the Strait of Georgia. The beach was a front yard that transformed daily, depending on the tide. In a big southeaster, wind shook the house and, combined with high tides, covered it with salt spray. There were unsettling nights when we feared that driftwood would ram the deck supports. On a perfect island, this site would face more south than east to make it brighter. And it would be much closer to the dock. But in our minds, the aesthetics of this site far outweighed the wind, the late-afternoon shadows, and the challenges of transporting household and building supplies by wheelbarrow over twisting trails.

Because I'm always drawn to a view, I am surprised at the number of islanders who turn their backs on scenery in favour of more practical sites. Jan and Sy, for example, chose a warm, sunny, south-facing site suited to gardening. Their comfortable two-storey house overlooks a small bay with a sheltered dock that they share with neighbours. They are close to the beach where barges can deliver heavy equipment and supplies and they can see people coming and going. But they did weigh views of Malaspina Channel against all these other factors in choosing this site. Jan reflects on their choice of a practical (but lovely) building site.

> We compromised the grand vista for the south-facing site. With more vision, I think I would have built on the west side of the island. But when we started we didn't have a lot of money for blasting and pouring and doing the work that would have been required. And I had just come from a west-facing house and it was so stinking hot that we always had the blinds down. Now you have the low-e glass and different kinds of window treatments. But this was thirty years ago, so this was the simplest place to build. And proximity to the dock was a major concern.

Jan misses seeing whales but comments that you can always walk across the island to enjoy the open water.

Other island residents choose sites away from views as well. Linda on Valdes grew up in a modest two-bedroom cabin, set well back from the beach on busy Gabriola Pass. Her parents "put the cabin where they did to get it out of the southeasterly that funnels in through the pass. It had no insulation and single-pane windows. I know it was common for early island settlers to build on sites protected from the wind rather than for the view." As the years went by her mom also enjoyed her complete privacy from passing boaters. And farther north, on Rendezvous Island, a sunny tree-ringed clearing is the site for Judith's home. It allowed her family to develop the gardens and orchards that would sustain them for years to come. They debated the choice. "I really liked the one on the north end with the beautiful waterfront. But Jeff could see a little bit beyond the superficial stuff. He saw the soil here—there's lots of it. And it is relatively flat, high enough up to catch most of the day's sun, and has good water catchment. It just needed some cleanup from past logging, so that was a good move. I'm glad he talked me out of the pretty lot."

For some people, a view of the sea is the last thing they want at the end of the day.

> Fishermen do not build their houses where they have to look at the sea. Not, that is, unless their cove happens to be so unprotected that they have to keep an eye on their boat. In that case, the window facing the sea will be small—probably the one over the kitchen sink—and the big windows will face the meadows or the mountains. "I'm going up and down all day long," explained one of Madrona Island's fishermen. "When I look out of my house I want the landscape to stay in place. You don't plan your picture windows to look on your workplace."[4]

One way or another it is the vista of the island and its surroundings, not the dwelling, that is the long-term focus in the island experience. An islander who took a long time to choose his site suggests, "You always build back from the beautiful spot...because that's where you want to look. That's where you can build the deck." Another says, "If you have a rugged site, as people have on the West Coast, especially waterfront, you don't take that as an adversity that you fight against. You take that as a starting point."

In the end, choosing a site is one of the most important personal decisions you make, since it profoundly influences how you see and engage with the island. The Islands Trust, in concert with the San Juan Preservation Trust, offers advice on siting that emphasizes the trust's concern about living lightly on the land. It begins with a reflection about building on the top of a ridge.

A notch in the trees on a ridgeline can funnel wind and increase its speed around your house, making decks less usable and damaging trees and shrubs. Siting down the slope can give your house protection you will later appreciate, especially during one of the islands' famous and occasionally destructive windstorms.

If your land is on the shoreline, you are part owner of a world-famous scenic and natural treasure. Because shoreline areas are especially sensitive, regulations may require that you set your house back from the water, retain some trees and shrubs for screening, and obtain permits for other types of shoreline structures.

. . . Siting your house away from the shoreline and screening it with vegetation can also make it more attractive and liveable. A bit of shrubbery or a few trees can effectively soften the outline of a building, and darker siding and roofing in natural colors can help to blend a structure into the landscape. Distance and screening will reduce glare from the water, and your water view can be beautifully framed with greenery. Careful siting and screening will protect a west-facing house especially from becoming so hot and bright you will have to close the drapes and shut out the view you love.

While shorelines and ridgelines are the most important and dramatic lines in the island landscape, less dramatic lines formed by forest edges and other changes in ground cover or terrain also affect the look and feel of your place. Seeing and appreciating the patterns in the landscape where forests meet field, field meets rocky hillside, or hillside meets sky will give you a better understanding of why the islands—and your own land—look so beautiful. Attention to all the lines in the landscape when planning buildings and other alterations will ensure that your land, and the islands as a whole, continue to work their scenic magic.[5]

Choosing a design

SETTLING ON AN ideal site raises a whole new set of questions about design. If you Google "gulf island architecture," numerous websites describe a vernacular style that embraces the landscape, makes efficient uses of interior spaces, features natural materials, involves straightforward but innovative construction, and integrates sustainable

technologies for light, heat, and other systems. Words such as *rustic,*
minimal, balanced, natural, green, and *personalized* abound. These
descriptors apply to the homes I visited as well. Designs for these special houses were developed on the backs of envelopes, gleaned from
magazines, or crafted by architects. But all capture the island essence
and reflect the personality of the owner in interesting ways.

One of the memorable island dwellings that I encountered was
designed and constructed by Rob and Laurie Wood as part of a 1970s
co-operative on Maurelle Island in the Discovery Islands. Built of
locally milled wood, this jewel box of a house sits on a bluff, high above
the water. On one side it overlooks the gardens, fields, and outbuildings that the owners rely on to sustain their independent lifestyle. On
the other, it looks west from Surge Narrows in the south around to
the Octopus Islands in the northwest. The house is spare, beautifully
proportioned, and functional. The interior feels like a ship, carefully
crafted, tiddly, efficient and comfortable in all weathers. Rob's training
as an architect is evident in the design, as is his love of the place and
of local wood and stone. "I deliberately set out to see if I could make a
house that feels good. A lot of people remark on it." Other people have
sensed how Rob's affinity for island living influences his design practice
and have commissioned him to plan houses on adjacent islands. For
example, he designed a house on nearby Rendezvous Island that reflects
his ethic, although the spaces are unique to the site and owners. That
house embraces different views, showcases art, and responds in distinctive ways to how the people Rob designed it for want to live on island.

Like choosing a setting, arriving at a design was the subject of
animated conversations. Some islanders favour simple, functional
designs to minimize the difficulties of construction and maintenance.
Others regard the process as a once-in-a-lifetime creative opportunity to build a striking residence, an architectural masterpiece, in a
spectacular setting. Resources, skills, and location all play roles in
selecting a design. In most cases, islanders describe long hours of
thinking through the dynamics of the site, the special needs of life
off the grid, their aesthetic preferences, and the personal dreams that
shape their choices. More questions emerge:

- What kinds of living, storage, and workshop spaces are desirable? And how can design respond to the character of the island, minimize disruption of the natural environment, and ensure the house is green, efficient, and easy to maintain?

- What systems, appliances, and other features are critical for a comfortable lifestyle?

- What regulations control construction and safety, and how are these enforced?

- How practical will the house be to build, given the challenges of bringing in materials, the skills required for construction, and safety issues (think steep roof angles, surrounding trees, or cliff edges)?

- How do hardscaping and landscaping—including patios, gardens, and outbuildings—complement the house, respect the environment, and enhance the experience of island living?

- How much will the house cost?

Islanders who are renovating also ponder such questions, although with less urgency. Moving into an existing house allows more time to consider options.

And you should also be attentive to how a house is likely to shape the feel of daily life on island as you contemplate design. Michael Modzelewski, who lived in Blackfish Sound, reflects on the ways his "shipshape" home suited his needs. "It was a small home—twelve feet across and thirty-four feet long. The surrounding immensity made a limited space not only tolerable but psychologically desirable. Like the animals with dens in the big woods, I welcomed this confinement, found it necessary to be able to leave the outer world completely, to nestle within a small, familiar space."[6]

Design also takes practical matters into consideration. Chic, for example, prepared plans for a house that perches high on a ridge at the top of thirty-seven-metre-high cliffs that surround his island in the San Juans. To ensure that he had anticipated structural issues, Chic ran the plans past an engineer. Doing so sent them back to the drawing board to redesign and reinforce the roof and foundations. "The engineer liked everything I did. Said it was all good. But in our location, there may be category 4 winds, so we've got a lot of shear and uplift. He said that our cabin, as heavy as it is, was not heavy enough to stay there if the wind blows beyond a certain level—it will blow away. Hard to believe, specially when we've lifted those logs and put them in place! If the wind gets a good grip, it can pull the overhangs away. It's about the site and how the wind gets under it." Chic went on to say that the engineer went through and added uplift resistance and specified tie downs. "We epoxied rebar into the bedrock on the footings—we had to glue the house down." Kathy adds, "We're ready for anything!"

A minor design debate among islanders, and a topic that seems to invoke laughter and disagreement among couples, is the question of front and back. Without the usual reference points of driveway, street, and suburban grid, arguments arise. Is the front of the house the side facing the water or the access path? Some people see the glorious water side as the natural front of an island home. After all, this is where the majority of time is spent. Others insist that the front of the house is always where you welcome guests who are making the way up a pathway or road from a dock. For them, the ceremonial place of arrivals and departures is the entrance, even if it is rarely used.

Getting organized

WHILE IT SEEMS tempting to break ground right away, islanders talk about the organizational challenges that crop up between choosing a design and starting a building project. Getting ready for island construction involves a number of interrelated steps: arranging permissions, assembling tools and acquiring all sorts of building supplies, designing systems to be integrated into the building, and accessing— or developing—skills. All of these are described as complicated, time-consuming, and particularly thought-provoking in the island context. As Chic comments, "You fall into bed exhausted and then, as you're waiting to go to sleep, your mind is processing the next steps. I have numerous electronic documents called 'next steps,' organized by what I'm working on, so I think things through. Sometimes I actually wake up and grab the iPhone and add some notes about something I'm afraid I'll forget."

ADHERING TO REGULATIONS Permissions, not surprisingly, emerge as the least popular first things to think about. But these are important, particularly considering the problems that you may confront if regulations are not properly addressed. And there are many regulations to consider. Federal and provincial regulations tend to relate to the protection of natural and cultural resources. For example, if the building site is located adjacent to a stream, riparian rights come into play. Protecting animal and plant habitats in many sensitive ecosystems in the islands is also a priority. And many building sites along the coast require a formal archaeological assessment to ensure that no traditional-use sites or human remains are negatively affected. If assessment reveals a conflict, various levels of remediation may be required to ensure that the traditional values of Indigenous peoples are respected. It's important to anticipate such investigations and include them in the building timeline and budget.

The Islands Trust in British Columbia also sets policy and regulations associated with land use in the Gulf Islands and as far north as Denman Island and east to Gambier in Howe Sound. The trust's primary roles are to foster the preservation and protection of ecosystems; to ensure that the scale, rate, and type of development are compatible; and to sustain island character and healthy communities. Island committees decide where and how lands are developed while the trust sets policies. For example, it does not support bridges, destination casinos, or finfish farms. And it develops designations and zoning for use and density, including residential, commercial, industrial, and agricultural uses, and protected areas for native species and habitats. Such zoning can stipulate siting, including setback from the beach, and the size and dimensions of buildings. Since different islands have different development goals in light of size, access, habitat, and availability of water, a starting point is to consult bylaws set by the local trust committee. This information is available on the Islands Trust website or at a local office.

Regional districts in British Columbia tend to oversee the permissions needed to actually construct and occupy buildings on islands. Working within the regulations set by the BC Building Code and by local bylaws, inspectors in some regions become regular visitors to islands in order to assess compliance and sign off on various stages. And since arranging travel to islands may pose significant challenges in the building timeline, coordinating inspections and occupancy permits becomes an important part of project management. Frustrating? Many islanders have encountered significant difficulties in reconciling the requirements of a code designed for on-the-grid houses with their island needs, realities, budgets, and timelines. As one grumbles,

> I've been hearing about this new, ridiculous, alternate-energy electrical code you're supposed to follow. They insist that you must have the same electrical capacity as you'd have in town, even though you don't want it or need it. That means that you must buy huge batteries, gigantic solar arrays, very fancy inverters—way more than what you actually want. But they insist that you have the capacity for dishwashers, hot-water heaters, power tools, ovens—things for which you can easily find low-energy alternatives. Because my house was built years ago I haven't had to comply and I'm very comfortable with my wood cook stove, little twin tub washing machine, solar or wood-fired hot water and LED lights. I use a small fraction of the electricity burned in a city home.

Clarifying expectations and coordinating permissions and inspections is a regular part of organizing for building in populous southern areas. Islanders in more remote areas, however, laugh when asked about this and report that they rarely encounter close scrutiny in their building projects. As one person said, "I suppose you're supposed to comply, but nobody comes out here and says, 'You can't do it that way.'" Building inspectors, for example, have never made the trip to a small island in the northern part of the Georgia Basin. The owners wanted the percolation for their septic field inspected but couldn't persuade anyone from the regional district to come by. "So we had a fellow who was sailing by come over, look at what we'd done, and tell us if it was right or wrong. He said, 'It looks good.'" They are philosophical. "The trick is to do it right even if it's not inspected; don't try to get around rules and regulations—they're there for a reason. You really need to abide by them so that things like the septic field work perfectly." On a different island I heard that "we had a copy of the Ontario Building Code, which we used as reference because we didn't want a house that fell down." On the wet coasts of British Columbia and Puget Sound, preventing rainwater and standing water from causing rot and infestation is a particular concern. Following codes and using appropriate materials can save endless repairs a few years later.

And it is worth noting that if you contract a registered builder to construct your island home, the builder is required to adhere to a home warranty process that involves a range of standards and inspections, regardless of the location of the structure. While this ensures a well-built house, the costs of compliance with codes and warranty inspections will be reflected in the overall estimates.

Other regulations? While no one I spoke with brought it up, it's worth noting that job sites are also regulated by employment standards, WorkSafe BC or Washington State regulations, and other health and safety considerations if paid contractors are involved. Insurance companies may have expectations regarding house construction standards. And they likely require fire protection and other systems that protect the security of an island home. And, of course, your own sense of appropriate approaches to construction should regulate what happens. Again and again I heard about the importance of safety on site. And Jan and Sy laugh when they say, "Advice for islanders: drink beer *after* the job is done."

ASSEMBLING TOOLS AND MATERIALS When islanders talk about organizational steps, they are much more enthusiastic about collecting tools—a large assortment of them. For novice islanders the list must be pretty daunting. An axe and hatchet, a Swede or bow saw, handsaws of various kinds, diverse hammers, a full suite of screwdrivers, socket wrenches, a vice, Vice-Grips, a hand drill, a brace and bits, chisels, a plane, levels, squares, measuring tapes and carpenter's pencils, a plumb bob, a chalk line, files, sanding tools, a box cutter, wire cutters, and good scissors all play valuable roles in building projects. And a chainsaw is invaluable—one islander says that she "loves the feeling of power it gives me."[7] If electricity is available, table, band,

and rip saws, routers, drills, and sanders (and tools to fix the generator) all save time and effort. The shopping list could also include good ladders, some kind of workbench, sawhorses, a wheelbarrow, a blowtorch, a concrete mixer, a post hole digger, buckets, trowels for concrete work, a come-along, jacks, clamps, a crowbar, wedges, a rod for hand drilling rock, an adze, a froe, shovels, rakes, a pickaxe, rope, tape, wire, chain, slings, lubricants, good gloves, a weed-whacker, and a few bungee cords. And a northern islander recommends a gun. Are all these necessary? Perhaps not, but it's hard to shorten this list when you consider the multiple specialized tasks involved in construction, particularly in a remote location with few hands to help out and bears lurking nearby. Chic grins when he says that "the whole purpose of the island is to allow me to buy any tool or instrument that I want. I can justify almost anything. Not a helicopter yet, but any other power equipment or tool. I have one each of all the tools, and then I have an overlap or a backup."

A copy of the current building code and a construction handbook are also worth their weight in gold. I still have my dad's Reader's Digest house-building manual. It is covered with dirt, grime, and what I suspect are specks of blood. Although hard to access on many islands, the Internet can be a great source of advice. What else? Depending on the project, plumbing and wiring tools, paintbrushes, scrapers, landscaping tools ... the list goes on and on. Many of these items can be acquired second-hand, perhaps from established or departing islanders. And all should be of good quality to withstand hard use. Chic observes that "you wear out everything—power tools, hand tools, gloves, jeans. That's one of the fun things about being out there. How many people actually wear out all their stuff? That's what's so healthy about this environment. It's not that it's hard work, it's just constant work."

Other useful supplies for a building site include a really good first aid kit, chairs for contemplating either the view or building progress, a camera, a diary for reflective moments, paper for lists, a cooler for beer during the day, and bottles of scotch and wine for evenings when progress is evaluated and plans are made for the next day. The tools to create a simple home are complicated.

Many islanders also find ways to bring such heavy equipment as excavators, concrete mixers, and tractors on island.

For example, Chic and Kathy wanted both a Jeep and an excavator that could play multiple roles in transporting gear, preparing their building site, and moving heavy timbers. Developing strategies to get them to Snowberry Island, with its high surrounding cliffs, kept Chic up at night. First came the Jeep. "It came over on a small launch with a drop-down gate. They pushed the barge up against the rock. I drove the Jeep up, pulling on the winch that was anchored to a fir tree high above at the same time as I was driving. It went right up the bank. We had some problems. The oversize wheels got underneath a rock, so we had to set up a come-along to get it up and over, but it got there." Bringing the excavator on island was even more challenging.

> We barged it over in October. It was very wet, there was a lot of moss. The excavator has rubber tracks and the rock was slimy—like a cat going up a tin roof. Kathy got it up. She took our Jeep and backed it down the other side of the island so the winch line came up over the island. So now she's a counterweight to the excavator. The excavator weighs 7,000 pounds. The Jeep doesn't weigh that much—it's only 4,500 pounds, but it has a 9,500-pound winch. She's pulling with the winch, but her Jeep is getting pulled uphill by the excavator. At least we're thinking the excavator's not going to fall off the island, but she's not even wearing a life jacket!

As a full collection of tools and equipment is being assembled, a space where it can be securely organized, stored, and used is needed. One of the first structures Mom and Dad built was a lockable A-frame shed (a little practice project) where their growing assortment of carpentry and other tools and equipment was stored between building sessions. Tools were always cleaned and put away at the end of a day and organized so that they were easy to locate. Once the house was done, their next major building project was a full-blown workshop and storage shed in the middle of the island. It became the centre for everything from beer brewing to engine repairs. A storage shed at the dock, a greenhouse, and a boat-building shed followed as the years passed.

Sourcing the various construction materials that come together in a house is one of the most challenging aspects of building on island, as is ensuring that everything is on hand at the time it is needed. Sy grimaces when he says, "You don't want to have to go back to a store, specially when you're building something. There are intricate parts of a building, and you have to have the right materials before you can continue on…so you get really good at remembering to get stuff." Every islander has a story about having to stop building for want of a nail or a piece of lumber. These stories usually go on to describe improvisations, long trips to the nearest hardware store, or expensive float-plane or water-taxi delivery services. Time and time again I heard that careful forethought, detailed lists, and inventory systems are critical, as is a willingness to adapt and change when problems arise. Elizabeth Arthur, who settled with her husband on a truly remote and undeveloped island in Stuart Lake in northern BC, reflects on the irony of how much stuff must be handled in order to create housing for a simple island life. "When we decided to move to the island and away from the life which centered on the materialistic world, I never imagined I would gain here such an intimate knowledge of things. Piles of boards, stacks of insulation, boxes of nails, cans of wood stain— they demand attention, not shrilly, but patiently."[8]

There seem to be as many strategies for acquiring building materials as there are projects. On islands that have multiple residents, a road system, and a marine loading ramp, bringing materials by truck on a barge is a relatively straightforward, if expensive, approach. The foundations of a house on an island near Silva Bay were done quickly when a concrete truck arrived by barge. And I talked with one islander who used squared pine logs from Ontario for his dream home. Barging his logs to the Gulf Island was the end of a long transcontinental trucking journey. Elsewhere, a 930-square-metre log lodge, deconstructed from a site in the interior of British Columbia and barged over on trucks, was reconstructed as a rather grand private home.

The busy commercial landing craft, barges, and other freight vessels seen plying coastal waters are often called into service to deliver vehicles, building materials, and heavy equipment. While Jan and Sy normally use their large aluminum skiff to carry bulky equipment and supplies to the island from nearby Saltery Bay, they turned to one of these more robust vessels when building their house.

That was major! We had our materials delivered to Mitchell Island [in the Fraser River estuary]: all the lumber, all the insulation, windows, doors, whatever. We collected the stuff over a period of maybe a month. Then it was loaded on a landing barge. The owner brought the barge up here and delivered it to a spot on the beach in front of the building site. We had all our friends organized for a work party, because usually when you get materials you have to carry them up by hand. But he had a four-wheel-drive forklift—it was the most amazing thing. He came in on a rising tide, going slowly. All our friends who'd come to help were getting quietly drunk, because there was no work to be done. They were just watching the forklift going back and forth. And now it's getting dark, the tide is high, and the operator is getting a little stressed and driving the forklift like a race car. The last time it was hard to get onto the barge, and he came aboard so hard he almost went off the end—there were sparks flying and we all went, "Whoa . . ." I wish I had a video of that. But everything was moved to the building site.

A key to minimizing costs when using commercial barges is partnering with neighbours to maximize loads. Nevertheless, it is estimated that using a truck and barge can double the cost of an island home. As Jan notes, "It's expensive. Everything is expensive. It's at least two and a half times as expensive as building on the mainland. That's our rule of thumb. Everything is costly to get over here." Other people, closer to supply centres, offer estimates of one and a half to two times the cost; the nature of the materials and the degree of organization all influence the price.

Another delivery strategy for islanders with difficult sites is slinging materials by helicopter. While relatively pricey, helicopter delivery is not prohibitive if supplies are barged to the island and the helicopter just flies out, lifts slings from the barge deck, and carries them over a short distance to the building site. Often only a couple of hours are needed if the sling weights and the reception area are well planned. Judith tells me that three houses have been delivered this way on Rendezvous, and their owners experienced a huge saving in time, injuries or backaches, road fixing, and vehicle repairs. Their difficult but impressive sites were all on the top of steep bluffs. There's something very appealing about having all your building materials neatly arranged on site over the course of a busy morning.

Other islanders take more modest—and physically demanding—approaches. Mom and Dad's method of transporting materials by boat and homemade barge on an as-needed basis is not uncommon. And as many islanders attest, it's remarkable what can be loaded onto a small commuter boat in calm weather. Emily and Tom laugh when they describe carrying a bale of insulation to Protection Island on their kayak. I've seen Roger's boat weighed down by twenty long sheets of aluminum roofing. These were as cumbersome to get on and off the boat as the boat was to operate with such a heavy load. And 6-metre laminated beams, a 431-kilogram centrifugal log splitter, water tanks, and a sawmill have all been balanced on Chic and Kathy's Sea Sport to make the 15-kilometre trip to Snowberry Island. "I'm going out anyway, so as long as I don't overload the boat and can plane on the way, I put stuff on top and head out. We buzz out there at 26 knots. It works great." He adds with a smile, "I did put a bigger engine—300 horsepower—on the boat. Another rationalized purchase—totally rationalized."

Getting materials from the landing area to the building site is another challenge involving strong arms and backs, wheelbarrows, and such invaluable equipment as power wagons, small tractors, four-by-fours, or pickup trucks that have been barged over for island use. David explains how he carried the lumber for his first cabin up a steep sandstone embankment. "There were no stairs, so everything was carried up on my back on an extension ladder over the steep part. Lots of bruises—and carrying the HardiPlank was a killer." Materials for their next house were delivered to a distant dock and transported in small lots along a narrow, hilly road. "I built outriggers for the quad—two-by-fours that would bolt onto the front and rear so I could carry my lumber through the forest."

Cranes, come-alongs, high-lead systems, truck winches, and roller systems are all put to work on various islands. These demand knowledge of the physics of dragging, lifting, and supporting heavy materials. At this point, questions about the merits of a building site that far from the dock or beach, or up a steep hill may resurface. Kathy and Chic tell funny stories about using either their small power wagon or a Jeep to haul materials up steep embankments and across their island.

One day Kathy spied this log that was floating in. It was about 42 feet long—nice log, very straight. The problem with anything that floats around here is that it's 120 feet below where we'd want to use it. We lassoed it and then put full power on the boat just to pull it off the beach. It's very hard to pull stuff when you're pushing against water. We got it off the rocks and towed it down to the dock. Then I had to lift the end onto the dock and use the come-along to pull it up across the dock. Since it was longer than the ramp, I cut it in half and we used the come-along to pull it onto the power wagon. The wagon is only 5 feet long, so we've got a 21-foot pole balanced on a 5-foot power wagon, and we have to go up a steep slope and then another hill and turn a corner and try not to dig it in.

I am struck by the number of islanders who mill much of the lumber for their houses on site. Recycled timbers from derelict canneries, wharfs, or camps nearby, or logs cut locally or hauled up from the beach all make appearances in island homes. The hard physical work of installing a mill or moving a portable one, sourcing found timber, getting it to the mill, and cutting dimensional lumber seems to be offset by the savings and satisfaction inherent in the process. For example, an Alaska mill attached to Joe Martin's chainsaw allowed him to rework timbers from an abandoned bridge on Kennedy Lake. He towed the lumber to Echachis, near Tofino, to create his home. And like Sy on his small island in Jervis Inlet, Chic on Snowberry Island worked with a portable mill to cut all the posts and beams needed for his home. He strives for close tolerances that suit his meticulous building style. "We've sawn a lot of lumber up there. The mill works pretty well. It saws a max length of eighteen feet six inches, so I took the ends off to get more out of it. I can mill eighteen feet six inches on a log and then move the log and saw the rest of it. You can mill pretty big things—my ridge beams are six by eighteen feet, so I mill them larger and then let them shrink for a while and then remill them." Time becomes a significant cost of the milling process as green lumber dries.

With so much complexity in sourcing materials, it's not surprising to see island homes that have been built from kits. Prefabricated components and comprehensive packaged structures are relatively quick to deliver and construct, and have the added benefit of making highly efficient and cost-effective use of lumber and labour. The *Private Islands* newsletter notes,

> Your housing is likely to be the most significant ecological footprint left on your island, but this is one area where it's easy to go green. Modular housing that's easy to transport and assemble and uses natural, green materials is not only good for the environment, but significantly less expensive than traditional construction. These types of ready-made homes and cottages come in an incredible variety of styles, from futuristic geodesic domes, to miniature Georgian estates, to innovative tree houses that won't even leave a mark on your forest floor.

It goes on to say, "Less construction time means lower labour costs, and the home's mass-produced kit creates an economy of scale. As many use eco-friendly woods, have built-in solar generators, and require a minimal foundation, modular housing is one area where going green is friendly to both the earth and your wallet."[9]

Sometimes fate delivers building materials. Years after our A-frame was completed on Bath Island, a barge carrying clear, twelve-by-twelve-inch timbers dumped its load in Porlier Pass in a January storm. Over the next few days, we rescued enough of its precious cargo to form the foundation of a guest cottage. I'm not sure it ever occurred to Mom and

Dad that we shouldn't wade up to our waists to secure many of these timbers and haul them onshore—hypothermia was not a named condition in those days. But we certainly knew we were cold.

Islanders everywhere tend to integrate found objects and recycle building materials as part of building projects. Windows from structures at Expo 86, beams from abandoned logging and fishing camps, and furniture made from twisted and weathered tree roots all add character and save money. A fallen cedar, cut into sections and towed from a local inlet, produced enough shakes for Joe's Echachis Island roof, but cutting them was so repetitive he found himself dreaming at night about endlessly working a froe and mallet. And Misty Lawson's parents used beachwood for their house, adding rooms over the years to expand their first small cabin. Because Misty's father was a thoughtful designer who took both sun and wind into consideration and a talented carpenter who anticipated drenching rains, the house has withstood its harsh West Coast environment for over forty years with no more than the usual maintenance.

An island couple that lives on the eastern seaboard takes great pride in their use and reuse of found materials.

The snug, two-room log house that we call home was a lot less trouble and a great deal less expensive to build out here on MacLeod Island than if we'd constructed it inland somewhere. Why? Because we cut and trimmed out the tree trunks for its walls two miles down shore and then leisurely floated the timbers to the cabin site behind our boat.

Not to mention the fact that most of our windowsill lumber was "scrounged for free" driftwood that we picked up on the beach. Or that five washed-up railroad ties serve as steps to the cabin. Or that the dozen creosoted planks which came in on the tide after one particularly severe gale were just what we needed to finish off other parts of the house. Or that old crates—tossed overboard from passing ships—are all we've ever needed in the way of dressers and drawers . . .

Many materials used in island construction projects do double duty. Packing materials are carefully tucked away to meet upcoming storage and transportation needs; ends of lumber are stowed for future construction; and left-over or used nails, screws, hinges, and other bits of hardware are stored with the knowledge that one day they may save the islander a half-day trip to a hardware store. Creative islanders take recycling seriously as it helps minimize the challenges involved in moving things on to—and off—the island.[10]

The ultimate act of recycling is moving an existing dwelling onto an island. Linda on Valdes describes how her parents acquired their home in 1947. "For fifty dollars they bought a small two-room float house [from a logging operation] and owners helped my dad to get it into position up off the water. It was on cedar blocks—what I would call shake blocks about four feet long. They just used sandstone rock under the blocks and that house sat there for sixty years. There were four of us in that house—no running water and no electricity, ever."

According to Jim Connelly, who works with the house moving firm Nickel Brothers in Victoria, staff are always delighted to see houses make their way from urban settings to islands. Barging an existing house to an island property has many benefits. Often the older houses available for moving from urban neighbourhoods are well built, with charming features. And the cost of moving is much less than new construction, even when a combination of trucking and barging is involved. But it is important to have the right site. The beach in front should be clear of rocks (Connolly calls them can-openers) that get in the way of positioning a sixty-metre steel barge close to shore on a high tide. And, ideally, the point at which the house comes ashore should be no more than four and a half metres above high water to allow a ramp to be constructed from the barge. The foundation must be pre-poured. And there should be enough room beside the foundation to receive a building of up to twelve metres wide (though Connelly refers to a house of this size as "hell on wheels"). Once the house is sitting on the site, it is rolled sideways onto the foundation and is ready for refinishing. There may be a bit of cracking and chimneys always need to be replaced, but on the whole it is a quick and satisfying way to create an island home and to give an old house a new lease on life.

DESIGNING SYSTEMS A third aspect of getting organized for construction is considering the systems you are prepared to create and sustain, far removed from easy hookups with mainland utility grids. Where will your water come from and sewage go? How important is electricity? And are creature comforts necessary or nice? In interesting ways, systems determine what will be distinctive about day-to-day island life. This is most often revealed in the ways kitchens and bathrooms are designed. If an outhouse, water jugs, a wood stove, and lanterns are sufficient (and permitted by local authorities), then life will be simple, uncomplicated. As Margaret McIntyre observes, "You know, it's funny how living this sort of life teaches you to distinguish between the important things and the unimportant...I can remember when a house without full plumbing was a thing unheard of in respectable society, and a hot bath in the morning was something indispensable to decency. Now we find that a roof over one's head and food in one's stomach are the real basic necessities of life, and plumbing of any description is a complete superfluity."[11]

Most islanders opt for the complications of indoor plumbing, hot running water, and some form of power to light the house, run appliances, and provide communication links. And most describe the challenges of planning, installing, and maintaining such systems with enthusiasm, since these choices require ingenuity, allow experimentation with green technologies, and reinforce the value of self-sufficiency that brings people to islands in the first place. Systems typically evolve over time in response to need, experience, and resources. As Rob on Maurelle notes, their nature and functionality shape the character and quality of island life.

Harnessing a reliable supply of potable water is high on most lists of necessities. Quality and quantity are both key considerations, particularly on the dry San Juan and Gulf Islands. The amount of water needed to sustain a home depends on many factors, including whether the property is occupied year-round or seasonally, how many people use the water, and how conscious they are of conservation. I grew up shutting the tap off as soon as my toothbrush was damp and not turning it on again until the final rinse. Water was used sparingly and then recycled, baths were only a few inches deep, and toilets were flushed on an as-needed basis. Many islanders cringe when guests happily treat water as if they were in their city homes where, Environment Canada tells us, they use an average of 250 litres per person per day.[12] This translates to 91,000 litres per year. Islanders get by on a lot less and are quick to adopt low-flow showers and toilets, low-volume washers, and minimal landscaping. Judith on Rendezvous comments, "I'm careful of how I use my water. The idea of using it just to flush the toilet is really hard to accept, so I don't do that." She prefers a water-free composting toilet. And as Eric Nicol, the much-loved BC humourist, reflects from his summer home on Saturna, "Because water is so precious you soon adjust to thinking of an Okanagan Chardonnay as a nice breakfast beverage."[13]

Nevertheless, given the sheer volume of water that tends to be necessary over the course of a year, the most relaxed islanders are those with deep and reliable wells. They are spared the seasonal worry of hoarding water and making limited supplies last, although islanders with wells are still respectful of fluctuations in the water table, as well as potential saltwater contamination in precious aquifers. And even these islanders need to design pumping, tank, and distribution systems that provide a high-pressure supply to their houses, fire hoses, gardens, and other work areas.

Despite some interesting experiments with water witching, many islanders can't locate a source or don't have the resources to drill for water. Instead they look to the sky, collecting rainwater off roofs and other surfaces during wet seasons and storing it in large cisterns usually located on high points above the house to allow for a gravity feed. The Islands Trust indicates that the average home is able to capture 91,000 to 105,000 litres of water a year with average Gulf Islands rainfall. This is sufficient to provide, per year, around 50 percent of the daily supply for a household with four persons.[14] And since water is used even as it is captured, a household's capacity to store 91,000 litres in multiple tanks or cisterns is generally regarded as more than sufficient. Of course, much depends on location, the number of people, the months they are in residence, and whether gardens demand water. Some islanders get by with 4,550 litres of storage on the wet West Coast; Roger now has 40,950 litres on Bath Island; other islanders have installed over 100,000 litres of storage in an abundance of caution. Rain barrels, connected with downspouts, are also useful elements in rainwater catchment systems.

Getting water tanks to islands always seems to involve funny tales (at least in retrospect) of small boats, high winds, work parties, and complicated methods of lifting these unwieldy objects to a high point of land. Chic recommends a flat site, backing into a hill so that attached hoses can be buried to avoid freezing, which is a key concern if no one is around to monitor things in cold winter months. And everyone recommends regular cleaning—roofs, gutters, tanks—to keep the system working effectively.

One of the tanks that still provides water storage on Bath Island is an enormous steel flotation pontoon that escaped from the military installation near Comox, to the north. Clair spotted the 7.6-by-1.5-metre tank drifting southward near Thrasher Rock one calm afternoon. As she didn't have a boat with a motor at hand, she rowed out, took the pontoon under tow, and spent three hours slowly hauling it back to the dock area. After some negotiation with the navy to acquire possession, Dad put all his engineering talents to work to lift the tank into position. Yet another block and tackle system was threaded through treetops to haul the tank up a cliff face and skid it to a position of honour atop the island. While corroded on the outside, the interior of that tank was clean as a whistle and, with a capacity of 15,470 litres, it more than doubled the island's water-storage capacity at the time.

Neighbours on Valdes Island tell a similar story of salvaging a pontoon that broke free from the Roberts Bank construction project.

We always wished that we had a big tank. Wishing was good, because one day this old fisherman said, "What's that big tank on the beach south of you?" It was very large; it had been the lead tank in the dredging unit in the river, so it had big bollards on it. It was made of riveted steel and would be like something you'd see on a box car. And very, very long. Round. It had saddles where the dredge line had hung. The tide and waves had pushed it quite far up the beach. We just had a little boat with a ten-horse engine. We had to go at night when the tide was out and put ground anchors out. We could shorten the lines and pull it to get it floating. We moved it right in front of our house for the winter. Big cables secured it to trees. It would pound in the storms and the whole house would shake. In those days we didn't have an immediate neighbour. So we used a manual hand winch, a Beebe winch, to pull it up to the top of our property. But because of the saddles, it wouldn't roll. We jacked it up on timbers to raise it off the beach. And then used the winch to drag it up through the neighbouring field. It was quite a project. Once we got it up, we pulled it sideways in behind a couple of trees and filled it with water from the creek. That's been a godsend for us because we had a source of water, not for drinking but for everything else—washing, gardening.

Gifts from the sea are part of island life. Their arrival is always unexpected. The trick is to secure found objects first and then ponder how they might be used.

Another option for sourcing surface water is channelling from a nearby stream. Both Helen Piddington in Loughborough Inlet (not an island, but certainly off the grid) and Margaret McIntyre on Nelson Island relied on this method. And on Maurelle Island Rob and Laurie dammed a swamp above their property to create a year-round reservoir and gravity-fed supply system. The big drop gives them great pressure, and there is no need to maintain pumps.

A particularly imaginative system of catchment and supply provides Jan and Sy and their neighbours, Bob and Sue, with fresh water. They recall that water was one of the first things they had to take care of when they moved their young family to their shared island at the mouth of Jervis Inlet in the 1980s. "None of these islands have groundwater and drilling is very expensive. So we got the water rights to a little spring on Crown land high up there on Nelson Island, just across the channel. It has about one hundred and eighty feet of head." Working side by side with Bob and Sue, they built a small dam and designed a catchment system that fills a 4,550-litre bag, the kind helicopters use for firefighting. And they bought hundreds of metres of coiled pipe to run down the slope, under the channel, and across to their island. "It was quite a production. We unfurled the pipe, pulled it with the little boat, and had a diver anchor the line all the way." There were problems. "Unbeknownst to us, it was defective line. So we had many, many leaks under the water—we could tell, since it was losing pressure." They replaced the whole thing with 2.5-centimetre municipal plastic pipe for potable water and since then it has worked well, although it has needed repair when boats have dropped anchors on it. And in the wintertime "there's oodles of water, but it has frozen. And there's always maintenance issues like cleaning out the dam, but it's sufficient for most of the year for two families."

Desalinization is a useful but still relatively rare strategy for generating fresh water when no other source is workable. The challenge seems to be meeting power requirements. But as solar-powered desalination becomes increasingly viable, systems that remove minerals from salt water through a series of membranes seem like a godsend to islanders. There are a handful of these systems in place in the San Juan and Gulf Islands.

And connection to city water is the easiest system of all. As Protection Island is located within the Nanaimo boundaries, the city ran a water line under the harbour and set up hydrants so that residents were able to respond to fire. According to islanders, it didn't take long for locals to figure out how to tap into the hydrants for domestic water, and now all island water is supplied through this system.

Some islanders, including my parents, create different water systems for different uses. Brackish groundwater from the hand-dug well was collected and stored on Bath Island. It required regular pumping and careful monitoring throughout the year but provided water for toilets, bathing, cleaning, and gardening in all but the driest months. Black plastic piping wound through underbrush from the well to the tanks and from the tanks to the houses and to taps in the gardens. These lines were fine, except for the occasional year when they froze in the winter then burst with the thaw. Roger still maintains the system but has switched to rubber-reinforced lines since they withstand freeze-thaw cycles more successfully. They could be buried to minimize freezing, but the work involved on a rocky island is daunting.

Mom and Dad also set up a rainwater collection system on the expansive roof of the A-frame. Broad gutters collected water that drained into a tank under the house. Hand-pumping it to a second tank suspended in the eaves was a daily chore. The rainwater was filtered and plumbed into a special tap in the kitchen. It was boiled before use but always had the vague taste of asphalt shingles. Mom and Dad switched to hauling containers of water to the island when they couldn't discourage birds from perching on the ridgeline.

A third system was set up in response to the ever-present fear of wildfire. Yet another tank was added to the collection on the top of the island and filled with seawater. Hoses ran from the tank to the various buildings on the island but were never put to use. And the seawater pump was kept in a shed close to the beach for quick deployment if a direct stream of water was needed. Seawater isn't ideal for many reasons but, in the absence of other water, it seemed like a reasonable choice.

Regardless of how they source water, islanders talk about the importance of supply management throughout the year. Monitoring volume and quality, topping up in wet seasons, caring for multi-stage filtration and purification systems, and taking conservative approaches to use all ensure that precious water flows from taps. And they tell stories of catastrophic water loss caused by leakage in fittings and pipes, failure of aging tank foundations, or simply forgetting to turn a tap off. Water is an ongoing preoccupation, and the increasingly dry conditions in parts of the West Coast are a major concern. If 2018 was one of the hottest years on record, what will island water tables and catchment systems look like in 2028? And how will this affect ecosystems and the threat of wildfire?

Systems for sewage and grey-water disposal are also important since most islanders set their sights higher than the basic outhouse and don't want to fling dishwater out the back door. Septic fields provide the most common solution, and islanders talk about the importance of both design and maintenance to avoid odour and overflow problems.

Grey-water recycling systems have real value on water-starved islands. Even fifty years ago Mom rarely allowed grey water to go into the septic system, at least in the summer months. Dishwater and bathwater were regularly carried by bucket out to the gardens where soap-tolerant plants thrived from this daily attention. And in the driest summers, salt water was carried in buckets to the bathroom to flush toilets on an as-needed basis.

Other forms of waste and recycling systems also need attention. What kinds of garbage will be generated and how can they be disposed of? Vegetable waste can go into compost bins (add these to the list of things to be built) to create a precious amendment for island soils. But grease and scraps of meat are more challenging to dispose of unless they are part of the dog's diet or slipped into the wood stove. Paper, cardboard, and wood go into the stoves, fireplaces, or winter bonfires, but plastics, metals, glass, many leftover construction materials, all those beer cans, and recyclable containers and packaging need other ecologically friendly disposal strategies. Islanders find themselves working hard to create and manage a number of separate waste-storage systems and to carry bags of garbage and recyclables to mainland depots. While everyone is attentive to recycling these days, the work involved in attending to waste generated in building and living on an island creates a great incentive to buy and use only the materials that are needed, or to grow food and make other consumables on island.

Some degree of electricity is also high on most islanders' list of necessities. At a minimum, twelve-volt batteries to charge cell phones or power radio telephones in more remote areas are valued for both safety and social communications. Small generators have been used for decades to charge batteries for these purposes. While Mom and Dad charged car batteries with a small generator attached to a noisy Briggs & Stratton engine, much more sophisticated diesel generators feeding banks of deep-cycle batteries now provide an intermittent soundtrack that intrudes on the peace of many islands. Whether or not these may be seen as disruptive, their use reflects the degree to which electricity is valued. Generators need a reliable supply of diesel that adds cost and complication.

Water-generated power is another option if a reliable stream is nearby. A hydroelectric system on Maurelle Island gives Laurie and Rob adequate power when water supply from their reservoir is plentiful. "We have one particular device—a micro-hydro wheel that we got about twenty-five years ago and it is unbelievably cost-beneficial. The amount of investment we put into it is a lot less than many of our other systems, and yet eight months of the year, day in, day out, we get all the electricity we need." When water to drive their Pelton water wheel dries up in summer, they switch to solar power. "We don't use as much power in the summertime." Helen Piddington, who lives farther north in Loughborough Inlet, writes about the ways in which the ubiquitous Pelton water wheel, first designed for use in nineteenth-century goldfields, has made life more comfortable.

> The powerhouse walls are of stone, the floor concrete. Two Pelton wheels sit side by side over a trough and a generator and an invertor are nearby. Water is piped downhill for a mile. It passes through a brass valve that shoots it onto the cups of one or the other wheel making it spin at a terrific speed and turn the generator. The resulting AC power is stored in banks of batteries, set up as 12 or 24 volt—we have both systems. When 110 volts are needed this AC power is drawn from the batteries and transformed by invertors into DC power. To me this is black magic but it works . . . the Pelton wheels run night and day, year-round.[15]

Not surprisingly, many islanders are early adopters of clean-energy technologies and have been experimenting with solar systems for years. Rob and Laurie used a rudimentary solar panel on Maurelle Island in the 1970s. "A friend who was a physics prof at UBC came to visit and saw us using kerosene lamps that were dirty, dangerous, unhealthy, and carbon-producing. It was definitely a problem. He gave me an obsolete solar panel and a fluorescent light that we've had for almost forty years." It was in their original shack and is now installed in their new house. The panel also allowed them to run a marine VHF radio. Rob says this raised eyebrows in the Maurelle co-op. "We were already starting to be bourgeois."

Today many island homes have multiple solar panels installed on south- and west-facing roof surfaces or integrated into adjacent landscaping, along with banks of batteries secreted in dedicated utility rooms. And as solar systems are getting both cheaper and more reliable, islanders talk about increasing capacity. Chic does not see power generation as a problem. "Lighting is a no-brainer. We live in a day when for 1 watt of energy you can have terrific light from an LED. And most of our electronics run on very little wattage. The computer I use runs on 5 watts—that's it. Just a small battery bank can actually power all your daily activities. If you want to run something bigger like laundry or power equipment, you need 15 amps and you can get that from a generator. Things are getting better all the time." His words are echoed by Sy. "Ten years ago, solar energy was ten dollars a watt, and today it's one dollar a watt—I can go out and buy half a dozen 250-watt panels, and that gives us a lot of power. We run our washing machines, our dishwasher during the daytime." And David and Suromitra, who have designed a sophisticated solar system to power their house and workshop, laugh when they point to their clothesline. "Our solar-powered dryer is the best thing in the world."

Wind power is also an option, but although I hear stories of experiments with windmills of various kinds, no one reports much sustained success. Variable winds and difficulties in maintaining towers, rotors, and associated hardware seem to make home-built solutions more trouble than they're worth. Years ago, Dad built a tower with a two-bladed propeller and placed it at the corner of the deck. I remember both the sound and the vibrations that shook the house when a southeaster came up, but I don't recall why he abandoned his new technology after just a few months.

Regardless of how power is generated, storage and distribution systems must also be planned and maintained. Rob describes their Maurelle Island approach.

An important component of homemade electricity is having a way of storing the power in a bank of batteries so it is available when you need it. The most common batteries are 12 volt just like in cars except bigger. Whereas a typical car battery is 80 amp hours we bought an 800 amp hour battery. From the batteries the power is "inverted" to regular household 110 volts for distribution in the house circuits. An additional advantage of an inverter is that at the same time as it is delivering power from the batteries it can also receive power from an auxiliary gasoline generator and use it to charge the batteries when the Pelton wheel or solar panels are low.[16]

Relatively stable and affordable propane for light, cooking, refrigeration, and on-demand hot water is another common island system. This is particularly convenient in areas where propane delivery barges can top up large tanks positioned at the shoreline. I also talked with people who set their 100-pound tanks on their ATV on the dock from time to time so that the delivery barge can come alongside to fill them. But where barge delivery services aren't available, hefting propane bottles in and out of boats, into cars, and back and forth to a filling station makes you very aware of how much propane is being consumed. Chic and Kathy were very pleased that they managed to transport a propane refrigerator to their cabin until they realized that its pilot flame was burning all the time, even, ironically, when it's very cold out. "You go through about 40 pounds a month. That's 40 pounds you have to carry."

How your island home will be heated is yet another question to address before building begins. Heat pumps or electric or propane space heaters work well for some people. I didn't speak with anyone who uses geothermal power, although it seems an appealing, if costly, possibility for living off the grid. "About the size of an average refrigerator and [easy to install], geothermal heat pumps use the temperature of the ground or water sources to regulate building temperatures, heat water, and provide air conditioning."[17] More typically, where wood is available in nearby forests or along beaches, it is used for heating and cooking, although there is much grumbling about the ongoing labour involved in collecting, cutting, and storing firewood (add a woodshed to the list of necessary structures). But even if they don't serve as the primary heat source, the fireplaces, cookstoves, and airtight stoves commonly integrated into island homes create a warm and welcoming environment and serve as backups to other systems.

Regardless of the heating system chosen, house design and construction can do much to minimize household heating requirements by taking advantage of passive solar power. Window design and placement, deep eaves that provide shade in the summer but allow in low winter sun, thick insulation, and good ventilation all help moderate temperatures.

Building in redundancies and having fallback options when systems fail is another part of systems planning. If pipes freeze, a bucket to carry water for flushing toilets is a simple remedy. And candles and oil lanterns come out when power disappears. Having a spirit of adventure in coping with such failures is also key. As one islander notes, "We don't need [kerosene lamps] often but I'm always glad to use them. Their smell, the pesky trimming of wicks, and even the constant washing and polishing of glass globes pleases me, for they make the room in which they sit seem the centre of the universe."[18]

Keeping all systems straightforward is a mantra for many islanders. Laurie, for example, takes a realistic view of maintenance challenges on Maurelle Island. "We know how all our systems work, but we're bad at mechanics. Other than the very basics, we need to get somebody else to fix things." Her friend Judith on Rendezvous sets out the consequences of complexity.

> Keep it simple. If you really want to live on an island, live an island lifestyle and make it as simple as you can. The fewer systems you have to break down, the fewer gizmos and gadgets you need to maintain or fix, the less income you need and the more time you will have to actually enjoy being on the island. Sitting in the garden in the sunshine, going for walks, collecting oysters—all of the island things that you like doing—you won't have time to do if you fill your life with all that urban paraphernalia.

Part of living simply is adapting to circumstances. "I'm always conscious of my electricity supply and battery condition. So if it's a cloudy summer day, I won't do laundry or vacuuming. I'll put these off until the solar panels are producing. My life is not so rigid or scheduled that I can't put off the laundry until the day after tomorrow when the sun is shining, or handwash an essential item, or sweep the rug with the corn broom if it looks really bad."

ASSEMBLING EXPERTISE A fourth aspect of getting organized involves thinking about the knowledge and skills you already have, the things you want or need to learn, and the expertise that you'd rather purchase. Margaret McIntyre describes the joy of tackling a simple building project when she and her partner moved to a remote cabin on Nelson Island in the late 1950s: "For the first time in our lives we experienced the thrill that comes from doing a thing by yourself, no matter how badly it is done. The most appallingly amateurish affair became a thing of wondrous beauty when it was the work of our own scratched and aching hands." She goes on to explain that "a supply of two-by-fours and shiplap had come up on the *Monstrosity* with our furniture. Some of this we decided to use to build the chicken house, and a long happy day was spent hauling it out of the hold, throwing it overboard, and towing it piecemeal round to our bay, where we beached it and carried it up the hill, one board at a time. This done, we assembled our tools and set to work."[19]

Clearly this first experience strengthened their confidence. McIntyre and her partner went on to renovate a small cabin and reflected that "nothing that we have ever done before or since has ever given us such satisfaction. Every time we came into it, we paused to beam delightedly around and exchange comments on its beauties. 'It's our home,' said Jerry proudly, 'we made it.' Possibly in those last three words lay its chief charms."[20]

The challenge and reward of creating a home through self-reliance, ingenuity, and hard work are a big part of people's attraction to an island. And it seems fair to say that those who are inclined to live on islands either bring a range of skills or are predisposed to acquire them, often on the fly. Roger, a specialist in adult education, describes living on Bath Island as lifelong learning. "You're on an island, and by definition that means there will be problems that you're going to have to solve, like right now. The knowledge thus gained is power for next time it happens."

Chic shares this view. "It's one of those life things—neither sequence nor outcome—it's all about process, about being here and doing it. It has a lot to do with the things we've talked about—taking time, late at night, to conceive methods to get materials to the island, or to raise beams. And that's a lot of fun. It's very gratifying to come up with things that work. And then you find things that don't work. I always say that the root of wisdom is making mistakes—and then you're left with knowledge."

David Conover also savoured the pleasures of learning as he settled on Wallace Island. "I found as I toiled, no greater thrill than that of learning a fresh fact, and putting it to use in the same moment. By blunting the [tip] of a nail, I discovered, I could drive it in without splitting the board. And to pull out a bent spike, a block under the hammer claws worked wonders, saving nails and hammer handles as well."[21]

Building foundations; integrating septic, water, power, and fuel systems; moving on to framing, roofing, masonry, wiring, and plumbing; and then installing doors and windows, finishing many kinds of surfaces, crafting cabinetry and countertops, connecting appliances and fixtures, landscaping, maintaining systems, and, of course, using tools and operating machinery—these tasks all require knowledge, varied skills, and a willingness to learn. And they present multifaceted organizational issues. Joy Orth emphasizes the critical role that the skills for self-sufficiency play in island settings.

> My problem is that I've never learned to adequately understand our electrical system. Yesterday I somehow managed to knock loose the lead to the house from our bank of batteries and can't seem to find the right connection to restore power to the radio and CB . . . It goes to prove that each member of a remote community should understand and know how to operate all the vital equipment. I've always resisted mechanical things so here I sit with my thin line to civilization broken . . . The most powerful tool any of us can own is the desire and determination of our own spirit to make things go—somehow—and to do it with good cheer.[22]

The complexity of house design and systems, time frame for construction, proximity to tradespeople, and degree of personal challenge all come into play as you think about the expertise needed to tackle an island house. Dad drew on years of working in the bush, along with lessons learned in building a thirty-six-foot sailboat, to guide their project, and Mom and Dad chose a design that was relatively simple to frame and finish. But Dad would have been the first to say that fine carpentry was not his forte. They were happy to order cabinetry for the kitchen and bathroom, as well as windows and doors, from Vancouver suppliers. They tackled all the other tasks. And while everything worked out remarkably well, I had to get used to hot water coming out of the cold-water tap in the bathroom.

Being captivated by the appeal of an island project but having little idea of what is involved is a starting point for several people. Geri comments that she was so entranced by the place and the idea of island living that she took little time to consider the practical implications that were to absorb much of her time in the following years. And a deep attraction to the island and a desire to be more self-sufficient brought Judith and her husband to Rendezvous Island. "The island gave us a sense of separation from the main society, like a moat, so that we didn't have someone telling us how and when and why to do things. We could be real human animals instead of tortured, social constructs. The beauty alone is enough to keep a person here." Settling in involved learning. "We just built the house—we didn't know anything. We went to the library and got a couple of books; we figured it out as we went along. You know, we didn't know how much we couldn't do—we thought we could do everything."

Across the channel on Maurelle, Rob was also figuring things out as he went along. "While I knew theoretically what needed to be done, I didn't have a clue how to do it. I didn't even have any tools when I came here. I got a level and square for a Christmas present. The first house we built, we didn't have a tape measure, so we took a six-inch nail and used it to measure out a six-foot-six-inch ceiling...that's thirteen lengths. I was so ignorant that I didn't know in Canada that a six-inch nail is only five and a half inches, so I built a six-foot ceiling."

Sy tells a similar story of building. "We were city people, so we had no background. My next-door neighbour helped—we learned plumbing with him. I got the Canadian [Electrical] Code book and wired it up ... so we learned electricity that way. It's not rocket science." Sy says that one of the most exciting moments during their long process of building water and waste systems, framing the house, acquiring fixtures, and learning plumbing, was the first time he flushed the toilet. He laughs when he describes the sheer satisfaction of seeing the water enter, swirl, and disappear.

Farther north, on Gilford Island, Yvonne Maximchuk writes about yet another plumbing challenge. "The old [hot-water] tank has packed it in, so I bought a new one. It sat in the bathroom for weeks, mainly because I didn't know how to make the little flare on the end of the copper tube to connect the tube with the fittings. I didn't have a flaring tool. Didn't have any solder to install the tap on the top of the tank. Didn't have a tap for it, either. And I didn't know how to solder. Too many other things to do, but the time finally came for it to be tackled." She goes on to describe the complicated tasks involved, the lessons learned and mistakes made, and notes, "What a long, luxurious, delicious, hard-earned bath I reveled in after the water was up to temperature."[23]

Knowledge, skills, and advice come from many sources. Certainly there are many guidebooks on how to construct a house, although few that directly address the additional complexity of island sites. And lots of information is available online. Web sources seem particularly helpful in thinking through the many green technologies that are revolutionizing power generation and waste disposal. And depending on where the island is located, courses, consultants, and contractors might play useful roles in developing house builders' knowledge and skills.

Time and time again islanders comment that friends, neighbours, and even passing strangers offer much appreciated expertise and help, often because visitors, too, are intrigued by the special challenges of building on an island and enjoy getting their hands dirty. There are also times when other people's advice isn't particularly useful. I am intrigued that two islanders who don't know each other and live at opposite ends of the Georgia Basin offer the same observation about the inclination of friends, and strangers, to suggest easy solutions to complex island problems, often preceded by the word "just." Both roll their eyes as they describe how people offer off-the-cuff ideas as if somehow the islander hasn't seen the solution after numerous hours of late-night pondering. Or as if the visitor's values and tastes are more appropriate. Comments such as "It's just a matter of blowing a hole through that rock" or "Why don't you just use tidal power?" don't begin to address the complexity of a problem. As one of these islanders says, "'Just' is a four-letter word." Since becoming an islander is a very personal journey involving complicated choices, it seems wise for visitors to be thoughtful in critiquing the approaches that the islander is taking.

Even if an islander does the bulk of construction work as part of a deep-seated desire to craft a house, there may be occasions when a sub-contractor or tradesperson is needed to take on difficult projects, provide specialized equipment, or speed things along. But finding people to play these roles can be tricky. Availability, cost, transportation challenges, and, at least in some cases, differing expectations about quality and timing are all described as problematic. In his account of renovating a cabin on Saturna Island, Eric Nicol observes that "island building contractors are a very special breed. Most of them are refugees from city conformism. They are, at heart, artists, like the rest of the poets, painters and pottery makers that populate the Gulf Islands." He continues: "If pressed, island building contractors will build 'to code,' but their hearts won't be in it. What gives them creative satisfaction—and hopefully will also please clients—is adding the byzantine touches that distinguish the cottage from the 'monster' house of the city."[24]

Adherence to schedules seems to be a key issue. One islander talks about the difficulties of coordinating work crews when one or more workers don't show up due to last-minute scheduling conflicts. More than once he has brought in urban crews for brief intensive periods, preferring to incur extra cost rather than deal with delays. Another islander, who has cooled his heels at the local marina waiting for absent workers on more than one occasion, expresses frustration.

"It's a big issue. People think I'm just a cheapskate with a radical 'do-it-yourself' attitude. But the energy that is required to contact others who have the skills, are willing to do it my way, are reliable and are honest is huge. You're not going to get all those attributes embodied in one person. Maybe I'm too cynical, but my previous attempts to buy outside help have not been successful." But he goes on to say, "I wouldn't mind hiring somebody to do my gyprock, starting right now. I did that wall there. It's going to be all right when it's painted, and after all this is just an island."

There are also many positive stories of working with tradespeople whose involvement made the building process much pleasanter, either by ensuring that a complex job was done properly or by taking on some of the many specialist tasks involved in building. And general contractors who specialize in construction in remote sites can bring a wealth of experience that saves both money and stress. Dan Sauve of DSS Construction has built a number of iconic island homes along the BC coast. He thrives on the complexity and creativity inherent in working on island, and comments that the key to a successful project is a strong relationship with the client. Clarity around expectations, effective communication, and mutual trust are all critical in dealing with the inevitable design and logistical problems—and opportunities—that will crop up. Clients who have a clear and consistent vision for their project, appreciate the challenges and costs of island construction, and are available for consultation are the most rewarding to work with. Dan recommends working with contractors whose teams are skilled in all aspects of construction in order to minimize the need for sub-contractors. Every time a specialist is involved, a day is devoted to transporting the person and their tools to and from the island. And Dan laughs when he adds that "it's important to specify when the contractor's role is complete, since island building projects are never truly finished."

How you assemble the expertise you need to construct an island house is determined by your skills, goals, and circumstances. And of course, there's a sweet spot between challenge and tedium, between fear and boredom that is different for every islander. Knowing your abilities, having a good sense of your limitations, and choosing the appropriate site, design, tools, systems, and supports are important first steps in ensuring that your island building process is a satisfying one.

Building challenges, building pleasures

AND FINALLY, IT is worth repeating that island construction is rarely cheap, mainly because the costs of delivering materials, as well as transporting, accommodating, and paying workers, can be prohibitive. But experiences vary. It is certainly possible to see island living as an inexpensive alternative to mainland living, particularly as property values and the costs of construction in urban centres escalate. Building a modest house, largely by hand using local and recycled materials, is part of a romantic island dream for some people, and where access is challenging and building inspection less rigorous, it may be the only way to go. Some, like Rob, take advantage of bartering to keep costs down. "We met loggers going into Waddington, at Bute Inlet—we became great friends and ended up doing a trade. One had permission to recycle bridge timbers from the company because they had spikes in them. I did 2,000 bucks worth of architectural drawings. I got 12,000 board feet of old-growth fir, all in trade, no cash."

But most islanders describe the building process as expensive. Dave comments, "Everything out here costs way more. If you get 10 yards of gravel dumped in your driveway in town, it probably costs you 250 or 300 bucks. If you get 10 yards here, it will cost you 2,500 or 3,000 bucks. It comes in individual bags and goes to a marine terminal. And then it goes on a barge. And a guy with a forklift brings it up." Joy Orth also notes the stress that goes with a remote island location:

> Everything we did seemed to take more money, material and time than we'd anticipated. Everything was going out—nothing coming in. Conditions were trying, nerves got edgy. We discovered there's a lot more involved in a move such as ours than simply finding a place you love and moving in. It takes real organization to live on the bounty of the wilderness

around you—especially if you feel you really should have more than an 8 by 10 cabin, oiled paper windows, and a sack of flour with a supply of jerky. It's easy to romanticize about the expectations of our early-day pioneers and mountain men. It's something else to try to approximate those experiences, even in a limited way."[25]

And Eric Nicol, on Saturna, reflects that "no matter how much you allow for unanticipated costs, these always exceed the estimate by roughly $100,000. But not to fret. You are choosing a very satisfying way of going bankrupt."[26]

With all this to keep in mind, it's not surprising that some prospective islanders are put off by the complications of actually building even something simple on their perfect island. But almost everyone who builds on an island describes the task of settling in as deeply satisfying. It's the "perfect excuse to be out in this pristine environment," according to Chic, and Kathy adds, "I will try anything if it is helpful." Roger speaks of the immense pleasure of getting jobs done, while Judith comments on her deep sense of integration with the land. For Elizabeth Arthur, it's also about better understanding how buildings work. "A house used to contain any number of secrets in its walls. Why did the water gush from the taps, just so? How did the floor support my weight; what was really beneath its surface? At what point had the doorways appeared in the walls? When I walked into a house, a peculiar weakness beset me. Because I could not fathom the reasons behind the shape of things, they had power over me."[27]

Rob Wood sums up the pleasures of building on island, particularly when creativity is not inhibited by mainland norms. "Dwellings made from local materials that blend into their surroundings with elegant simplicity invariably possess a timeless quality that expresses unique, personal joy and pride in the instinctive process of human nest building." He goes on to say that "fantasy alone could not possibly have replicated the depth of pleasure the actual experience would turn out to be. It's almost as if all my previous adventures had been preparing me for this. What an incredible bonus the Canadian wilderness offers for those brave enough to commit to living beyond the grid. It allows absolute freedom to manifest this basic human impulse unfettered by all the conventional codes and standards intended to protect us from our own mistakes."[28] Sy shares Rob's pleasure in creating an island home near Nelson Island. "It's a labour of love."

There's a wonderful reciprocity about building a home on an island. Even as you make your imprint, the island changes you. All the stories I heard about the creativity, ingenuity, learning, and satisfactions inherent in building something special were really stories about people beginning the process of becoming islanders.

(5)

ON ISLAND TIME

Despite our new address (Bath Island, Gabriola, BC), family dynamics looked similar as we settled on island. Mom created a welcoming home while Dad focused on earning a living and the heavy work of maintaining property and boats. And Clair and I went to school. Like everyone else in the Pacific Northwest, our attention was captured by distant events: John F. Kennedy's assassination, the beginnings of space travel, the tensions of the civil rights movement, and the growing war in Vietnam. The whole family was excited when the *Readers' Digest* Condensed Book arrived each month. Clair and I succumbed to Beatlemania and smoked our first (and last) cigarettes with Gabriola kids in the woods beside the schoolhouse. Mom twisted her hair into a French chignon, bought pedal pushers, and studied *The Joy of Cooking* for new ways to prepare oysters. Dad celebrated the Lions' first Grey Cup and pondered the wisdom of building boats with fibreglass. CHQM filled the house with Vancouver news and easy-listening music, unless I thought I could get away with switching the battery-powered radio to CKLG or CFUN. Even from an island, we were caught up in the dynamics of the 1960s.

But little in this new life was particularly normal. We no longer had electric lights or appliances. Without a dial phone, communications were limited to mail or stilted conversations on the radio telephone. Beach and forest, not road and fence, bounded the house. Boats replaced cars for local errands. The first task every day was lighting fires for warmth. We learned to cook on a wood stove. With no grocery store around the corner, we were increasingly reliant on fresh foods from the garden or ocean. Dad turned his back on the forest industry to work at Withey's Shipyard in Silva Bay and experimented with cottage industries to generate income. And going to school involved daily boat and school bus rides, new friends among the island kids, and homework by propane light. And we all had to learn new skills, new routines, new approaches to daily life.

MEMORIES OF ISLAND life are so embedded in cycles of activities repeated over time that it's hard to distinguish one year from the next, or even one task from another. Overlapping daily routines, weekly chores, and annual activities are integrated with the rhythms of tides, moon, and seasons. Punctuated by unexpected incidents, these make up the patterns of island living. And time on island takes on special qualities, remote from the more scheduled mainland routines.

When Margaret McIntyre moved to Nelson Island with her partner in the late 1950s, she celebrated the "never-ending miracle of being perfectly free to do exactly as we pleased." She marvelled at a new sense of time.

> We never seemed to get used to the fact that time did not mean anything. We could rise at any hour, knowing that there were no appointments to be kept and no buses to catch … we woke to a world as pure as the day on which it was created, and our nerves no longer frayed by the clash of conflicting personalities. The clock stopped, but it made no difference. We knew that daylight was the time for waking and dark the time for sleeping, and we ate when we were hungry. We began to forget what day it was, but that did not matter because all days were alike. For us, time had suddenly ceased."[1]

Of course, "doing exactly what they pleased" involved tackling myriad tasks that left Margaret and her partner exhausted at the end of each day.

The dream of complete detachment from the tyranny of clocks is achieved by only a handful of remote islanders. Most find themselves balancing ongoing mainland connections with a remarkable range of tasks distinctive to being on island. There is a persistent tension between structure and autonomy and between linear and cyclical concepts of time. Can you put off the dentist appointment because the water tank has sprung a leak? Does this require a trip to the nearest hardware store, four hours away? When will the tide be low enough to adjust the anchors on the dock? Interweaving new cycles and tasks with ongoing commitments and coping with the unanticipated create the fabric of island living. And since my mom maintained that early morning was the best time of the day, we also adapted to living with the hours of the sun. Up at dawn, to bed (if only to read by propane light) at sunset. Long days in the summer, short days in the winter.

Creature comforts

BEING ON ISLAND involves rethinking creature comforts that city-dwellers take for granted. Staying warm is more complex, putting food on the table involves new skills and management strategies, and tasks such as laundry present unexpected challenges. These distinctive chores become part of the daily pattern of island life.

The rituals of heating houses that lack furnaces and baseboard heaters demand significant time. Clair and I focused on collecting wood for fires. Surefooted, we scoured beaches for substantial pieces for the fireplace and smaller bits to tuck into the cookstove. Long-burning bark and desiccated, creosoted, or sap-laden sticks that would catch quickly were treasures. Damp chunks were useful for slowing a fire, and cedar was prized for kindling and hot flames. Every piece was unique. Most were rounded and buffed by unknown voyages. Some had been buried for months, even years, in the tangled driftwood apron that wrapped around the island, only to be revealed as storms and high tides rearranged the shore. We developed judicious eyes, dallied to avoid other chores, and were easily distracted by beach treasures. Occasionally the tide served up a wealth of new wood, and we'd fill extra boxes in the hope of getting the next day off. And even now, when I walk on driftwood-strewn beaches, I'm quietly assessing the wood supply.

On her own during weekdays, Mom also roamed the beach to assemble piles of firewood at trailheads. When these reached respectable heights, she made multiple runs with the garden tractor and trailer to add to woodpiles near the house. We stacked fireplace wood by various sizes and types. Special pieces for hot and cool fires were segregated. And we all knew how to use the chopping block, axe, wedge, and hatchet to deal with unwieldy pieces or to cut kindling.

Current wisdom warns that the salty coating on well-worn pieces of beach wood creates acidic fumes that corrode cookstove, fireplace, and chimney components (as well as lungs). For this reason, many islanders prefer logs harvested from local forests. But dealing with logs in the bush is challenging. David Cox on Read Island writes about the difficulties. Once the tree is down, he and his wife have to "cut the branches off the trunk with a chainsaw. Then we would cut the trunk into rounds. Then we would have to move heavy rounds of wood out of the forest through impossible terrain to the shore with no machinery to help us. Once at the shore we would lift the rounds into the boat and out at the other end. This doesn't include getting them up to the house, splitting and stacking them."[2] Instead, Cox prefers logs that are adrift. Finding them is the easy part, he says.

> When we see a log out on the water we get out the binoculars. Is it float-ing high in the water? If so, it's not waterlogged. Is it less than ten inches in diameter? Anything larger is harder for us to handle. Does it have a lot of knots? Knots make it difficult to split and sometimes it's just not worth the effort. What kind of wood is it? If it's fir we're happy. Hemlock is good, too. Cedar is good for kindling as it burns fast and hot. However a good cedar log is prized and we wouldn't cut one up for kindling if it could be used for lumber. If all the questions are answered satisfactorily we rush to the boat armed with lengths of rope attached to log dogs ... and head out to salvage it.

If the log has a brand on it, you should be attentive to salvage regulations. According to the BC government's *Marine Log Salvage Procedures and Guidelines*, a registered timber mark, log brand, or ownership tag is evidence that the log is the property of another, and furthermore, "when an identifiable log is recovered, the salvor, as a precaution and evidence of good faith should at the earliest opportunity notify the identifiable owner that he has recovered his timber, provide the location where the timber is being held and ask for instructions on the ultimate disposal."[3] It is an offence under the Criminal Code of Canada to remove the identifying marks.

Once you've determined if you can use the log, the harder part is dealing with it once it's on the beach. Cox uses a chainsaw to cut three-metre sections but cautions that "cutting at awkward angles while slipping and slithering over kelp-covered rocks" is dangerous. So is using a complex block and tackle high-lead system to move heavy sections up a cliff. And the final steps of cutting rounds and splitting and piling the wood take strength and coordination. Judith describes how to tackle a large round, using special tools to penetrate its dense surface.

> The maul is similar to the sledge hammer, a heavy axe but with a striking surface on the back side of the blade. The wedge is a wedge, made of heavy steel for splitting or of plastic to assist with falling a tree with a chainsaw. The splitting maul first strikes the block with an exploratory blow or two to see if it will split easily. If not, the indents left by the maul blade are good starting cracks for the wedge, which is tapped in gently at first, then beat mercilessly with powerful blows from the back of the maul or with a sledge hammer. You have to be careful: a dropped wedge or a six- or eight-pound maul can break a toe.

As many islanders attest, firewood, whether from the beach or the forest, warms you twice: first when you collect it and second when you burn it. And it has insulating value. On MacLeod Island off Cape Breton, it does double duty as a protective wall alongside the chicken coop. "Before we burn it (last, at the end of the season), we leave that firewood stacked through most of the icy weather on both the inside and the outside of the ten-foot-by-fourteen-foot building that houses the rabbits and chickens. Which means that the wood serves a several-months-long 'apprenticeship' as insulation before it finally winds up in the stove, heating our cabin!"[4]

Having the right tools makes wood collecting easier. Judith was wishing that her quad was in working condition when I talked with her. "Not having it is really difficult right now. I have to bring my firewood in, one wheelbarrow load at a time, which I'm doing, but with a barely healed broken leg, it's very, very slow." And after several years of hard work on Read Island, Cox comments that a mechanical splitter is one of his favourite purchases. One way or another, the firewood routine is onerous. Cox offers a wry reflection on the process. "Burning free wood…is likely the most labour-intensive heat known to man."

Hand in hand with gathering firewood is using it wisely. We quickly mastered the art of starting and managing fires. The fireplace was straightforward. If winds were strong, we held flaming paper up the chimney to start an updraft. A handful of cedar kindling, set over scrunched paper, burned brightly for the crucial minutes it took to layer on more substantial pieces of dry wood. Building a good fire quickly became a matter of pride. On a good day the fire burned steadily and heat seeped into the room. On a bad day, we added more paper and kindling, embarrassed at a failed attempt. There were also protocols that go with starting fires: poking someone else's fire was not good form. But once fires were started, everyone kept an eye on them as the day went by.

The cookstove required greater finesse. Not that it was hard to start. We'd clean out yesterday's ashes, lay out newspaper and kindling in the firebox, open the vents, strike a match, and replace the lids. In the enclosed firebox, often warm from the previous day, flames wrapped around the wood. Creating the right kind of heat was trickier. If warmth in the kitchen and heat for the water coil in the firebox was the only need, we'd adjust vents and add chunks of "normal" beach wood every hour or so. "Hot" wood was required to take the oven above 350 degrees, to use the top of the stove as a grill, or to bring a canning kettle to a boil. Cedar was ideal. Pitchy or creosoted wood really got things going, but you had to be cautious about starting a chimney fire. And slow, long-burning fires to last through winter nights or while everyone was outdoors required dense bark, damped down with closed vents. A bark fire glowed as if fed by coal, and the stove radiated heat. It was also useful to know how to make the transition from one kind of heat to the other. Adjusting vents, changing the type of wood, and letting the fire die back a bit became as natural as turning the knobs on an electric stove.

Mom mastered cooking on the wood stove with ease. She knew the hot and relatively cool spots on the stovetop and moved pots and pans to adjust temperature. A kettle simmered off to one side. The cast-iron stovetop, scrubbed and oiled daily, sometimes served as a cooking surface. Puddles of pancake mix, toast, grilled sandwiches, even sausages sizzled, unbounded by pots and pans. The oven yielded bread and cookies, along with cakes and pies for daily desserts. Roasts and holiday turkeys were every bit as beautiful as those produced in mainland stoves. And a pair of sad irons sat on the back of the stovetop, ready for pressing clothes. Eventually Mom and Dad bought a propane stove. It was a blessing on hot summer days but never as satisfying to cook on—or to sit by—as the hospitable wood stove.

Farther north in the Stikine River estuary Joy Orth also treasured her wood stove at the centre of her island home.

A good stove is like the sun. It pours life into the food it touches ... Our wood cookstove has given strength to my cooking which it has never had before. The food prepared on it has a richer texture, a more delicate flavor, a more nourishing effect. The most important difference between a wood cookstove and most other stoves is, I think, the care which it requires: care returns itself in care. A heat which is built slowly and patiently will burn more steadily than one which is ignited in an instant. Pushing a button or tossing a match onto gasoline is easy: the energy in gas and oil lies close to the surface. The wood which has been a shorter time growing, clutches its growth more shyly. But once you touch that growth, it spends itself with radiance. I like the stove because I can cook so well with it. I like it also because of its history, and I like it finally, because it was so hard to get here.[5]

Island approaches to heating and cooking vary from rudimentary to sophisticated. In their early years on Maurelle, Rob and Laurie Wood had a fifty-five-gallon steel drum "hippie stove," adapted with a door and stovepipe. In many off-grid homes, airtight wood stoves have replaced both cookstoves and open fireplaces, which look lovely but aren't all that efficient. One way or another, most islanders rely on some wood for heat, atmosphere, or as a backup to other systems. Many, however, also use propane or electric heaters, stoves, and other appliances. And islanders with robust energy generation systems have furnaces, stoves, and other appliances that would make a mainlander envious. At the heart of one of my favourite island kitchens is an enormous red Aga cooker with both propane and electric components. Its low-intensity propane flame burns continuously to warm the heavy cast-iron components and make its hobs and specialized ovens available for cooking at any time. It consumes more fuel than standard gas stoves but plays double duty as a heat source. Fortunately, fuel trucks are barged to the island community a couple of times a year. In high summer, when the gas barbecue is in frequent use and the sun heats the house, the Aga's propane components are shut off and its electric unit serves the kitchen's needs.

Sourcing food, like generating heat, takes on distinctive island qualities. One of the biggest challenges is ensuring that ingredients are on hand. Many islanders look locally for fresh food. Mom would set out at first light to jig for cod or catch small salmon to serve on toast at breakfast. Clams were indispensable. She made a memorable chowder, using lots of clams from nearby Saturnina Island, along with bacon, onions, potatoes, canned corn, and evaporated milk. And occasionally she'd experiment with deep-fried clams or clam fritters. Oysters were a favourite. And since they grew in great quantities in a muddy bay on Saturnina, we'd transplant dinghy loads to a pocket bay on the north side of Bath Island for quick access. There's nothing better than opening a raw oyster on the beach and slurping it down, although impressing our cousins every summer by eating really large ones took courage. Small oysters basted in barbecue sauce on a charcoal grill were a summer treat. We rarely ate mussels, as they weren't popular in those days. But when tides were really low, scallops and abalone became part of our diet. Islanders a bit farther north talk about eating halibut and prawns to the point that they are no longer a delicacy. And islanders near the northern end of Vancouver Island feast on eulachon when these oily little fish head upriver on spring spawning runs.

While seafood is available year-round, fresh vegetables and fruit are more seasonal. Mom's garden yielded lettuce, spinach, beans, peas, tomatoes, onions, Swiss chard, potatoes, carrots, and zucchini. And ratty Brussels sprouts and cauliflower were harvested in the fall and winter. Herbs, strawberries, raspberries, rhubarb, and wild blackberries were there for the picking, along with apples in the late summer and fall. Gardens are important on many islands, both for food and a sense of self-reliance. David Conover found great pleasure in the garden that he and Jeanne managed to create on Wallace Island. "I liked the feel of the soil and of growing things. Everywhere else, Nature defied me, but here in this twenty-four by forty patch, I was king."[6] And on Maurelle Island, Laurie's large enclosed garden provides approximately 60 percent of their food and is the treasured heart of their homestead. A huge amount of work has been involved in clearing the land, creating deer-proof fencing, enriching the soil, planting, tending, harvesting, and getting ready for yet another growing season. Rob reflects that "if the garden were just about the economics of producing food a person could be excused for wondering whether the cost of the vast amount of labour that goes in is justified."[7] But he goes on to talk about the therapeutic value of working the land, of being self-sufficient, and of eating fresh produce, and comments that "this source of happiness and meaning is the essential motivation and reward for our alternative lifestyle."

Hunting for deer, elk, and game birds also puts food on island tables. Residents of Sidney Island near Victoria have a regular supply of venison as they work to reduce the number of deer that overrun the island and transform its ecosystem. Farther north on remote Blackfish Sound, long-term islander, fisher, and trapper Bill Proctor writes about his approach to cooking a venison roast all day at low heat in his wood stove. "Prepared this way the roast is always tender and tasty, never tough. I like to make venison stew and I boil the bones for soup stock. The rendered fat makes the most beautiful white fat and I use that for frying and making gravy. Venison burgers are great, too."[8]

Gathering wild greens and berries is possible on many islands. Depending on the location and season, there may be nettles, blackberries, huckleberries, salal berries, Oregon grape, rose hips, thimbleberries and salmonberries, dandelion leaves, miner's lettuce, and even wild strawberries available for nibbling, cooking, and in some cases canning.

Fishing, hunting, gardening, and gathering shellfish and berries offer many rewards. Convenience is one, since the alternative is a long trip to the market. Freshness is another—the flavours of almost anything harvested locally have a special piquancy. And satisfaction is yet another, as Richard Nelson notes in *The Island Within*. "There is a special intimacy in living directly from nature, nourishing my body with the same wildness that so elevates my spirit."[9] This is echoed more prosaically by Bill Proctor, who says that "all this food from the land and sea keeps down the grocery bills and I think has helped keep me healthy in more ways than one. I get lots of exercise going out and finding my food."[10]

Islanders also talk of the pleasures of preparing foods from scratch. Mom was known for her baked beans, beef stews, and soups that simmered over long days. Her yogourt was rich and flavourful, as was her bread. Bean sprouts provided freshness year-round. She made some form of dessert every night and always had cookies and cakes on hand. One of my favourite concoctions was ceviche made with rockfish and lime juice. I was less fond of Mom's attempts to cook dogfish. And as she lived in an era that celebrated convenience foods, she was also happy to experiment with everything from cake mixes to instant potatoes if they promised greater efficiency or enabled her to tackle something interesting in the kitchen.

Mom cooked with seaweed with mixed results. Her jars of preserved kelp rings looked lovely but didn't get used up very quickly. And she nibbled on dulse that she'd collected when the tide was low, although we rarely followed her lead. Other islanders treasure these free gifts from the sea. Joy Orth seems to have had more success with pickles than Mom. Orth says, "The long bulbous type of kelp called bull kelp, because of its resemblance to a bull whip, makes excellent pickles when picked early in the year while the crop is young. After soaking, the tender rings cut from the stipe, or long stem, can be made into sweet or dill pickles, full of minerals." Seaweeds have multiple uses. "They are dried and added in winter to stews and soups… Sometimes after a good southerly blow and a high tide the beach will be littered with seaweed torn loose by the sea and swept over to us. Then I descend to the beach with my plastic bags to gather mulch for the garden. It adds precious minerals as well as making a weed-free protection for plants."[11]

A flock of stately Barred Rock chickens eventually offered us yet another source of food, along with constant amusement as we got to know the ladies and their vicious rooster. Their coop was located at the centre of the island, surrounded by chicken wire on the sides and across the top to discourage predatory mink and eagles. Clair and I shared the daily chores of collecting eggs, setting out feed first thing in the morning, and closing the coop door as darkness set in. And Mom added hauling bags of feed and butchering and plucking non-laying hens to her repertoire. Today Roger maintains an elegant coop for his "chooks," conducts regular battles with predators, and minimizes time off island to ensure the chooks' well-being. As he says, "they have no idea that I make considerable sacrifices for them." Other islanders also value chickens and their eggs, but with mixed outcomes. An even greater battle with mink takes place on Sidney Island. Frank and Geri have tried numerous chicken coop designs to discourage persistent marauders. Judith on Rendezvous has recently lost two batches of chicks to mink and says, "What I need is a really skookum run that's absolutely bomb-proof. I'm really missing the chickens and the eggs.

And I love goats, but I'm not sure that I want to get into that. I also like to be able to just pick up and go away for a week. I could leave chickens for a week, but I couldn't leave a goat."

Avoiding spoilage is another distinctive chore. Propane fridges are common and have probably improved significantly from the small model that provided unreliable cooling for milk, cheese, and meat in Mom's kitchen. But, like other off-the-grid appliances, they require a special knowledge of their workings. And they need propane that has to be carried to the island. Customer service is a long way away. On Saturna, Eric Nicol laments that his propane fridge "knows only two temperatures: room, and that of liquid nitrogen."[12] And David Cox on Read Island describes "burping" his dysfunctional propane fridge by inverting it—a much more effective strategy than following instructions for cleaning the gas line provided in the service manual.[13] Chic and Kathy on Snowberry Island laugh at the irony of carrying heavy propane bottles to the island to heat their fridge element in order to cool food during chilly winters. Sometimes keeping things outdoors is the easiest strategy of all.

Cold-storage spaces or root cellars provide a simple alternative or backup to fridges. On Maurelle, Rob and Laurie dug a deep pit in a hillside, as did Margaret McIntyre on Nelson Island. "The rocky nature of most of our property prevented us from digging storage pits anywhere near the house, but the shores of our little lake were full of these primitive refrigerators, the tops covered with boards and weighted down with stones to keep wild animals from helping themselves to our stores. The need for an extra half-pound of butter meant a mile climb up the rough hillside."[14]

Mom and Dad came up with a simple but seasonal strategy for storing perishables that wouldn't fit in the fridge. A wood and mesh box outside the back door kept things cool on spring, fall, and winter days. And they kept a freezer in a garage at Page's Marina at Silva Bay for purchased meats and fresh-caught fish and prawns. Bringing frozen supplies to the island was part of the daily after-school routine, along with collecting mail and buying milk from the tiny store at the marina.

And a few islanders do without refrigeration. One I spoke with said that her parents would hang salmon and venison. "There was no refrigeration. The venison hung until it grew a second coat of green hair. You'd just whack that off and eat the meat inside. That's why we're pretty healthy today—we ate a lot of that stuff."

Another regular cycle of island life is laundry. This may not be a distinctive chore for islanders with electricity and water to run washers and dryers. If these utilities aren't on hand, however, it takes effort to wash heavy, often very dirty clothes and find ways to dry them. For the first few years Mom handwashed all our clothes, carried them up the steep stairs to the second-floor deck, and strung them on a clothesline. It was a notable day when she acquired a gas-powered washing machine with a wringer. And it was a frustrating day when the tether securing the long clothesline to a distant tree gave way under the weight of newly washed sheets and towels.

Bath Island laundry was heavy work. But it seems downright simple compared with Margaret McIntyre's approach on Nelson Island in the same period.

> One day a week was devoted to washing clothes. No electric washing machines and dryers here. We carried our laundry up to the lake, built a fire in the open, placed a large square galvanized washtub firmly on it and filled it with water. Dirty overalls and wool socks all went in together, along with sheets, towels and tablecloths, and the lot was boiled furiously until the water was the consistency of pea soup and everything in it reduced to a uniform grey. After this we rinsed the mournful-looking results out in the icy waters of the lake and hung them over the branches of the trees to dry... Ironing was something we never bothered about except on rare occasions, when we used a flat stone heated in the oven and wrapped in paper."[15]

Most islands I visited had sufficient electricity to run a small washing machine. Clotheslines remain popular.

Provisioning

ENSURING THAT FOOD, gear, building materials, and other necessities of island life are on hand normally involves trips off island and seems to take an inordinate amount of time and physical effort. Roger on Bath Island describes the tasks involved in provisioning as "gruelling." Local marinas and weekly community markets on adjacent islands can take care of some needs while providing opportunities to socialize. But even the simplest approach to island life requires trips to town. And there is considerable pressure to accomplish as much as possible—and as accurately as possible—in busy days off island. As Linda on Valdes observes, "It's difficult. To grocery shop, you go to Nanaimo, you buy your food, your feed. Then you take the ferry home, and everything gets carried down to the wharf and into the boat. And when you get to the island it's got to be carried out of the boat and up to another vehicle and driven across the island, and then you unload it into your house. It all seems uphill. Everything: your fuel, your propane, and food."

The inventory of supplies needed for island life is long and constantly in flux. Despite a fairly common interest in sourcing foods locally, cooks go through volumes of non-perishable goods that are produced elsewhere: flours, rice, sugar, spices, legumes, powdered milk, and leavening agents, along with such prepared foods as pasta, canned meats, and dried vegetables, and staples including cooking oil, lard, vinegar, mustard, sauces, dried fruits, and nuts. And toiletries, propane, boat gas, mantles for propane lights, animal feed, hardware, lumber, and the occasional bottle of scotch or gin are needed, along with screws, drill bits, sandpaper, and caulking. Endless lists, on scraps of paper or in meticulous journals, keep islanders organized. Suromitra on her remote island laughs when she says, "I've always got a list going—the moment something gets used up, it's on the list. You've got to be thinking ahead and noting things for the next trip. Funny things happen—we bought Worcestershire sauce last time but forgot to cross it off, so now we have two bottles. And we forgot to buy butter because it's so self-evident. We have a list for when we leave the island as well—even something as silly as unplugging the smoke detector, because otherwise that battery will die...Little things."

Almost everyone emphasizes a reliance on lists. "I live to make lists" says Caroline Woodward, lightkeeper on Lennard Island, "for the illusion of control and for the simple joy of crossing out completed items with a bright highlighter pen."[16] Maintaining a record of brands, dimensions, sizes, volumes, and other specifics prevents confusion at the store and worse—bringing home materials that have to go back. Wallets contain fabric and paint chips just in case they're needed. Smart phones contain pictures that save a thousand words. And like Suromitra, a number of people keep lists of provisions that are already on island so that they don't replicate things already on hand. Relying on memory is a faulty approach to provisioning.

A notebook that contains every conceivable island detail—from house plans, dimensions, model numbers, maintenance schedules, work lists, materials lists for projects, and inventories of hardware to current shopping lists—is a constant reference for Roger, whether he's on Bath Island or in town. "If I'm in Home Depot in Vancouver, I have the dimensions of a window that needs replacing." Being organized can save precious time and careful attention to detail can save repeated trips. But not always: David, whose island is a half-day journey from Campbell River, talks with some frustration about how easy it is to take delivery of tools and appliances that are missing parts or are incorrectly assembled. As just one example, he put clear instructions on the order form and double-checked with the shipping agent that a new fridge would have a right-hand door. Once it arrived by water taxi and was hauled across the island on an ATV, David opened the box to find that the door was hinged on the wrong side. It had to go back.

Actual provisioning tends to be a weekly or monthly task, depending on proximity to stores or the urgency of needs. Acquiring all the things on lists and taking care of such personal matters as haircuts, banking, and checkups requires organization, particularly if a ferry trip is involved. Sandy Oliver, who lives off the coast of Maine, writes that "living on an island takes a lot of work. Think about the effort it takes to go to the mainland, the planning it takes ahead of time,... planning the errand route to be the most efficient it can be; watching the time so that one can be back at the ferry in time. Always paying attention."[17]

Mom fell into the habit of shopping in Nanaimo every Thursday unless the weather was truly awful. She'd load the boat with storage bins, garbage, and propane bottles and head for Page's Marina, where the family station wagon was kept. It would start after a few tries and Mom would dash along Gabriola roads to ensure a place on the ferry. The twenty-five-minute ride to Nanaimo was an opportunity to chat with acquaintances, to catch up on news. Phillip Vannini, who studies the impacts of ferries on islands, equates the Gabriola ferry to a floating community hall. "Its influence can be seen in the social interactions of Gabriola Islanders, their relationship with time, the arrangement of space and development on the island, the ritual of commuting and communication, and the dialectic between islanders and non-islanders."[18] Conversations begin in the lineup and continue until the ferry pulls into its Nanaimo slip.

Once in Nanaimo, Mom followed her weekly routine, often beginning with a visit to the lumberyard where entire sheets of plywood would be placed in the back of the station wagon. Salespeople knew Mom and always ensured that her lumber was true and clear. She had a sharp eye for pieces unlikely to meet my father's exacting standards and was happy to sort through pallets to find choice two-by-fours. Sacks of cement and boxes of nails went on top of the lumber, as did bags of feed and other heavy materials. Late morning involved a visit to the library to choose books that we'd all devour in the following days. An eclectic mix of biography, world history, mysteries, and Harlequin romances found its way into her well-worn book bag.

Mom devoted the middle of the day to more pleasurable or personal activities, including art lessons, visits with friends, or appointments. Grocery shopping took up the hour before it was time to line up for the 3:15 ferry. Dairy products and meat went into a cooler, while other groceries were organized in cardboard boxes or heavy-duty totes.

As Clair and I would also be on the 3:15 ferry, we'd all return to Page's, unload the car, transfer things to the freezer, and carry the collection of food, propane, chicken feed, books, and other supplies down the long, often slippery ramp to the boat. Lumber and truly heavy items were left for a weekend trip. If it was raining or snowing, a tarp protected boxes and bags. The tarp also kept crows and gulls from raiding groceries. Once home, we'd unload, carry everything up the ramp to the tractor or wheelbarrow, and follow the trail across the island to the house. Roger, who now has his own provisioning routines for Bath Island, speaks from experience when he says, "one false move on an icy dock and the entire load goes in the water."[19]

Chic and Kathy on Snowberry Island know the hazards of docks. They often use a power wagon to transport supplies from their dock, up the steep trail to the top of a thirty-seven-metre bluff, and then across the island to their cabin. The power wagon is a motorized wheelbarrow with a little Briggs & Stratton engine and a four-speed transmission. It is one of Chic's favourite island tools. "I can load a thousand pounds or more on this thing and go right up the ramp." Chic recalls a story, which now makes him laugh, about bringing the wagon onto the dock to fill it with supplies. "It wasn't a low tide and the ramp wasn't that steep. We were loading stuff. I shifted something, and suddenly the wagon started to flip over into the water. I lurched to grab one of the handlebars, thinking 'This is not going to end well,' and just about went into the water myself. So I kicked back and managed to twist the wagon so that it came back down on the dock. In the meantime everything in it catapulted into the water." As if that wasn't bad enough, they were uncertain what had disappeared.

I had no idea what went overboard. We carry a lot of stuff to and from the island in plastic bins. We kind of stage stuff to get it from point A to point B. So there I was, wondering what went into the water. I'd brought over some saw blades, tools, and nails for putting shingles on—sixty-nine dollars for a little box of stainless nails and it turns out to be on the bottom. Several bottles of wine also went over, along with my very nice hammer drill. These cost a couple of hundred of bucks, and I'd tossed them in at the last minute. All that stuff is now thirty feet down under the dock. We can recover it—the wine will be fine, not so much the hammer drill.

Other islanders use golf carts, four-by-fours, old trucks or SUVs (usually unlicensed and beaten up), or bicycles to transport goods from dock to house. A Protection Island resident writes, "Island living requires considerable schlepping." She goes on to say that she longs for the days when she could drive her car into the carport and from there carry bags into the kitchen. As an islander, she now has to "haul everything out of the boat, load it onto the bikes (or into a wheelbarrow) and cart it the last kilometre home. Those wire panniers on the back of my bike have a CostPerUse that's infinitesimally small, so indispensable are they."[20]

The process of moving goods on and off island entails more risk on Echachis, where everything is loaded or unloaded over the bow of a boat that is heaving in the surf. Not surprisingly, things and people get wet in the process. On Read Island, where the Coxes also come into a beach, they have the additional step of loading things into a carefully engineered twenty-four-metre funicular on steel rails to deal with the steep embankment between house and shoreline.[21] And in light of all the work involved in transporting goods to Wallace Island, David Conover writes, "Every item not only had to be practical but must pay its way in usefulness."[22]

Islanders in truly isolated locations make seasonal trips "out" and return laden with bulky cargo, carefully balanced in the holds of boats or planes. Far away, off the coast of Scotland, an island resident laments the pressure of shopping only a couple of times a year. "We did not shop, we raided the stores. You have so little time and there are so many things [we] needed. You had to know what you were doing and what you wanted. We just spent a fortune stocking up."[23] Some islanders rely on coastal steamships to drop off supplies from time to time. They are among the earliest "online" shoppers, placing recurrent food and equipment orders by radio telephone or mail. For those who now have a satellite connection, Web-based order forms must seem like a breeze if delivery arrangements to an island address are straightforward and affordable.

Personal shoppers and sympathetic clerks in local stores may also process telephone and online orders and transport them to a water taxi or local freight boat. Many remote islanders look forward to social interactions when supply and mail vessels arrive. And opening long-awaited purchases is an opportunity to enjoy a bit of retail therapy, to vary the menu, to get on with projects.

It was always exciting to receive the *Sears Wish Book* every season and pore over it, choosing clothes that seemed more desirable than those in Nanaimo stores. We'd fill in and mail the order form with a cheque, and wait for packages to arrive by mail weeks later. On one memorable occasion my parents ordered Mustang Floater Coats in floral prints for my sister and me. We'd hide these thick, cumbersome jackets under the steps of the church where the school bus picked us up on Gabriola. There was no way we were going to appear at school in such odd-looking garb when all our friends had matching shoes, coats, dresses, and purses.

Some reluctant shoppers appreciate the willingness of fellow islanders to take care of a few chores when they venture into town. On various islands listservs coordinate shared shopping. But as David Cox notes,

> the protocol is to offer first before someone has to ask. Actually, asking is not so good. Waiting for an offer and then accepting is the proper protocol. Should someone be going to town and they do not offer to pick up something, it is assumed that they have way too much to do and no face is lost. And, once in a while, if something is more pressing than a loaf of bread, it is okay to ask if someone is going to town. But such an imposition must be reserved for really necessary things such as a part for the boat motor.[24]

Judith, on nearby Rendezvous Island, says, "I can generally figure out some way of paying them back for the effort."

Many islanders have guests well trained to bring things along when they arrive. Boxes of wine, dog food, spare engine parts, and apple pies have all been part of cargo that we've taken when we've visited island friends. And when you run out of something, you improvise or do without until the next provisioning trip. As one islander comments, "There's very little in life that is truly necessary—most things are just nice."

Provisioning is possible year-round when towns are nearby. People in remote settings, however, must also anticipate the possibility of being cut off as winter sets in. Joy Orth's family makes "every effort, these last few years, to have all [provisions] in by the end of October. You may have plenty of time after that—then again, you might not."[25] A couple that lives on an island off the coast of Nova Scotia makes sure they augment local foods before winter sets in.

> No matter what we *think* the next few months' weather might be like, we've learned to stock up in November with enough "bought" goods to run us through the winter: extra grain for the chickens, pellets (stored in garbage cans) for the rabbits, 30 pounds of salt mackerel and 15 of salt cod (available from fish plants and storable at room temperature), powdered milk, flours, 15 pounds of butter (refrigerated outdoors by nature), rice, raisins, six gallons of kerosene for the lamps, extra matches, saw blades and radio batteries. All this, in addition to 124 pints of assorted home canned vegetables, 24 pints of wild berry purees and heaping mounds of turnips, cabbages, parsnips, carrots and potatoes.[26]

Some islanders enjoy provisioning as an opportunity to connect with urban life. Others loathe it. These people dread the time off island, the ferry ride, the traffic, the stress, and the consumerism inherent in malls and grocery stores. Phillip Vannini observes that "few conversation topics bind islanders together more than 'going to town.' Wherever or whatever 'town' may be, going to it is like descending down [into] the abyss of hell. I have actually known islanders who occasionally take a day trip to Vancouver just to feel better about their life. Actually, I have done it too, at least twice. Such trips are completely unmotivated by anything other than absorbing as much noise, traffic, and busyness as you can in less than ten hours. Just to take it all in—and then to feel refreshed upon coming back home."[27]

An inevitable outcome of provisioning is garbage: packaging, plastic, glass, tin cans, and returnable wine bottles and beer cans, and, over time, worn-out stuff. Some people quietly confess to disposing of non-biodegradable garbage in incinerator bins or in burial pits far from their homes. But for most, getting rid of garbage goes hand-in-hand with off-island trips. Elizabeth Arthur describes the work involved in moving garbage from her island in a northern lake. "The black bags of garbage, packaged on the island, carried to the beach, loaded in the boat, and now transferred once again, entirely filled the back of the truck. It strikes Bob as absolutely ridiculous to lug our garbage all the way to the town dump, but I don't want to fill the island or the lakeshore woods with junk."[28] And, of course, many materials can and should be recycled. Carefully sorting waste materials and hauling them to the nearest recycling depot frequently enough to minimize unsightly piles is one more chore. The organizational and physical effort of recycling is a constant reminder of the waste generated in contemporary living, and inspires many islanders to consciously avoid importing potential garbage. Minimal packaging and large-volume purchases offer an economy of scale. Some islanders purchase only things that are strictly necessary; others only replace things when they are no longer useful. For example, on Lennard Island, Caroline Woodward wears old clothes "until they are worn out completely and then I cut them into rags for the engine room clean rag bin."[29]

Minimizing or repurposing garbage and recyclables dovetails with the desire for greater simplicity that attracts many people to island life in the first place. In *Off the Grid: Re-assembling Domestic Life*, the authors reflect that "one of the great appeals of off-grid living is that it allows you to practice a form of voluntary simplicity based in frugality, sustainability, self-sufficiency and resilience. The 'voluntary' part refers to a deliberate act of choice: an awakening leading to a lifestyle conversion." They link this awakening to a critical awareness that global society has spun out of control. They go on to say that "simplicity consists of voluntary choices, such as to buy less, consume sustainably and ethically, eat more local and natural foods, reduce clutter, recycle and re-use, practice creativity, take a more active role in self-education, use renewable energy resources, prefer smaller-scale forms of living, and develop skills based on the values of self-reliance."[30] In the 1950s, when Margaret McIntyre lived on Nelson Island, she noted habits that remain common today. "There were economies practiced by the islanders which we observed and imitated. Planks and pieces of finished lumber washed up by the tide were carefully dried and stacked for any future building. Iron dogs, spikes and odd pieces of metal found on old logging sites were straightened out and saved; cardboard cartons and string that come with the groceries were stored away...A glass jar was never thrown away. The prodigal waste of civilization never touched the island. There was a use for everything."[31]

Nevertheless, islands can become the final resting place for diverse stuff. There is a remarkable collection of old moss-covered trucks in the woods on Valdes (and many other islands, I suspect). Linda notes that these were gifts to her parents from relatives who no longer needed them. "We'd float them over on a raft made out of cedar logs—all the trips were scary when the raft carried a big old truck or car. They were ancient when they got here and they usually didn't stand up too well on the old logging roads. Steve, my husband, is a pretty good mechanic, so we went through quite a few, but not so many as my mom. We had an endless supply." And as Tom Barchyn on Protection Island wryly observes, once something is on island, it takes a lot of effort to get it off. Piles of unused building materials, derelict equipment, cracked tanks, desiccated hoses, stained plumbing fixtures, and other scraps of domestic life are tucked away in old sheds or disappearing into the brush. Some people see potential in such rubbish. Helen Piddington has lived with her family in remote Loughborough Inlet long enough to accumulate such stuff. She writes, "I used to be bothered by all the junk that lies about in heaps. Now I realize how valuable it can be. One never knows what will be needed to improve repairs or deal with emergencies."[32] And swapping is part of the island sharing economy, as is scouring beaches for detritus that might come in handy one day.

Changing seasons

TIME ON ISLANDS is also devoted to seasonal chores. For example, as winter slips into spring, islanders turn over the vegetable gardens that put food on their tables for much of the year. There are a number of on-island solutions for enriching soil and providing water. Wheelbarrow loads of slippery seaweed cast ashore by winter storms, for example, substitute for bags of fertilizer and expensive seaweed supplements available at garden centres. It's important to rinse salt from mounds of odorous weed before turning the satisfying goop into the soil, along with crushed shells, compost, chicken manure, sawdust from the workshop, and ashes from the firebox. And cisterns, rain barrels, and other dedicated tanks provide precious water that is carefully meted out when the soil goes dry. Grey water of various kinds may also be cast onto the garden, though it's important to be attentive to soaps and grease that can damage plants.

My mom was always careful to keep handfuls of seeds from various annuals as summer turned to fall. These were nurtured in her small greenhouse the following spring in anticipation of warm weather. Experience taught her which plants would thrive during the island growing season, which would withstand salty air, and which would mature in a timely way. In addition to her vegetable garden, she tended garden beds along the trail to the house, and tucked roses and shrubs here and there as the mood struck her. Some of those old leggy roses still add colour along pathways today.

There were no deer on the island in those days, but they now swim to the island and regularly raid Roger's garden. And their frustrating presence on other islands is lamented in stories of lost crops, decimated shrubs, and strangely shaped trees. A creative gardener on Nelson Island locates her garden on a dock anchored in the middle of a lake, thereby solving her water problems and discouraging deer from feasting on her plants. I love the notion of rowing out to a garden.

Spring is also a time to ensure that equipment and systems are shipshape. Hauling boats, painting their bottoms, replacing zincs, tuning engines, and checking docks, anchors, and mooring buoys takes energy and time as days grow longer. So does examining water tanks and lines, spring cleaning, checking chimneys, and renewing woodpiles. Spring is also a time to deal with the wear and tear that wind and lashing rains inflict on houses. Checking the roof, downspouts, caulking, and paint is all part of the spring routine. As Geri observes, "Houses weather differently on islands." And as spring turns to summer, it is time to recover trails from the encroaching forest and begin at least some of the new construction and landscape projects planned on winter evenings. The garden demands ongoing attention, and it's suddenly more appealing to be out fishing and harvesting shellfish. Water tanks are topped up, and strategies to battle dreaded summer fires reviewed.

High summer, when most islands are at their most alluring, should bring more time for play, but many islanders reflect that the "easy" life that mainlanders associate with island living is elusive. A reporter in Australia pours cold water on the romantic notion that islands are about leisure. "Just quite simply, living on an island does not measure [up] to what most people's expectation of living on an island is. People buy the dream, the aspiration that they're going to sit on the front verandah drinking pina coladas at 4 o'clock in the afternoon when they realize, 'Hang on, I've got to go and turn the septic system on. Hang on, we've run out of milk.' Right? It's those sorts of things people forget."[33]

Expectations of endless playtime are dispelled early in most islanders' experience. For enjoyment Jan does walk the paths that run through the forest and overlook Jervis Inlet, but she says, "There's no sitting around during the day. We go down to the dock sometimes— it's nice in the evenings." And while David and Suromitra take time to explore local inlets, they say that summer days fly by with all the tasks they set for themselves. Kathy has a similar experience on Snowberry.

"We spend the bulk of our time doing projects rather than just sitting around reading. Sometimes we'll take an hour to walk to the end of the island." Like many islanders, Roger doesn't recognize the dichotomy of work and play, since he sees island chores as a form of recreation. Nonetheless, he loves fishing and boating, and laments that his time on the water is reduced to transportation. It's only when visitors place him in the role of guide that he takes "time off," explores the Flat Top islands, and has fun in kayaks and dinghies. "It's not very often I get to sit on the deck and contemplate the achievements and glories of island life, or have pleasant conversations about Descartes and the meaning of life. It's more like owning a farm. The work is continuous and unrelenting and it never stops. Some of my friends call this place a 'boot camp' because they get recruited for the heavy lifting." And even caring for the welcome guests who arrive in July and August involves time and work to provision, plan, cook, and entertain.

As the warmth of summer gave way to the shorter days of fall, Michael Modzelewski felt re-energized. "Autumn on the island was my favorite season. The summer heat and procession of people had vanished, and now the air was knife-edge keen. There was great reach and clarity in the sky. The blue was so transparent that the planets were still visible at midmorning. The north wind infused me with endless energy. I worked with arms and back all day, and then fully charged, wrote and read into the night. I'd snatch a couple hours sleep, then burst out of bed at sunrise to have at it all over again."[34]

The fall is harvest time—a time for picking and preserving foods that make the long winter more palatable. In addition to preparing jams, jellies, and preserves, Mom canned endless jars of salmon in her pressure cooker. She also made wine and beer. There was always a carboy with something brewing adjacent to the stove and a stash of bottles of what I suspect was rather awful wine for sipping on winter evenings. Other islanders dry or smoke fish, and fill freezers with a wealth of locally sourced foods.

The fall is also time to anticipate problems that winter may bring. It is wiser to deal with dangerous trees, broken branches, wobbly drainpipes, loose shingles, vulnerable water and fuel lines, and loose treads on slippery ramps in the pleasant days of autumn than in the throes of a winter storm. Water lines should once again be checked and where not needed, drained. Piles of brush and other debris can be burned; working boats winterized; recreational boats, summer toys, and furniture put under shelter; tools cleaned and stored; gutters cleared; and dock lines replaced. One islander is pleased that he has deliberately designed his home to minimize maintenance. Another confronts the need to fix the slumping foundation of a forty-year-old cottage before she can realign and replace a leaking shingle roof with metal panels. "I have to start with the building structure itself. I can't do anything until that part of the house is levelled." She is very aware that these jobs need to be done before the rains.

The final months of the year bring shorter days along with extended storms, rain, occasional snow, and, for some islanders, a sense of despondency. "Winter works a darker magic. Surf rages beneath the seaward cliffs and cloud hangs low over the inlet walls. It is the time when spawned out salmon are dying along the creeks and whispering dune grass of the estuaries lies flattened in the rain."[35] Time is spent on contemplative or creative indoor activities: writing, sewing, painting, reading, rug hooking, cooking, keeping fires burning. Winter months also provide opportunities for socializing. Judith enjoys time with old friends. "I love the winters. All the summer folk have gone—they're wonderful people to have around. They are pretty intense socializers. It's lovely to go out to dinner, meet all these interesting people, and learn all kinds of stuff. But then they all go in September, and we're left with the people who are here year-round, my old friends forever. Then we do more gentle socializing and there's some community get-togethers, the book club, the Christmas parties." She smiles as she adds, "In the winters, all your canning is done, all the gardens are put to bed, the firewood is in. You light the fire and it's just fantastic. People sit around, drinking coffee and telling stories. It's a good time." Winter also brings many lovely—but brisk—outdoor days when the sun is at low angle and high tides stir up beaches and deposit new logs and castaway treasures.

Some of my favourite memories involve Christmas. Every year we roamed Bath Island as well as nearby unoccupied islands in search of a small tree to fit in the corner of the living room. As not many were perfect, we drilled holes to insert temporary branches. Scrambling over beaches, bushwhacking, debating the merits of various specimens, cutting the perfect tree, and hauling it down a slippery beach was fun and certainly more adventurous than driving to the local garden store. It would be lovely to have a picture of us heading home with a tree lashed in the dinghy. I also remember the occasional snowfalls that transformed the woods and beaches, the warmth of the kitchen as the turkey roasted for hours in the wood stove, and Mom's insistence on best clothing, candlelight, wine, and immaculate manners as we celebrated this holiday on our small island.

Judith also remembers Christmas at Surge Narrows fondly. "It was a beautiful summery day one Christmas, and we stopped in at Surge Narrows and picked up Christmas presents, sat on the dock, and opened them. It was great. Our kids just grew up thinking this was the way everyone did it."

The unexpected

WHILE ISLAND TIME is shaped by predictable and pressing daily, weekly, and seasonal routines, many islanders observe that they never know how a day will turn out. On Wallace Island, David Conover reflected on the pleasures—and challenges—of planning how precious time should be used each day. "How wonderful to dole out time instead of being a slave to it. The chores came first: the woodpile, boat, lanterns, stuck drawers, and broken tools. The greatest bugaboo ... was estimating the time for a job. Hauling materials took nearly as much time as building... Even doubled, my calculations were often faulty. For an island is always working against you, forever trying to escape by foiling your plans."[36]

Jan and Sy have lots of stories of unexpected events that demanded immediate attention.

You think you know what you're doing when you get up in the morning. Then you find out that the decision has been taken out of your hands since something has to be done *right* now. We have some water tanks out behind the catchment system for emergency water. The other day, I went by to check that mosquitos weren't breeding. Both of the tanks, six thousand gallons, were empty. Gone! Obviously we had a leak. So obviously we had to fix it. That turned into a three-week project, since we cleared around the tanks and cleaned inside. You think you know what you're doing when you get up in the morning, but you don't.

Being flexible about the unexpected was also important when fifty guests were invited to the island for their daughter's wedding. Days before the big event, Jan and Sy became concerned that the road from the dock was slippery. "We thought of all the incoming non-islanders and decided this would be a good time to put down gravel. Amazingly the barge, equipment, and operators were available at short notice, and we had a load of gravel delivered. Of course it was a short tidal window, but the operators were good and got eighteen dump truck loads of gravel offloaded! That was five days before wedding day, but it all got done on time." Then, of course, things started to break. "The day before the wedding, when guests were arriving, the dishwasher broke down. Not really a problem, they [dishes] could be done by hand. Then the generator broke down. Again, not usually a problem, but it was overcast and there was very little solar gain. We borrowed a thousand-watt generator to make coffee for the masses and play the tunes for the dancing." The wedding itself was lovely—and memorable. "The ceremony was going smoothly, and everything was perfect until a bee flew down the dress of the officiator (who is allergic to bees). The groom, being helpful, tried to get it out, and the bride, groom, and officiator suddenly collapsed in hysterics. The bee flew away, and the ceremony continued with just an occasional giggle surfacing."

The perpetual need to cope with the unexpected is echoed by Yvonne Maximchuk, who says that the beginning of each day is her quiet time. But things rarely stay quiet. "Something is always happening. A neighbour needs a hand or to borrow something, or the boomstick has come loose, and so on. I noticed from the start...that life is like this . . . I make a plan and by 9 AM my plan has vanished like an unweighted prawn trap caught in the tide. I just try to stay with the outline as the details get coloured in by unfolding events. A day that turns out as planned is rare."[37]

Roger adds to this theme. "Problems crop up every day and because you're on an island, it's probably wise to deal with them right away. You just have to find time by rearranging the other things you'd planned to tackle." He also reflects that coping with the unexpected involves learning. For example, when his engine blew up one winter, he found helpful advice through an online forum about Ford motors. "I was down at the marina in the engine room with a blue tarp over some two-by-fours, and it was snowing. And I'm not sure whether the gaskets go on this way or that way. So I take a photo and post it, and get a reply straightaway. It gave me a lot of comfort. And I'll know what to do next time"

The vagaries of wind, temperature, sea conditions, and fog also inject uncertainty into island routines. As Caroline Woodward on Lennard Island writes, "So much of our life is about the weather." Of course weather, along with other natural phenomena, has always been part of island cycles, of island pleasures. In 1873 Celia Thaxter reflected that what is happening outdoors "becomes of the first importance to the dwellers on the rock; the changes of the sky and sea, the flitting of the coasters to and fro, the visits of the sea-fowl, sunrise and sunset, the changing moon, the northern lights, the constellations that wheel in splendor through the winter night—all are noted with a love and careful scrutiny that is seldom given by people living in populous places."[38]

Wind in particular, and its influence on sea state, shapes time on island. A gale-force wind in the city might rattle signs, blow off your hat, or send you running for shelter. A windy day on island threatens your moorage, prevents passages, brings down trees. David Conover dreaded long stormy stretches. "Around us six-story firs whipped and groaned like dark pendulums against the sky. The nights were always the worst. Snapping limbs brought us bolt upright in bed . . . Close and warm inside, we could feel the shack quiver like a ship in a storm, hear the wind wailing against the walls and rattling the door."[39]

Weather reports and your ability to read clouds, light, water conditions, and air pressure help anticipate disruptive weather. But changing conditions can still upset carefully laid plans. Bill Proctor, who lived on Swanson Island off the east coast of northern Vancouver Island, describes the extreme conditions that affected life over one year in Blackfish Sound. "It blew northerly gales for sixteen days without let-up. That year there was 31 feet of snow on the flats at the head of Knight Inlet and sustained winds of 100 miles an hour ... And in August of 1976 it blew northwest gales for twelve days non-stop. In the morning the wind would be down to 30 knots and back up to 40 in the afternoon ... Our faces were so windburnt we all looked like tomatoes. The other extreme I have seen was fourteen days straight of fog, with no breaks."[40]

Farther south on Nelson Island, days of unexpected wind also took their toll. Margaret MacIntyre notes that severe weather damaged floats, washed away dinghies, and drove logs into the sides of fishing boats. "The men living on the outside [of the bay] had spent night after night sitting up to guard their boats and watching to see that the mooring ropes and cables held during the storm. The Dutchman had broken two ribs when he slipped on the wet planks of his float. His woman had bound him up with strips made from old sugar sacks and the next day he had gone out and split half a cord of wood."[41]

Weather not only disrupts plans, it unsettles your sense of well-being. Michael Modzelewski, who also loved living in Blackfish Sound, recalls a particularly bad stretch of weather. "There was no let up in the storms. Day and night, night and day, winds and rain raged. After the constant confinement, I felt victimized, rendered powerless by the power of the weather. Never before had I encountered such raw, walloping forces."[42]

Disruptive events are counterbalanced by unforeseen pleasures. Dropping everything to go for a swim, follow a pod of orca, watch a wolf on the beach, or marvel at a canopy of stars—these are the kinds of experiences that sustain busy islanders and remind them why they chose an island life. On Bath Island we watched sea lions wrestle octopus, crowds of eagles swarm a beach, and otters do a sinuous water ballet. Farther north, Ralph Keller, who is a long-term resident of Read Island and runs the Discovery Island Lodge, sees pleasure in both the unexpected events and quiet beauties that surround him.

With the hindsight benefit of forty years of remote island living, I can safely identify the appeal: anything can happen at any time. The most mundane day can turn into the adventure of a lifetime. You can head out by land to visit a neighbour and come face to face with a pack of wolves who refuse to get out of the way. Or a major storm will knock over thirty trees across the road, barring you from the government dock, and requiring days to clear away.

While looking out the window, drinking your morning coffee, you might see a large male cougar amble by just a few feet away. Perhaps you glance out and notice seventy or eighty Pacific white-sided dolphins stampeding around the bay. Or you drive the boat to town and along the way encounter a group of humpbacks breaching. And if you get lost in the fog, you can spend the night—God knows where—on an isolated point waiting for it to lift so you can get home. High adventure waits around any corner...whether you're watching wildlife or out in a storm...you just never know. That isn't usually what attracts people to island life, but it might be what keeps them here.

The combinations of daily and seasonal, expected and unexpected, difficult and pleasurable often mean that there is little time for rest. While no one seems to be complaining, a common theme in all my conversations with islanders is the unremitting work that takes up island time. Roger, who loves his island life, nevertheless reflects that "it's always been work, work, work. It's incredible that I've filled up thirty years just working. And if you walk around the island you don't see much evidence of it." To Jan on her small island off Nelson Island, it's "a lifestyle." Most islanders link hard work with satisfaction, although Roger comments that balancing the expected and unexpected can be wearing. "There are times when things are going sideways simultaneously—sometimes I wonder, 'Shit, do I have another crisis in me?' That's the problem when there's no relief. Things come in waves: the boat leg is broken, the water tank is falling over, there's a leak around the skylight in the A-frame, and the deer are eating the garden. It looks like there might be a water shortage..." But he adds that "there is also immense pleasure in getting the jobs done." And he's still there, thirty years later.

Rob Wood spent hours clearing the site for his house and continues to work his land on Maurelle. "You just go out in the morning and start dealing with what is most obviously in need of attention. Then one thing leads on to the next. At the end of the day you're tired but satisfied by the visible progress; you're energized by the combination of vigorous exercise, fresh air and the energy of the land itself."[43] This is echoed by David on a nearby island. "Every day there's something to be done, and you do it—and in contrast to my job [on the mainland], the accountability chain here is really short. At the end of the day, something is done and it's great. It gives me satisfaction." And a resident on Gambier Island in Howe Sound reflects that the calmness of being on island—when everything is working—can't be matched.[44]

Annual cycles of leaving islands as summer draws to a close or for an extended winter holiday are also accompanied by distinctive routines. Again, lists play important roles in ensuring that nothing is forgotten. The last thing in the world you want is to be most of the way to the airport and wonder if you've shut off the garden hose. Roger, for example, maintains a checklist of things to monitor if he is departing Bath Island for more than a day. It includes

> turning off the propane, shutting down the water, locking the shed, making sure the bathroom window is closed, making sure the chooks' feed trough is filled up, and this and that. There are about thirty things. Locking the sheds, for example, is crucial. I have my valuables distributed so if I have a break-in in one shed, it doesn't necessarily involve the others. And I've learned the hard way that the only way to do this routine is by myself. There are people who want to come and stay here, but I don't want them to because they're never going to be as conscientious as I am about shut-down arrangements.

He starts to deplete perishable food stocks well before departure so that the fridge is left empty. And he has a firm rule that no fires will be left to die down after he has departed—a lesson learned when he returned from two weeks off island in midwinter to find that a burn pile was still smouldering and had migrated through brush for almost twelve metres.

Even as you plan to depart, you start lists for returning. David tries to be as thorough as possible, given that his island is hours away from the nearest stores. "Home Depot, Canadian Tire, Thrifty's—everything that we need is written out, and part of the fun for us while off island is going through the list, crossing things off, putting things in the tubs, getting ready."

Islanders are as attracted by warm vacations in the depths of winter as anyone else. There are logistical challenges in taking time away from islands, however, particularly if no one is around to keep an eye on things, feed the chickens, and look after the dog. Who will check the house and docks after a big blow? What happens if water lines freeze or otters take up residence on your boat? Do you want someone to stay on island or does that complicate things? Many people living on the remote coast are leery of being away, as odds are that something will go wrong. Helen Piddington writes that "this explains quite simply why we don't go off travelling together as friends and family are always urging us to do. And also why we don't jump at offers to campwatch for a month or more."[45] Instead, she and her husband take turns being away.

Patterns of island time

THE IMPULSE TO move to an island is almost always connected with a desire to improve the quality and quantity of your time. People choose islands, large and small, to escape urban pressures, spend more time in nature, exercise greater independence, be more self-sufficient, savour a special place, move at a slower pace. Such words as *idyll, retreat, respite, adventure, sanctuary, refuge,* and *haven* convey how island time is experienced. Phillip Vannini, who studies life on ferry-dependent islands, observes "a more relaxed attitude toward everyday routines and a slower pace of work, ... a less hurried disposition towards interacting with others, the ability to make time for the appreciation of nature and its rhythms, and a sharp appreciation for peace and quiet."[46] But there can be no universal experience of island time on Gabriola—or anywhere else—and stereotypes don't always fit. A sense of time is always personal, always a result of the rhythm, speed, and duration of activities that make up one's life in a particular place.[47] Being on island time is a way of living, a state of mind that varies from person to person.

And, of course the ways in which islanders on Gabriola, Salt Spring, or Quadra experience the pace, rhythm, and duration of time differ in interesting ways from those of people who live on islands off the ferry grid. Residents of ferry-dependent islands travel in cars that can pull up to the back door. They can make quick trips to local grocery and hardware stores. Their creature comforts are relatively easy to arrange. If contractors and tradespeople don't live on island, they are a ferry ride away. Power and all its conveniences are readily available, and in some cases island-wide sewer and water utilities are available. Clinics, schools, libraries, clubs, and even restaurants and fashionable shopping may be right around the corner. Ferry-dependent island lifestyles are special and distinctive (and complicated by ferries), but they don't require the same skills or investments in time as life on islands without ferry service does. The extra boat ride, the hours needed to create and maintain systems from scratch, the difficulties of construction, the challenges of provisioning, and the details—and rewards—of day-to-day self-sufficiency set residents of such islands apart. Things are more complicated, risks are greater, and there are more concerns to juggle. And the farther you get from the mainland, the more distinctive the patterns of island time become. From his home on Read Island, Ralph Keller reflects on a key difference between ferry-served and more remote islands.

There are islanders who live on islands supported by ferries, electricity, and larger communities. Then there are islanders who live in very remote, often hostile environments. Here in the Discovery Islands we deal with massive storms, the world's most powerful tidal rapids, and powerful, frigid outflow winds from time to time. We have faced tragedy and death within our community. Island life isn't always just quirky and eccentric; it's dangerous—and people die in terrible ways. Outer islanders take real risks to live out here and sometimes they make mistakes. That creates a powerful connection to the land that sets us apart from others.

People on islands not served by ferries have much in common in how they experience island time. Tides, weather, and seasons set the cadence. The forest, shore, and surrounding water set the stage. Few people are involved in decision making. Careful planning is valued, as is the ability to deal with the unexpected. Cycles of daily, weekly, and seasonal practices that are the essence of life on island are often satisfying, occasionally overwhelming. Activities are physical, strenuous, skilled. And few islanders find time for recreational activities. When pressed, they tend to smile and say that projects are their recreation or that they take only occasional moments from urgent chores to engage in the activities that brought them to the islands in the first place. Sailboats languish at the dock. Kayaks are launched only for sunset paddles. Deck furniture is rarely occupied midday. It is only when guests are present that islanders put down their tools.

And just as islanders are glad to set their own pace and schedule, they recognize that fellow islanders may make different choices about time. In some cases this inspires grudging admiration. The builder of a complex island house described working with a carpenter from a nearby island. "I think it's philosophical—this fellow is anti-system. He'll be on his way to work for us and everyone else would be here. But if he sees a pod of killer whales on the way here, he's going to stop and look at them. He doesn't care how late he's going to be for work. He'll grasp the opportunities that are presented to him. He knows that his philosophy doesn't quite fit with yours, but he knows what's important in life and if you don't understand that, that's your loss." Some people are accepting of this way of being; others find themselves at odds with others around their sense of time.

Islanders also reflect on how focused they feel when on island. Rob, for example, comments that "living off grid is not so much about solar panels and baking bread as about paying attention and being fully present in the moment. This honest sincerity builds on itself to form an authentic sense of community... it's enjoyment of the beauty and adventure of the place that counts."[48] On nearby Read Island, David Cox writes that "one of the weird differences between living in the woods and the city is one's increased ability to be more present in the moment. This altered state of being may just be due to aging and failing memory but I prefer to think of it as the beginning of some sort of better late than never enlightenment. I am no philosopher, but going to the woods at least increases awareness of the senses and probably, by extension, one's sense of being."[49]

And on Snowberry Island, Chic emphasizes that pleasure lies in the activity itself. "There isn't any timeline—it's all about the process. Being here and doing it."

It's tempting to generalize island time as cyclical and autonomous, as fluid and benign, in contrast to mainland schedules that are linear, externally imposed, and rigid. Few people, however, live on island without some synchronization with the rest of the world. Balancing the distinctive patterns of time on island with ferry, work, and school schedules, medical appointments, and tax deadlines is a dance that requires constant attention to rhythm and footwork. Many enjoy the tension, the movement between different types of time. If nothing else, it reminds them to value the sense of place, the sense of time, and the sense of purpose that an island brings to their lives.

(6)

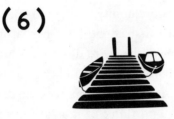

CONNECTIONS

The pay phone at the store at Page's Marina in Silva Bay was my connection to normalcy. Over the years, I spent hours and many dimes in that narrow glass and aluminum box, talking with friends about teenage preoccupations: school, boys, fashion, family, music, plans. As an adult, I've looked fondly at that phone booth on annual visits to Silva Bay. Sadly, like many pay phones, it disappeared in 2017 and with it went one more link to my island days.

Life on the island was busy. Dad and Mom had projects that kept us at home on weekends. Few friends were able to get to the island without help. And the radio telephone was *never* used for chatting. So, for the most part, our lives divided cleanly into self-contained times on island and social times when away. But I don't ever recall this as an issue, perhaps because school provided almost daily opportunities to connect with friends. My sister and I found lots of ways to interact with Gabriola kids when we attended the two-room schoolhouse in Grade 6. And we developed a much wider circle when we made the daily three-hour round trip to Nanaimo for junior and senior high. Five days a week, we took our boat to Silva Bay. That was the unique part of our travels. The balance of time was spent with almost thirty Gabriola kids on the bus, ferry, and second bus that delivered us to school in Nanaimo. In that time, there was lots of talk and laughter. There were interesting times when the old ferries, including the tiny *Neena* and the trusty *Westwood*, broke down or ran into the dock. And I still remember how excited all the kids were when we slowly went aground on a point in Descanso Bay one foggy afternoon. Ferry rides were also a time to read, do homework, or knit—I estimate that I spent two thousand hours riding to and from Gabriola on those school trips.

Developing relationships with Nanaimo friends took a bit of time. We arrived late at school and had to dash out at the final bell to catch the bus back to the ferry. Lunch was the only time we could interact outside of class. We didn't play team sports, belong to after-school clubs, go shopping, attend movies or parties, hang out downtown, or take part in any of the other late afternoon, evening, or weekend activities that occupied other adolescent girls. And I think we were generally perceived as different. People knew us as "island" girls. Even today, I meet people who assume we were connected to the lighthouse on Entrance Island. They had no understanding of where our island was located, nor were they particularly curious about what was involved in living there. But our boating skills were recognized. The write-up in my 1970 school annual says that I'm a master navigator who has been "accumulating sea hours by circulating her island in her row boat." My sister's write-up notes that it's hard to get in touch with her and predicts she will be "the most famous girl map maker."

But we did develop good friends who enjoyed our relative eccentricity, shared the challenges of growing up, and welcomed us for overnight stays to attend dances or tournaments. Their parents were also happy for us to stay when storms prevented a return home. During the summer holidays, friends would make their way to the island. And, of course, we'd talk on the pay phone whenever the opportunity presented itself. We were the same as all other adolescent kids in the 1960s, yet apart, different.

MANY PEOPLE WITH little experience of islands assume that residents tend to be isolated, reclusive, disconnected, and that the insular nature of islands limits their interests and restricts their world views. Islanders defy such stereotypes. The ones that I've come across are welcoming, engaging, friendly, perceptive, witty, and happy to share their experiences. They enjoy the company of friends and strangers, rely on fellow islanders for support, and participate in diverse off-island activities. They are attuned to world and cultural affairs and thoughtful about the ways in which being on island shapes their perspectives. They are connected.

At the same time they treasure life on island. The privilege of spending time in a beautiful place, the inherent autonomy and independence, and the pleasures of connecting more deeply with themselves are mentioned repeatedly. Solitude, for many, is a positive experience, deliberately chosen. They value being alone to think, concentrate, consider priorities. They enjoy their own company and the company of the few people around them. And they talk of their seclusion as a springboard to self-awareness, intentionality, creativity. They are strong and confident individuals.

Finding balance

IF THERE IS a unifying thread in islanders' thoughts about social connections, it's the complementary nature of solitude and socializing. In many ways the existence of one enhances the value of the other, as long as they stay in balance. Islanders negotiate a personal equilibrium between being on and off island, between connection and disconnection, and between self-sufficiency and reliance on off-island services and entertainments. Balance is, in part, determined by the location and nature of the island: Is it remote or close in? Easy to access or precarious? Networked or isolated? But context doesn't always determine the degree of connection: extroverts may live on remote islands and introverts on islands close to more populated areas.

A constantly adjusted balance between social and solitary works well for Judith on Rendezvous Island, as she told me while we sipped tea in china cups, sitting in comfy chairs in the midst of her orchard. "This is wonderful, it's absolute heaven. People coming to see me is really nice. This is probably my favourite activity in the whole world, sitting here, talking." But she also needs time by herself to think, and laughs as she considers the scope of our conversation about her island life. "We're talking about a whole lot of stuff here that I'm going to have to process—I'm going to need a week to do it!" If she visited with people every day, such interactions would be less of a treat. "It wouldn't be special—I'd get overloaded pretty quickly and wouldn't appreciate conversations near as much. I would start gasping for days alone. Now, whenever anybody shows up, I'm glad to see them."

Time to process, to ponder, to come up with new perspectives is a widely valued outcome of being on island. In his insightful book *Islands*, John Fowles writes, "One of the reasons I love islands so much is that...properly experienced, they make us stop and think a little: why am I here, what am I about, what is it all about, what has gone wrong?...Islands strip and dissolve the crud of our pretensions and cultural accretions."[1] Roger reflects how conducive islands are to creative thinking. His reasons include "closeness to nature, the surrounding water, the absence of irrelevant distractions, but there's something more to it than that. If you're walking around the island and see a seal suckling a pup or a carcass ravaged by turkey vultures, these create 'aha' moments of amazement that, in a way, grant permission for more unorthodox or eccentric approaches to your project."

Other islanders savour opportunities to regroup. Linda, who now divides her time between Valdes and Gabriola, goes to her childhood island when she needs time for herself. "I think the island is a part of who I am. I do retreats sometimes. I've had enough of my social being and I retreat to recharge my batteries." She never feels isolated. "It is totally my choice to be alone." And Joe Martin values the strong spiritual connections he feels on Echachis. "Being solitary is sometimes really good—all around the island you see the remnants of the ancestors, particularly a lot of whale bones...and there are graves, some skulls. Being there can be very spiritual. At times when I was troubled, I'd sit there and think about things my grandmother had told me—it helped."

Comfort with solitude, combined with a desire for autonomy, makes many islanders "fiercely independent, often foolishly so," observes Ralph Keller on Read Island. He goes on to say, "There are three elements at work here. Islanders are independent because, as you well know, they have to be. Perhaps more significant is a sense of protectiveness brought on by love for our surroundings. Then, living remotely as many of us do, we are isolated from mainstream thinking and become (to a greater or lesser extent) socially inbred. As a result, our philosophies and values can appear a bit odd to others." People moving to islands can find it challenging to reconcile their treasured independence and distinctive approach to daily life with the needs and expectations of family, friends, colleagues, and community.

Couples, for example, may find themselves negotiating a mutually satisfying balance between independence and collaboration, solitude and connection. In many ways, they have to reinvent their lives together. They must agree on big decisions. What is their perfect island? What will their home look like? What will they bring with them, and what will they leave behind? And how they will cope with myriad tasks? At the same time, the dynamics of day-to-day relationships shift. Couples spend more time together. They contribute different skills. They must trust and rely on each other in new, at times hazardous, circumstances. They distance themselves from other valued personal and professional networks. And as each partner encounters both joys and frustrations in island life and makes sense of newfound solitude, the other is called on to be respectful and sympathetic. The balance that works for one might not be completely satisfying for the other. Sustaining a relationship in such a setting takes work. Joy Orth found her life on a northern island both joyous and difficult. She reflects that "isolation strips a relationship down to its skeletal foundation: none of the trappings of civilization are left to obscure your vision. It can be chancy, and not easily handled. Anyone anticipating a drastic change in lifestyle that will take them away from accustomed activities, especially when isolation is involved, should be aware that there will be major psychological adjustments to be made."

I was too young to appreciate the adjustments that both Mom and Dad must have made when they left Vancouver behind. I don't recall anything other than enthusiasm, a calm process of figuring things out, and mutual satisfaction in leaving the city. My dad was the dominant personality, full of big ideas, enormous energy, and dogged determination to build things right the first time. He was charming, commanding, and not always patient. He loved to laugh but had an impressive repertoire of curses when things went wrong. My mom played the quieter role of quartermaster. She ensured that everything from building materials to food and the comforts of home were on hand. They always observed happy hour (gin in the summer, rum in the winter) and took time to walk the island, savour its features, and dream about next steps. They didn't argue, at least not while my sister and I were around. They made decisions efficiently, though I don't know how they negotiated their differences, and they accomplished a great deal, working side by side through long days. Did they have fun? Did they share the same goals? Did Dad worry about whether Mom was happy in this new life? At times I wonder if Mom enjoyed her island-bound role and the constant demands of keeping everything moving along, but she never expressed any frustration. I wish I could ask both of them how they managed their relationship over their twenty-four years on Bath Island. Would they tell me anything other than it was a good life?

When one islander first visited the island that her husband had purchased long before they met, she was very aware of how much the place meant to him. But first impressions were not encouraging. "I had never done this kind of thing. The first time I came here we had been together for a year. I thought, 'This is awful.' We came on a little boat and it was pouring rain. I fell coming ashore at the cliff face and shed a few tears, and thought 'Oh man, if I'm going to stay with this guy I'm going to have to like this!'" Over the next few months they worked together on a rudimentary cabin and she learned to pee in a bucket. Her husband reflects that building the cabin was an important first step, "because we actually figured out what worked for us... A couple will get an island and only then realize that they won't get along. One of them loves it, the other hates it, and they'll divorce." Both laugh as she adds, "and how things change... I love it here." She emphasizes that "you have to really love spending time with the person, because there's nobody else, there's no escape. Ten acres of forest, no shopping, no restaurants, no manicures, no movies." Her husband agrees and says, "As a couple, you've really got to like each other, because if you don't like being together, this is hell, you're trapped." They now balance careers on the mainland with island time. And when on island for extended stays, they rarely invite others along—being together in a special place is their shared priority.

Geri laughs as she recalls a few of the trials involved in building a home on Sidney Island. But she describes working together with her husband, Frank, as a wonderful experience. They shared an equal commitment to making a life on island, along with a common vision of what they wanted to accomplish. And they were happy to get their hands dirty on the many projects involved in building and landscaping a home. "There's nothing we like better than getting outside and doing something." And they came to understand each other's perspectives on the many decisions involved in the process, although she says that she had to rethink her "urban sensibilities" as they planned their off-the-grid systems. The experience has given them more time to be creative together, more time to talk and laugh away from the demands of busy professional lives.

Being compatible is also key for Caroline Woodward on Lennard Island, where she works alongside her husband as a lightkeeper. "It's a risk to expose any relationship to such intense solitude and more than a few have confided that they could not do what we are doing as a couple. Frankly, we're the first-born from families of four siblings. We both come from small rural communities. We're very similar in so many ways. We have rousing, infrequent fights because we're both always right, of course, but we've been loving partners, best friends... since 1986. We count our blessings to have found each other. It doesn't get much better and we both know it."[2]

Much farther north on a remote island in Stuart Lake, Elizabeth Arthur and her husband, Bob, tested their relationship almost to the breaking point. Throughout Arthur's book about working together to build a house, it is evident that they have a loving marriage and shared goals. "Bob brings me coffee in the mornings and tells stories to make me laugh, imperiling the coffee mug. In the evenings I read P.G. Wodehouse to him, while he continues to work as long as it is light."[3] With the house completed, they left the island for their first winter but stayed through the second. But as summer days gave way to ice-bound winter, they began to feel isolated, bushed. Both were hypersensitive to their hard and insular world and to each other.

> The question of how much hate our love can absorb and still survive seems to be answered by how much it has to ... Our life on this rock has been a flow of years condensed into months. Our proximity to one another has allowed no other choice. We have spent more time together in two years than many couples do in ten. And in this winter we have attained a degree of mutual awareness that hovers always on the edge of painful intensity ... The island itself is a magnifying glass for our emotions. We are stranded here, cast away onto a small platform beneath the sky.

Arthur was horrified that their constant proximity could lead to confrontation. "A breakdown is on its way ... and there was no cortisone to cure the condition, and once the outbreak reached the surface, we scratched and scratched until the brain was bleeding, and still there was no respite from awareness."[4] They got through a difficult period, but the experience became part of their decision to leave the following year "and never again live so closely together that we're compelled to tear ourselves apart."[5]

While the rebalancing inherent in moving to an island can involve stress, many couples see it as a positive change. They have more time for each other. They work together to create and celebrate a distinctive home and lifestyle. They enjoy a stronger and more immediate connection with nature. And they leave behind stresses and worries inherent in urban existences that they haven't found satisfying. And some recognize that each person brings particular skills to the partnership.

Balancing solitude with social connections is further complicated when children are part of an island family. On one hand you give them the gift of a remarkable lifestyle, embedded in nature. All these years later I feel privileged to have grown up on Bath Island. I can still picture the sandstone radiating heat in high summer, the twice-daily march of tide across the broad sweep of beach. And I remember orcas rolling in kelp beds and the ever changing colours of coastal mountains as the sun makes its way across the sky. Memories also focus on activities: building things, night crossings by boat, finding treasures on the beach, reading by propane light.

My sense of privilege is echoed by Misty Lawson who began life on an island near Tofino. "I was born on that island with just my family around. I have always felt connected to that place. It grounds me, it's good for my soul." Even though she has moved closer to Tofino where life on another island is somewhat easier for her young family, she still feels a powerful affinity with her parents' island and emphasizes that she "wouldn't change a thing" about her experience growing up. While visitors who described mainland living gave her a sense that her life was somehow different, she says that when she was growing up, "the island felt like the most normal place in the world." And her connection with family is equally powerful. She feels privileged that both her parents were at home as she grew up and that then, as now, her family was close and supportive.

Misty and her siblings were home schooled, since "trying to get to school in six- to seven-metre seas was much too difficult." Lessons were based on their strengths, and they were encouraged to follow topics that excited their curiosity. Their parents allowed them to choose their learning paths and in doing so, developed their critical thinking skills and their appreciation of experimentation. And in addition to traditional lessons, the island itself was a remarkable schoolroom. Her parents involved the kids in all aspects of island living and trusted them to take responsibility and to look out for one another. "We were always on the buddy system, on the island and on the water." By the age of nine, Misty was piloting their boat by herself on the difficult crossing to Tofino. "I remember my father asking me to pick up some friends. I was so nervous, and had to stand on a crate to see over the centre console—but I did it." She goes on to say that her own children are encouraged to be independent and responsible in boats and on island as it is such a wonderful way to experience life.

Island childhoods seem to foster confidence and self-sufficiency. Linda recalls that, from the time she was a small girl, she could explore her family's large property on Valdes on her own. While her mother limited beach exploration because of strong currents in Gabriola Pass, she "taught us that there was nothing in the woods to be afraid of. Everything is good. I never felt any sense of harm—I still don't." She continues to treasure the solitude. "I led a life that was largely with my mom. And when I was young, my dolls were my companions. They were all named, and I cherished them." Linda also loved to read and rarely felt constrained by being on the island. "I didn't. There was so much to do—that was just life, because to sustain life in this kind of a situation, we had to work at it. There was always stuff to do."

Jan and Sy recognize that living on island gave their daughters a remarkable range of skills at an early age. The girls were three and five when the family moved from Las Vegas to their remote BC island and built a house. Like my sister and I, their girls played important roles in construction, if only to fetch, carry, and hand tape measures, saws, hammers, or nails to carpenters at the right moment. And they became accustomed to commuting by boat to get to school. Over time they developed good boat-handling skills and made the passage on their own. Sy speaks proudly of his daughters' seamanship and describes a time his eldest took the boat into Saltery Bay. "There was a lot of activity: loggers, fishermen. They watched this little girl docking the boat, and called out, "Nice job, Skipper!""

Once they were ten years old, Judith's kids also made the passage to school on their own in a twelve-foot skiff. "I had another boat at home so that if they got into trouble I could go get them. And neighbours were watching them all along the way, and the school teacher made sure they came in. Their instruction was to go straight to the VHF—before they even took off their coats—and call to let me know that they got there."

On Maurelle, where Laurie and Rob were part of a collaborative community for many years, children had a degree of freedom and a sense of connection rarely experienced in more urban settings. They roamed the island and felt welcome in all homes. Rob calls them "free-range kids." He reflects that "part of the reward...of living on the remote coast, especially in a tribal situation, was that through experience we learned to trust a sixth sense that provided access to a collective heightened awareness of our surroundings. Between all of us parents someone would in fact know pretty well where the kids were and what they were doing."[6] The experience shaped their characters, their relationships. "Certainly the children benefited tremendously from their happy experiences of growing up in such an adventurous physical environment and acquiring deeply ingrained self-confidence and self-reliance. They also benefited from their tribal experience of belonging to an extended family, acquiring a deep bond and love for each other."[7] While those kids now make their lives a long way from Maurelle Island, many remain firm friends and still return from time to time.

Nonetheless, being on island can limit play, friendships, and the development of off-island social skills. This is particularly the case on truly remote islands or islands without a community. It was a standing joke in my family that Dad chose an island as the ideal place to raise two daughters. Prospective boyfriends had to be pretty special to brave both the passage and his cool reception. There were lots of times I wished I'd been included in friends' weekend activities, could act in a play, or join a team. I'm sure my sister did as well. Were we lonely as kids? Sometimes. But I'm not sure our vexations were all that different from our friends' as they also stretched teenage wings. In some ways we avoided the social dilemmas that many teens face because we were rarely placed in difficult situations. And we were always busy and focused on island things. When we finally headed off to new lives in Victoria and Vancouver, we had lots to learn about urban dynamics, telephones, electricity, and dating.

Jan and Sy laugh when they recall their daughters' opinions of life on island. "Of course, when they were growing up here, they just wished they lived in a normal house in the city." But they are glad to also say that "they both really like it, they really do." One of their special memories is trick or treating by dinghy along the shore of adjacent islands. And good friends near Powell River welcomed the girls whenever weather or activities kept them on the mainland. These friends also collected the family's mail, received phone messages on their behalf, and lent a helping hand whenever there was a work party.

On Rendezvous, where Judith raised her kids on her own, she was aware that there were times when they felt unfairly distanced from friends. "Mine were the only kids here, which was kind of unfortunate." She smiles ruefully when she adds, "Sometimes in the winter the Bute wind blew—high pressure, beautiful sun, ferocious squalls, incredible cold, frozen lakes—and we couldn't leave the island because the water was just too horrendous. But we could hear on the VHF that all the kids on Read Island were having skating parties or going to someone's house because they have a southern exposure and with the sun blasting like it's summer. And we'd be sitting here shivering—that was bad."

While her life on Valdes differed from the lives of Gabriola and Nanaimo friends, Linda doesn't feel that she missed much because she lived on an island.

> My mom was really good. She believed in education so if I needed to do research, if I needed to be in Nanaimo at the library late, she would make that happen. When we were young, she would take us places. When *King Tut's Treasures* or the *Bounty* came to Vancouver back in the '60s we went over to see them. And I had an uncle that lived in North Van, so Mom would take us over there in early December. He had two girls who were around my age and took us to all these shopping malls. We would see every Santa in the Lower Mainland.

Linda recalls the daily effort of rowing across Gabriola Pass to Degnen Bay where there was a school bus stop. The family had a boat with a small inboard motor, but it was heavy and difficult to launch when the tide was low. "My mom had a double-ended clinker-built rowboat that was light enough that she could pull it up and down on skids. She would have to work the tides, crossing at a point that the current would sweep us toward Degnen—she knew the back eddies." Despite dealing with a notorious stretch of water, they never had an incident of any kind. And Linda recalls how comfortable she was in the boat. "Believe me, I was a cherished child. She'd wrap me in blankets. I'd have a hot-water bottle at my feet and

I'd have an umbrella over my head—and she'd be out there rowing in the rain and snow."

Collaborative thinking helped sort out access to schooling in the Discovery Islands. Laurie recalls,

> When we first moved to Maurelle, the school on Read Island was closed. But there were other people that had moved to Read so we met up with them. There were a few kids on Maurelle of school age and maybe fifteen other kids on the other islands. As parents we persuaded the school board to open the elementary school at Surge Narrows. But we didn't have fast boats then. We just had the sailboat and slower boats and had to deal with tidal rapids. We got together and bought a float house and boarded the kids on Read Island—they had a four-day school week. We all took turns as house parents for a few years.

When islanders replaced their old displacement boats with planing hulls with powerful engines to negotiate the rapids, life became easier. The school board agreed to provide a daily transportation allowance and closed the float house. Some continued to share the task of getting kids from the outside islands to school. Judith had a standing arrangement with a nearby family. "We still did a lot of exchange—I'd bring two kids home with me and the next night my two would go home with them. That gave us a break from commuting every day." The school at Surge Narrows now operates three days a week. "It starts at 8:45 and ends at 4:00 PM. We'd really like to go back to the four-day week because they're very long days and it's a lot to pack in for the kids. But they all do well and they don't seem to be suffering from it."

As kids transition from early grades to senior ones, from childhood to teen years, many make their way to larger schools in nearby communities. In the Southern Gulf Islands, for example, kids who attended elementary and middle schools on Mayne and Galiano take the MV *Scholarship* water taxi to Salt Spring for high school. And kids on Gabriola and surrounding islands begin the daily ferry trip to Nanaimo when they get to Grade 8. This makes for long days. At the same time, stepping into a larger community context draws attention to island kids as somehow different. High school students who live on Cortes, for example, think it's cool to grow up on Read Island. Judith laughs when she says that her kids "always said they were from Read Island because nobody knew where Rendezvous was. But Read had real cachet about it. So that was good." Kids from some island families, however, also begin to recognize that they haven't grown up with the same resources as town families. "The thing was that we didn't have any money. We were poor—I was really scraping the bottom of the barrel when it came to money. So I think they noticed. They didn't have stuff."

Like Judith who sent her kids to the school on Cortes, some families opt to board their kids in town once they are in middle school or high school. Other families move off island to stay connected with their teens. As one parent comments, "I know my kids. My daughter in particular resented being on the island, particularly as a young teen. She really wanted to be with her friends. We did board her for a year and then thought, 'We didn't have kids just to ship them out.' So we bought a place near town and stayed with them in the winter and continued to spend time here in the summer. When the kids were done we returned to the island."

Other important family connections on island are with animals: dogs, cats, horses, and other pets. David Connover's cat, Kiki, was an accomplished mouser, an efficient watchdog, and a valued companion. And our perpetually friendly golden retriever, Pilot, was a constant source of amusement and camaraderie, although his inclination to swim two kilometres to Silva Bay rather than stay on the island was a nuisance. More than once we arrived at Page's Marina at the end of a day in town and found him tied to a tree, delighted that he had joined us without invitation. We also had three cats that were great company.

Horses are more challenging to get to islands as this normally involves an expensive combination of trailer and barge transport. But not always. When Laurie's daughter wanted to keep her horse on Maurelle Island, Riskie made the trip in the cockpit of their catamaran. Judith, who was on the dock at the time, laughed when she told me that "they walked the horse down the ramp at Herriot Bay. At the bottom of the ramp there were these two guys sitting on the rail. They saw the horse coming down—you should have seen the look in their eyes! It was astounding. The horse walked down that ramp and just stepped on the boat and stood there. Laurie and Kirsten, her daughter, are horse whisperers—it's just amazing what they can do with animals. And off they went. They were sailing. I think the horse had to duck when they tacked." Rob describes the trip. "There were some quite big waves, and as the boat rocked gently from side to side, Riskie swayed her bum to help keep her balance. Her head was up and her ears pricked, which showed she was enjoying herself."[8]

Island communities

IMAGINE A CONTINUUM with total solitude on one end and a tight-knit community on the other. This describes the variety of social possibilities that people on islands off the ferry grid may experience. And their position on that continuum is, to a large degree, self-selected, a personal balance between independence and reliance. Decisions on the nature and location of the island play an important role. The more remote, the more insular. On shared islands, your physical distance from neighbours shapes social dynamics. And if you own an entire island, the scope of your community is reduced. Elizabeth Arthur and her husband, Bob, chose to own an island in the middle of a remote lake. Interactions with community occurred only when the couple left to provision, work, or take a break. Frank and Geri, on the other hand, chose a property that is part of an island strata corporation. They collaborate and socialize with other residents on a regular basis. Islanders' inclination to interact, whether they are part of a community or off on their own, also plays a role. Most islanders are somewhere in the middle of the continuum. But all have differing notions of what ideal community relations should look like.

Nonetheless, almost everyone requires some assurance that a community can be called on, whether to help kids get to school or deal with an emergency. Positive relations are important. An islander in New England writes that "the people you squabble with one day may save your life the next. When your car goes into a ditch, or your outboard quits halfway down to Mount Desert Rock, or you awake with chest pains in the middle of the night and need to get to the mainland fast, it's your neighbors who will bail you out. And you will do the same—not just out of neighborliness, but because a refusal to help threatens the safety of the entire community."[9] Roger on Bath Island recognizes the importance of staying in balance with neighbours on the other Flat Top Islands and on Gabriola, although much of his off-island time is spent in Vancouver. "I need to be able to come and go without any difficulties. Generally, people like the owners of Page's Marina are so decent and nice, and I want to maintain the reciprocity in our relationship. I don't like to be the guy who's on the wrong end of that teeter-totter." He also keeps a low profile "for my own need for security, to avoid break-ins, and not to piss anybody off." He laughs when he says, "I've been much more careful in my behaviour than I normally would be. I have not gone to meetings and made high-power speeches and dominated conversations and things like that. I don't write inflammatory letters to the paper—I don't write any letters to the paper. I don't know all that many people, but I do know some key people like the fire chief. And just lately I've been going there more often and am discovering people at the market or even in the thrift shop who are delightful."

Negotiating shared services also brings island communities together, whether on a single island or across an archipelago. Organizing a school at Surge Narrows, constructing a breakwater on Sidney Island, managing a community garden on Protection Island, or critiquing the actions of regulatory agencies on any one of a number of issues are all good examples. A recent study of life on Quadra and the Discovery Islands highlights the dynamics of collaboration. While islanders strive for balance between independence and community, some also experience strain.

Being part of a tight-knit group where almost everyone has a strongly held set of personal and political values can create some social tension. If your home community hosts less than a hundred people, many of whom you will almost certainly need to interact with in order to access food, transit, and support in emergency situations, then the risks of conflict manifest differently than they would in a mainland region with more people and public services. [Islanders] regularly navigate social spaces where they respect and depend deeply on others who they may not agree with politically, and want to function as a community while maintaining a sense of individuality and living their personal values in an authentic way.[10]

While most island communities take shape as people with common interests come and go, some are more deliberately formed around idealistic aspirations. Laurie and Rob are the last remaining members of a collective that bought a logged property on the southern end of Maurelle Island in the early 1970s. Rob describes how they came together. "We were part of an intentional community—I suppose you could call it a hippie commune, although a lot of us were sophisticated professionals, middle-class certainly. It was an attempt to avoid what we saw as the inevitable collapse of civilization. We thought we'd try to set up an alternative non-consuming society. We were idealists and had admirable ideals." The ten families lived together for ten years. "The kids grew up as a family and still are an extended family although not here anymore."

Rob regrets that they entered into a common living arrangement without thinking through some ground rules. "We were all anarchists— none of us liked bureaucracy. We wanted to be free of all that. We thought we could do it better. We instigated a system based on consensus. We all had to agree to everything. But that turned out to be an opportunity for some to power-trip, to veto. Nobody went for that behaviour and the rest of us ended up doing our own thing—we gave up trying to cooperate." If they were to do it again, Rob would follow rules set out in the legislation that governs collectives in the province. "We didn't know about it. Our co-op was actually relieved of its legal status because we didn't have meetings. We paid our taxes and thought we didn't have to do anything else." All that remains of the collective are acrimonious annual meetings in their lawyer's office.

"The whole thing went 'poof.' If we'd gone by the rules, it would have been better."

Few islanders choose to connect with one another so formally, but there are many stories of people helping one another with projects, work bees. Chic has met people in his professional practice who know island lifestyles and have specialized skills. "People love the idea that you're building a cabin off the grid, on the islands, in a spectacular location. It's a fun thing to talk about. So it's not hard to engage people in the process with whatever skills they offer—I've had people come by who do solar, plumbing, and electrical systems. I've worked with architects and engineers and other folks who know the islands." Sy and Jan enjoy having Bob and Sue as island neighbours as they tackle many projects together. And they have brought mainland friends together for a number of work parties. David talks about the invaluable help of a neighbour and friend in construction projects on his rocky island property. And Roger always welcomes an extra hand with the heavy tasks on Bath Island.

Recognizing other people's right to be eccentric or to hold opposing views is part of successful island living. A resident in the Discovery group study offered thoughtful advice. "You've got to accept [your neighbours] for ... who they are, and go with the flow ... and they've got to do the same." Another suggests that "focusing on commonalities rather than differences can be a good tool for approaching difficult topics."[11] Islanders are cautious as they negotiate contentious issues, express differences. The desire to avoid conflict can mean that the community lacks a political voice or enough volunteers to tackle major projects. Rather than formally addressing issues, they tend to build understanding, perhaps consensus, on community matters during conversations at the dock, at parties, or while people are helping one another. The happiest circumstance is when the island is home to "well-balanced, emotionally secure, intelligent people who gladly share information and expertise, and ... who are a joy to be around."[12]

On Protection Island, Tom and Emily value community. They appreciate that most residents collaborate—formally and informally—to source off-island products and services, organize events, and maintain the community garden. A listserv helps plan barge transportation or shared travel expenses for tradespeople. And the Lions Club coordinates many valued initiatives. Tom and Emily also recognize that socializing is an important island dynamic. "There's a lot of activity— we can't do it all. In the summer there's something on every week. We do a little bit, including kids' things like the gardening program and story time at the community library...If you go out walking it's not like in the city. When the baby was first born, I walked with her every day—the forty-five-minute walk often turned into two hours if the sun came out because everyone wanted to talk."

News spreads quickly on shared islands, particularly if there is a concern about someone's well-being. One islander observes that "there's a lot of gossip: everyone knows your business. People care— they're trying to help, but they're not really helping." This is noted in many island communities. "That small town surveillance is what people love and hate about small island communities. People look for isolation, a refuge, but what they often find is the opposite; if you share a small island with other people, it's hard to avoid them."[13] Emily agrees. "This is a difficult place to be a recluse. You'd be more successful in the city where you can be more anonymous. It's hard to hide away."

And even if someone favours solitude, occasional opportunities to connect with like-minded people, to share experiences, to take a break from day-to-day chores are important. A wonderful example is the Ladies Book Club that has been bringing the women of the Discovery Islands together once a month for over thirty-five years. Judith says,

> It's at a different place every month. That means that we're going up to Owen Bay, or they're coming out here, or we're on the south end of Read. People get to places where they wouldn't otherwise ever go. And they visit each other's houses—you get to know each other that way. It's during the day—you usually get there at eleven or noon and it's over by four. We chitchat and visit for an hour or so and then somebody says, 'Let's talk about the book.' It's almost something to hang the conversation on, and brings

out good thoughts about our lives generally, how we relate to what we're reading, and whether it has any application in our lives. Mostly it's about getting together. And there's the adventure of getting out in the boat. A lot of the women don't get out much on the water because you get into this little shuttle back and forth to town and that's all you seem to do.

As this monthly gathering connects people in such important ways, CBC has featured it as one of the most interesting book clubs in Canada.

Most of the people I spoke with enjoy getting to know islanders who live nearby. Kathy ranks new relationships high on her list of island benefits. "It's the people. Even though you come here for the nature, the beauty, the people that we've met are wonderful. I didn't have any idea what I was in for, but we have common interests. You meet people you would never meet in your other life." David says much the same thing about getting to know island neighbours. "We've become great friends and the wonderful thing is we would never ever have met if it weren't for this island. We always get together; we've worked together on projects. It has been so much fun, and I've learned so much from our neighbours."

Staying in touch

THE TOOLS ISLANDERS use to communicate with one another also influence where they are on the continuum from solitude to tight-knit community. For many years, the VHF radio has been the only way of calling out unless you used a ham radio. Since radio telephones are intended for use aboard boats, many islanders maintain the fiction that they are afloat. The VHF goes on in the morning and off at night, a constant chat line that connects the local community. And hand-held radios are standard gear on hikes, boat rides, beach walks. You squelch the white noise, filter constant messages, listen for personal calls, check marine weather, and always focus on calls for help. Marine radio operators monitor protocols for use. And depending on the privacy level selected, everyone within listening distance hears one or both sides of a conversation. Caroline Woodward describes efforts to stay in touch with her husband by radio telephone while he worked on Egg Island as "exhausting." Others tell funny stories of odd interpretations that arise from half-heard conversations or picking up nuances that suggest a visit or helping hand would be timely. "You didn't socialize by radio, but you listened carefully. You didn't have to guess what your neighbours were up to because you knew, and if there was a way you could jump in and help, you did. Someone would listen and think, 'She sounds like she's having a hard time. I'm going to go visit her tomorrow.' They'd show up apparently on a whim, but they'd be there to make sure you're okay."

Not surprisingly, Facebook and other social media are now in active use and facilitate both casual and formal communications across island communities in new and helpful ways. News is more effectively shared, events organized, collaborations arranged. However, it isn't synchronous and doesn't tend to capture all that is going on. And you have to be online, often sitting at a screen, with some regularity to participate. Some islanders still prefer the VHF radio as a primary means of staying connected, seeking help. Judith describes the VHF as an early form of social media. "It was more sociable, more reliable, and more helpful. The phone operators knew all the people on the coast and made a real effort to reach people." She tells a story of a time when her VHF was down because the batteries were low. An operator asked a tugboat skipper to relay a message that her mother needed to speak with her, and he sought her out to ensure that she made the call. "The radio phones were a constant presence. And because you were listening to both sides of conversations a lot of the time, you'd hear if your neighbour needed something and you could jump in and say, 'I've got a part for your generator' or 'I'm going to town tomorrow, I can take you or pick something up.' That happened all the time. And that's all gone because we're not listening to each other anymore."

The advent of new communications technologies, many people argue, is changing the very quality of islandness. Being on island has lost some of its insularity. Community dynamics have changed. Communication to the mainland and around the world can now be instantaneous. You're no longer tethered. The people you're talking with don't know if you're on a beach, in a boat, or in your house. Information is available at your fingertips. You can be coached through engine repairs or recipes by distant experts. And you save money and time through online searches for off-island products and services. Fewer trips to the mainland are involved. Virtual visits with mainland family and friends are easy to arrange. Browsing big department stores and specialty shops is possible at any hour of the day or night. Gifts are selected, purchased, wrapped, and delivered with just a few keystrokes. And by the time couriers figure out how drones can deliver pizzas and packages across intervening channels, island lifestyles—at least those near populated mainlands—will look very different.

At the same time, communication technologies allow islanders to work remotely, generate income, and maintain professional connections while enjoying their distance from the rat race. These technologies are functionally transforming the nature of solitude and community, of mental and physical separation. Some islanders say the ability to be in constant touch with the surrounding world is liberating,[14] particularly if it allows them to be on island while staying in touch with family and workplaces. As Geri notes, "My cell phone is my lifeline." Others look doubtful. I suspect my sister and I would have had a different on-island experience if we'd shopped online and carried smart phones everywhere we went.

As people settle on island, relationships with friends who don't see the appeal of island life can change. I know that a number of my parents' friends and relatives thought they were crazy walking away from an upwardly mobile life in West Vancouver. With little knowledge of the beauty of the island or why Mom and Dad yearned to carve out a new lifestyle, they watched with puzzlement and concern. And because Mom and Dad were no longer readily available for dinner parties, cruising weekends, and other gatherings, because communication was by letter and radio telephone, my parents lost touch with many people. Mom, in particular, spent a lot of time by herself while Dad, my sister, and I went off to work and school. And while she never commented to us about being lonely or feeling isolated, she would light up whenever guests came down the path for a visit. Dad, on the other hand, would put down his tools with a sigh. He'd socialized with colleagues and friends at work all week and treasured his weekends as a time to get things done.

A number of islanders comment that some friends "get" what they are doing, while others don't. Certainly, we all know people for whom islands hold no charm. Caroline Woodward sees this at play. "When I first told people I was moving out to the 'lights,' their reactions were either shared delight or sheer fright. No in-between emotions or opinions were ever registered."[15] And a friend of mine rolls her eyes and says that she can't imagine anything worse than spending more than a day or so on an island, away from the amenities of city life, separated from her friends, and reliant on boats for access. For her, island living equates to isolation, boredom. The concerns that such friends express, often with predictions of injury, penury, or loneliness, can play a positive role. David Conover writes that "in a way, these objections were helpful. We had convinced ourselves that to know the problems we were going to face was half the battle."[16] They moved to their island equipped with reference books on everything from business management to sheep husbandry to parenting.

On Bath Island, Roger observes that visitors sometimes get restless, despite their initial enthusiasm for an island experience. "For some, the idea of living off the grid with marginal WiFi and no hot showers is on the edge of craziness. They come with a romantic vision of being on island, but after three days they have to go." He observes a rural/urban divide among those who get it and those who don't. The ones who don't may become the friends that islanders connect with on occasional town visits. Or not at all.

Roger also observes that, as much as he enjoys company, visitors require organization and some degree of work. He lays in food, beer, and wine early in the summer to accommodate spontaneous day visits. And he makes special visits to Vancouver to collect guests from the mainland or from around the world. Typically, it takes a full day to cross the strait, tie in on the south arm of the Fraser, negotiate Vancouver traffic, buy provisions, and retrace his steps with a boatload of guests. He is glad that there are two houses on the island. A rudimentary telephone line, strung through the trees, with very old dial-up phones at each end, provides connection. Guests can settle in on their own, help themselves to a stocked fridge, gaze at the view of Vancouver, the beach, the strait, and appear at lunch or happy hour. He often hosts academic colleagues and encourages them to use their time on island to write. "This is a place where people can come and focus. That whole romance of island living—that whole notion of a rock surrounded by water—creates a setting for intense ruminations about life's projects." And welcoming as he always is, Roger says that after busy social days he feels "a strong need for alone time on my island."

Geri and Frank treasure their time alone on island and describe their quiet mornings and evenings on a patio overlooking Haro Strait as magical. They also mix happily with the interesting range of permanent and seasonal residents on Sidney Island. But they comment that spending so much time there tends to change relationships with family and friends on Vancouver Island and beyond. Even though they are easily reached by cell phone, people know that they're "away" and don't reach out in quite the same way as they would in town. It can be difficult to be available to aging parents or friends in need. And while some friends are regular visitors, others find the journey to the island too complicated, too time-consuming. From Frank and Geri's perspective, the gradual distancing of relationships is one of the few downsides to being on island.

Over the years, Rob and Laurie have learned the importance of socializing as a counterpoint to treasured solitude.

> One of our greatest joys and also one of our strongest assets is hospitality. We built our new house and garden bigger than we needed for ourselves because we love sharing our home with others, and the more time goes by and the more we invest in the place the more people seem to enjoy it. Also, as the world gets more hectic and artificial, people are starved for the peaceful ambience and silence we take for granted, not to mention Laurie's sumptuous gourmet meals with fresh seafood and organic

garden produce. The ultimate goal is for the homestead to become more sustainable by strengthening both its internal and external relationships. So if, as well as making it more productive, we can entice the world to come and visit us, then so much the better.[17]

If you find yourself a guest on an island, there are a few things to keep in mind. First of all, do your best to get there on time and without a lot of complication. Missing a connecting ferry will leave your host cooling his or her heels at a busy dock. Wear shoes that don't mark the boat. And if you're arriving on your own boat, do your homework to ensure that you can sort out secure moorage, perhaps in a nearby bay. Not all island docks can accommodate all vessels in all weathers. Contribute food and drink whether you're expected or not, but don't leave a lot of food—or garbage—behind. Use water sparingly. Don't even think about smoking or leaving a candle unattended. Keep your dog away from chickens and clean up any leavings. Offer a hand on any tasks interrupted by your arrival, but don't do anything that might result in a trip to a clinic. Amuse yourself (and your kids) while the islander takes care of daily chores. Put fishing gear, kayaks, and toys away after you've finished playing. And, as you would in any home, help with cooking and washing up whenever it seems appropriate. Above all, engage in the island and its charms—that's what your host is hoping you'll do.

Earning a living

MANY ISLANDERS ALSO connect with others as they find ways to generate an income. And unless a job is easily transferred to an island office or workshop, this may involve a lot of adaptation. As Misty Lawson says, "Living on an island is a full-time job. So it's hard to work full time as well, specially from an island." Dad took a job in the local shipyard, drawing on shipwright skills he'd gained in building Whereaway and other boats. And he and Mom dreamed up ways of earning money. We all did stints on a knitting machine to craft classic dark navy sweaters that were sold by Bosun's Locker in Victoria. We raised chinchillas for a while although never earned the promised fortune that made these dear little animals so popular in the early 1960s. And for two memorable summers Dad rigged *Whereaway* as a troller with a new cockpit in the stern, gurdies on the deck, and trolling poles aligned with the mast. The boat drew some surprised looks from sailing friends as Dad joined a small fleet from Silva Bay to fish near Princess Royal Island at the mouth of the Kitimat Canal across from Haida Gwaii. My sister and I each took a turn as deckhand. After a few years working locally, however, Dad returned to the forest industry. I don't know if it was the draw of reconnecting with old colleagues or the possibility of a better income that shaped his decision. From around 1966 onward, he worked with a forestry consulting firm four and a half days a week in Vancouver. On Fridays and Sundays he crossed the strait on *Whereaway* when the weather was good. And when it wasn't, he rode the old *Princess of Vancouver* from Nanaimo to downtown Vancouver. It became routine during winter months for us to make late-evening trips to the Gabriola ferry to pick him up. And we'd reverse the process on Sundays. His work was interesting and enabled him to travel internationally. Mom went along occasionally, but for the most part, she spent time on her own on the island with her two daughters. And since Dad was home only on weekends, that was family and project time. Mom was always cheerful, always creative. She had her own chores to do and sewed, knit, painted, gardened, read, wrote letters, and had tea with other islanders. While my dad was clearly the head of family, in many ways it was my mom who held everything together. I'd love to know what she enjoyed, what she found difficult.

On Rendezvous Island, Judith was also on her own with two children, and she did many jobs to generate an income. Postmistress at Surge Narrows, kayak guide, coordinator/cook for a community meal at the weekly market on Read Island, and substitute teacher—all these roles kept money coming in. And for a number of challenging years, she farmed oysters on the east coast of Read Island.

When my husband left, I took over our oyster farm in Evans Bay, nine miles from here. That was a bit of a run for me. I had a larger boat at that point, an oyster boat, but it was still a pain. I did that for years. It was beach lease, so I could only work when the tide was out. That meant that I was out there at two in the morning in the middle of winter, in the rain, picking oysters. Ralph and Lannie Keller on Read were so kind to me. They offered me a place to stay. It was pretty obvious that I couldn't stay in any of their actual lodgings because I stank so much of beach mud. All I had to do was walk into a building and people could smell me for days. So they let me use their sauna at the dock—it was fantastic because it was such a tiny space. I could heat it up immediately if I came off the beach at 3 AM when the tide came up. I didn't have to do the run home in the dark. I would fire up their stove and crash for a few hours. And then I'd get up in the daylight and organize the delivery of whatever I'd harvested during the night. At the end of the winter when they wanted to use the sauna again, they'd take the pressure washer and wash me out and that was the end of that!

We laughed as she described her oyster farming, but her tenacity stays with me. "I did that for quite a few years while my kids were in high school—they were off on Cortes boarding. Because I was my own boss, I was able to do whatever I had to for the kids. If they needed me for some reason, it was no problem." She adds,

I was very fortunate. I was good at growing oysters but not at marketing them, so I ended up with all these over-sized oysters. I was able to deliver to a good buyer on Cortes. He looked after the oysters from there; he trucked them down to Vancouver and sold them off. He was pretty flexible if I didn't have product. I was just a little corner of his business. But that got lonely. There was a lot that I needed to learn. So I ended up taking a day job with an oyster farm at Redonda Bay. They had oysters on floats and could work them regardless of tides. I learned a lot, and it was sociable because we all stood around the table dealing with the oysters. The paycheques came in regularly, so that was good.

But ongoing work at Evans Bay and long hours in two jobs took their toll. "My body was so stressed out by it. I was in terrible shape, hauling buckets of oysters up this long muddy beach with every step going squelch, having to pull my feet out of the mud. It was so physically demanding. So finally I decided I'd had enough and sold out just in the nick of time. I was lucky to be able to sell the place before the market for large oysters disappeared."

Raising sheep provided income for David and Jeanne Conover on Wallace Island and for Linda's parents on Valdes. Wool was a hard-earned product. "Their backs would be filled with clamshell grit off the beach. How did they do that? They were so hard to shear." And Linda helped with slaughtering the animals for meat. "My earliest job from the time I could walk and carry was emptying the blood pans. And we had the effort of getting them all the way into Nanaimo. Dad had a little open boat, what we used to call a 'putter,' a clinker-built putter. We'd take the carcasses to the butcher in Nanaimo. We just carried them up to the butcher shop in sacks." Linda's mother also gathered salal and delivered it to a buyer on Gabriola. "That's what my mom did—she put me through university by picking salal." When Linda returned to Valdes after attending university in Vancouver, she worked with the sheep and served as a deckhand on a troller on the West Coast in the summers. "It was a way to make money. Let's face it—living on the island is a luxury lifestyle. No matter how simple things are, life is expensive because there's so much you need. There's all the fuel, the boats, the maintenance. Plus you have to have a vehicle in both places."

A number of islanders commute to mainlands on an as-needed basis if on-island communications don't meet work needs. On Protection Island, Emily and Tom both do contract work that requires only occasional trips to nearby Nanaimo. But they value the city's proximity. "This place is special in that you can make a regular life in town with relatively little inconvenience. You get the advantages of an island, but you can still make a go of it in the city. And we wouldn't be able to work at home if we didn't have good Internet, so that's a reason that we're not on a more remote island."

Other islanders use a mix of planes and boats to connect to the city when necessary. Suromitra told me that "one time I was working with a Vancouver law firm. We drove the ATV to the dock at 5 AM, jumped in the boat, and went to the ferry. I took a taxi to the airport and was downtown for a meeting in Vancouver by 9:30—in my high heels. Then I took the plane from Coal Harbour around 3:30ish and was home for dinner. It can be done, but I wouldn't want to do it every day." She recognizes that being able to deal with unexpected issues in a demanding job while on island is important. "Thank goodness we can do conference calls. Being available and accessible gives you peace of mind. All the same, time here is pretty sacred. The office knows not to call in July unless something is burning down." Even as Suromitra and David savour their island time, they find it productive to think about work. "This is actually where we've both had very good ideas because you don't have the clutter. You can come up with new things."

A few islanders regularly divide time between their home on island and a mainland apartment or house to stay professionally connected in the same way that Dad eventually did. Roger is proud that he never missed lectures at UBC despite some daunting conditions crossing the strait. Frank and Geri use both their plane and boat, depending on weather, for the short hop to Victoria where they stay engaged in professional activities for several days of the week. And Chic and Kathy and David and Suromitra take more seasonal approaches to island living, given their busy professional careers in nearby cities. All talk about the pleasures of coming "home" from work stints.

That is not to say that islanders are always happy with their balance of social connections on island. Some experience moments when things go out of whack and solitude slips into loneliness. This may be an opportunity to learn about themselves as they work through the discomforts of isolation, or a time to get off island. And many talk about the value of stepping away for a refresher, to pursue diverse interests, to reengage with family and friends, or to escape a cold and windy winter. Caroline Woodward deals with long shifts and uncertain passages in her lighthouse assignments. She reflects that "sometimes...I need to escape the island just to see other people...

who understand that just to yak about the books we're writing or reading, and kids and pets and gardens, is a sociable mental health break for me. I usually fumble some appropriate social filters in place so that I don't blurt non-stop like [a] garrulous Yukon trapper."[18] All the islanders I talked with spoke of times when unrelenting work, unexpected events, or oppressive weather strains an otherwise happy balance in their on- and off-island connections. But they don't dwell on such moments. The overarching narrative is that being on island is a deeply satisfying way of life. But then, of course, I was talking to the converted.

(7)

NOT QUITE PARADISE

What could possibly go wrong? As it turns out, a few things.

My hands, for example, remind me of boating mishaps. The tip of my right thumb is crooked where it was caught between *Molly*'s bow and the dock. Clair and I were nosing *Molly* in between boats because visitors occupied our normal spot. I was perched on the forward deck and fended off in the exact spot that the bow nudged the wharf. Since the end of my thumb was partially detached, Dad whisked me over to the Royal Vancouver Yacht Club outstation on Tugboat Island, found a doctor aboard one of the vessels, and asked him to stitch me up.

On the back of the same hand is a curved scar from one of my first dates. I was going fishing with a boy who was spending the summer on Gabriola. Once *Molly* was loaded, I cautioned him not to start the engine. A strand of seaweed, wrapped around the propeller, had to come off first. But as I reached over the stern to remove the weed, he pulled the starting cord. A deep cut from the blade required multiple stitches and permanently cooled our relationship. I don't really recall if it was his horror at the blood or my contempt for unboatsmanlike behaviour that got in the way of our budding romance.

These were minor incidents. A small scar on my left hand is evidence that things can truly go wrong. And that trouble comes in pairs. This calamity began in late January of 1970. Mom went to bed early, commenting that she wasn't feeling well. She was in such pain by the middle of the night that I called Dad in Vancouver on the radio telephone. He arrived by float plane at first light, injected Mom with some kind of painkiller, and off they flew to the city. Mom had a successful operation for an internal malady. And since Dad drove Mom to southern California to recuperate once she was able to travel, my sister and I were left on our own for several weeks.

Being on our own wasn't an issue as we were so comfortable with island routines. I was attending Malaspina College in Nanaimo, and Clair was corresponding with companies about job options. The weather was typical for that time of year. Overcast, cold, and occasionally stormy. As January stretched into February, mid-terms were scheduled, and on one of the exam days a big southeaster blew in. I would have preferred not to head out, but I had to write that test, and the wind and waves weren't anything I hadn't encountered before. So I set off for Silva Bay first thing in the morning, taking waves on the stern quarter. About halfway across the kilometre of open water between Bath Island and Silva Bay, a sloppy breaking sea sent enough spray into the boat to douse the engine—on one of the few days that I didn't have a dry spark plug. Try as I might, I couldn't get that engine started. And while I was trying, the wind pushed *Molly* toward the shore of Tugboat Island. The oars weren't much help once I gave up on the engine since the seas were big and the boat was heavy. I don't recall if I tried to set the small anchor that was kept in the bow, and it certainly didn't occur to me to put on a life jacket. But I do recall thinking that once the boat beached I could step ashore. Instead, as *Molly* got into the surf, she slewed sideways and flipped, trapping me underneath as she moved along the beach in the surging swells. A propane bottle became a battering ram inside the boat. I honestly don't know how long I was trapped in that overturned hull, but eventually I slipped under the stern as the boat stopped moving. There I was, soaking wet, standing on the beach.

I was fortunate that I went ashore on Tugboat Island, one of the few islands occupied year-round in the Flat Top group fringing Silva Bay. A trail took me to the caretaker's house and I still remember how taken aback he was to find a bedraggled and shivering girl on his doorstep. I used his phone to call the staff at Silva Bay Resort where I worked on weekends. They collected me, popped me into bed in the lodge, and called the doctor. No one talked of hypothermia in those days, but they knew I needed warming up, along with a single stitch on the cut on my hand. My new navy blue leather trench coat, earned with wages from waitressing, was ruined. And the windshield and deck of the boat were gone. *Molly* was hauled off the beach by shipyard staff later in the afternoon. Ironically, Malaspina College was closed that day due to snow.

We didn't tell Mom and Dad about the accident when they called from California a few days later. There was no point in worrying them. But once home, they were horrified and talked of selling the island. They didn't—*Molly* was repaired, and life went on—though we all had a better sense of how things can go sideways.

EXPECTED TO HEAR lots of stories about problems and disasters when I spent time with islanders, but only a few were offered. And those generally related to accidents or ill health. Nevertheless, when problems crop up in these glorious places, they take on whole new dimensions, particularly if emergency attention is required. Again and again I heard about the importance of caution—in planning, in action, in follow-up. For all their spirit of adventure, islanders are very aware that they place themselves in harm's way with some regularity. They take precautions. And when things go wrong, impressive coping skills kick in.

Recently Judith, for example, was hauling her boat up on a float on Rendezvous Island. The surface was slick. "As I pulled, my foot on the float slipped and went under the boat. So when I fell backwards my body twisted and the leg didn't—it went crack, crack, crack. It didn't hurt, it just cracked." On her own, she secured the boat and made her way to her ATV. Despite increasing pain, and no doubt feeling nauseated and dizzy, she managed to get to her house, splinted the leg, and called for help. A long day later, she had surgery, a cast, and a dilemma. Where to go? How to keep an eye on her island property? Friends, of course, came to her aid. She spent a week or two back on island with company but ended up going off island for a month. Then she returned to her place, limping. "I'm coping pretty well. I have difficulty walking when I get a bit tired. I can't move very fast and have trouble going downhill. But functionally I'm managing just fine." The garden did not achieve its usual glory that summer. Problems with the ATV engine were irksome, and the tenuous nature of island living was highlighted. As Judith says, "That was a nuisance."

Taking care

CHIC ON SNOWBERRY stresses the importance of being attentive. "It's not the risks you're aware of but the ones that you don't think about, that you stumble into, like doing something too quickly with a tool. Safety first, that's the biggest thing." David echoes the need to consider the implications of actions as he walks about his remote island property. "The opportunity to hurt yourself here is an order of magnitude more than in town. You're operating chainsaws, you're wandering on slippery rocks, you're driving a quad. You constantly think, 'Hold on, let's not do that, let's not do this.'"

People talk about a heightened sense of their surroundings. Helen Piddington in an isolated stretch of Loughborough Inlet, for example, describes the value of listening. "Everyone is aware of sounds that are important, and any change in them is immediately apparent: an unusual cry from a child, a different rhythm in an engine, the whoosh of an overheated chimney. These can be vital warnings. So it is for us when we hear the groans and boomsticks at night. Are they breaking apart? Must we get up? Why does the dog bark? Is it wolves? Bear?"[1] A sudden squall, the mournful note of a foghorn, a change in the cadence of waves on the beach all portend conditions that pose problems, unsettle plans. The smell of smoke, the glow of a flare, a faint mayday on the VHF demand immediate action. And a knock on the door in the middle of the night sets your heart racing. I remember this happened one winter night. A houseboat had broken loose from its moorings in the Fraser River and drifted for a day before occupants used its woefully underpowered outboard to beach it on the island. Or so they said. Mom made them coffee and let them use the radio telephone to arrange a tow at the next high tide. It still seems improbable that they found their way across the strait.

Many islanders have safety habits, sometimes from learning things the hard way. Such routines are sensible anywhere but seem particularly valuable when help is some distance away. After a couple of painful incidents when rusty nails penetrated shoe leather, we never left a nail, screw, or spike sticking out of a board on a building site. We tried to prevent chimney fires. And we always stood off-centre when a line or cable was under stress. We stayed away from unstable land and side slopes when driving the tractor. And we always tested the stability of beach logs and rocks jumbled at the head of a cove before putting weight on them. Ladders were positioned carefully and, ideally, someone braced the bottom if the footing was wobbly. And widow-makers—branches or trees that might come down on your head—were removed or given a wide berth.

Roger says, "I'm impressed by the fact that your family lived here all those years without any big evacuations." He, too, is attentive to safety, particularly as he is often by himself. He carries a portable VHF if he's tackling a hazardous job away from the house. And he thinks through the implications of putting himself in difficult places. For example, he recently reroofed the A-frame. "I have a pretty impressive set of aluminum extension ladders that I used during the roofing saga. Some of them extend out to thirty, maybe even forty feet. And it's bloody hairy when you're on top of a ladder. At the top of the A, the sense of exposure is incredible. But I tie the ladder off. I try to observe the rules I know about." Roger is also cautious around chainsaws.

I've had many situations where I'm up a ladder and I really want to trim a branch. But it involves leaning just a little bit farther over. I've now got a light saw that I can actually hold with one hand, which has solved part of this problem. But I have a rule: when I'm here by myself I don't use chainsaws. Every now and then I break the rule. When a tree comes down over a path, it's just a matter of snip, snip, snip. I don't necessarily wear all the gear that you're supposed to wear, but I'm very bloody conscious of the fact that I'm alone. If I fall off a ladder with a chainsaw in my hand and I've got a big laceration, the ambulance on Gabriola is not going to be much use to me.

Finding the balance between enjoyment and caution, particularly with kids, requires both rules and trust. Roger enjoyed a three-week visit with a young grandson from New Zealand. "He wouldn't put shoes on, he loves going barefoot. There are prickles, but I thought, 'Oh well.' And we worked on various jobs where hammers were being dropped, there were rocks to trip over and nails to step on. I said to his mother, 'If he leaves here without a foot injury it will be a miracle.' He obeyed me on other issues like not running on the slippery ramp, so I overlooked going without shoes. He went home without injuries."

For his guests Roger has a couple of firm rules designed to avoid fire and injuries. "Things like smoking. I hate smoking anyway, but I've had visitors who arrived here unannounced, who think that my no-smoking signs don't apply to them. That's when my underlying authoritarian nature comes out. And I've had a few issues with alcohol when guests are in cut-loose mode." There's a bluff near his house that offers a memorable view of the setting sun. "I've thought about putting up railings, but I want to sit there with an unencumbered view. But I'm pretty watchful when people are running around. I usually set the chairs well back from the edge. I warn people about the drop-off. It's a bit of a horror to think what would happen if somebody went off onto the rocks. And some of my hippie-dippie buddies think this is a good place to smoke dope. That's another area where I'm extremely conservative. So I've had to stare a few people down on that issue."

Being attentive is also key for Chic and Kathy on Snowberry. "Kathy and I have kind of a pact that our number one thing is safety because we realize that we're one accident away from being completely out of this environment, this lifestyle and things we do. Literally one wrong step and you're toast, you're not able to do the things you need to do to stay in this environment. It all depends on physical well-being."

Being proactive about safety was also important to Michael Modzelewski during his time in Blackfish Sound.

The only danger I felt was the threat of a careless accident. An islander constantly uses tools—axe, chainsaw, fire, fishhooks—that can reverse into self-inflicting weapons. Before every activity, I consciously scouted for potential dangers. Once you inform your body that there is no hospital nearby, you suddenly possess amazing coordination. Each move is deliberately sure. There is no slack in you, for all systems are alert. It's exhilarating to live tuned to such a keen awareness. In dangerous undertakings, like falling a crooked tree, I discovered that I could split my personality. One part of me chopped the tree, while another 'me' stood by, on guard.[2]

Dealing with crises

THINKING THROUGH PREVENTIVE measures is important. But when things happen, it's also important to have coping strategies in place. Skills for dealing with injuries are invaluable. Judith, who trained in first aid during work in the oil fields in the 1970s, recommends additional training in wilderness first aid. "I was doing a lot of kayak guiding so I needed to keep my certification up. We realized that the industrial first aid doesn't cut it out here, so we started to do the wilderness first aid courses. They were fantastic." And, of course, having fully stocked and maintained first aid kits in the boat, in the workshop, and in the house is important. The Internet can also be a source of advice if problems are puzzling. As Judith says, at least it "gives you some more information before you go hightailing it off to town."

On the wild West Coast, people get in trouble quickly as they move in and out of boats in the perpetual surf. Joe came up with a great way to deal with shivering guests on Echachis. "I built a sauna above the high-tide line and always leave it prepped to start, in case of cold. One time a fellow tried to get into the boat wearing a backpack and they both went in. I just managed to get him out. All our stuff was in the water. I helped the guy, paddled to shore, and went and lit up the stove. In twenty minutes it was hot."

The prospect of house or brush fires scares everyone. But I was impressed with people's readiness to deal with fires on islands with communities. Sidney Island has a pumper truck and convenes island-ers from time to time to go over firefighting protocols. On Protection Island, locals have an organized fire response team that accesses city water. On Rendezvous Island, every household has a similar system of pumps and hoses so that any islander can locate and use neigh-bours' equipment as needed. And residents on the other Discovery Islands collaborate with one another to deal with fire. Judith plays a lead role. "I'm compiling a little directory of all the fire pumps in the whole community so we can give it to people. That way they'll know where the other pumps are kept, how to access them, their size, what kind of fittings they have, and so on. So if there was a call for a fire on Maurelle, everybody would grab their pumps and go. And if the Coxes hear a call and can't get to their pump, they can come and grab mine and take it over."

Roger has also thought through contingencies. "I do have a Bath Island fire department. It's a wheelbarrow with a Honda pump and an intake that I can set up specially so that it will stay underwater when it's just me here. Really, for the pump you need three people: one per-son on the intake hose, one on the motor, and the other fighting the fire. If I'm here by myself, I have to improvise, so I've tried to do that."

My family battled a frightening house fire on Bath Island. It hap-pened at Christmas 1967 during one of the deep freezes that flow out of mainland inlets. A foot of snow blanketed the island, the tree was up, the house was decorated. And fireplaces burned day and night to keep the chill away. Before going to bed one evening, Mom and Dad banked the living room fire. Late that night, floorboards underneath the hearth began to smoulder, and we awoke to smoke-filled rooms. The area around the boxed-in chimney was starting to burn. Dad used an axe to open the wall and a fire extinguisher to kill the flames, Mom tossed valuables outside into the snow. Water was flowing slowly in semi-frozen pipes, so Clair and I ran buckets up from the well. One of these buckets had been a rock-filled base for the Christmas tree, so the tree was tossed aside, baubles splintering.

We put the fire out. But foam, water, and charred wood marred the living room, hallway, and closet adjacent to the fireplace. The house reeked of smoke and was as cold inside as it was outside. Thank goodness for the little guest house on the far side of the island. We settled in and spent a couple of gloomy days restoring order in the main house. We were lucky that whole place didn't go up and that no one was hurt. The floor, hearth, and panelling were repaired, and I doubt that Mom and Dad ever banked the fires so enthusiastically again. The lessons? Fire extinguishers are invaluable and must be quickly accessible and fully charged. An axe is handy. Stoves, fireplaces, propane systems, candles, lanterns, cigarettes, and anything else that involves combustion should be treated with great care. A year-round source of fresh or salt water for both house and brush fires makes a big difference.

Islanders are cautious about other hazards as well. For example, wild animals deserve respect as you move into their terrain. Cougars, wolves, and bears are accomplished swimmers and appear from time to time on many islands along the coast. These remarkable animals are an integral part of the natural environment that attracts people to islands. Ralph describes a close encounter on Read Island. "One winter our water lines had frozen, and my wife was washing our son's diapers in the creek before bringing them into the house and boiling them in a big pot on the stove. She was busy rinsing. When she looked up there was a big male wolf—they just stared at each other for half a minute or so and then he left."

Not all encounters are so benign. Bears will root through garbage or break into houses if they scent food. And cougars will go after pets, even people, if cornered or starving. Islanders talk of their efforts to avoid confrontations by keeping food secure, controlling dogs and cats, and walking and working in the bush with caution and lots of noise. And some keep a gun on hand. On more than one island, cougars and bears have been shot out of fear that they will harm children, pets, or livestock.

Only a few islanders expressed concern about security from human intruders and vandalism. The ones who did were on islands shared with others or adjoining parks that attract day visitors. Roads give access to their properties, as do common docks and public beaches. Tom and Emily see a bit of mischief on Protection Island.

Problems are mostly in the summer with off-islanders. Some people come here to party. Usually we'll find that golf carts have been moved or used for joy-riding. Just people being silly. And there have been drug addicts who figured that island life is kind of fun. They took my friend's kayak. We found it on Newcastle—the police dealt with the guy. And when our kayak was stolen last summer, it was left on the other side of the island. We put a note on the listserv and had quick responses about its location. There are lots of eyes on the island and people know each other's boats and kayaks. They keep an eye on things.

No one spoke of personal threats, but more than one said that it was a comfort to have a gun on hand. "I always have a loaded gun. And that gives me some security. I've never used it, although I did have an experience. I hadn't been here very long at the house, and my husband was at work and these people were trying to break in in the middle of the night. They were drunk. I let the dog out of the house. She sounded very ferocious, so they hit the beach at a run and left." Dogs play similar roles on other islands, though the ones I met were always very enthusiastic to greet me.

It's not unusual for boaters to come ashore to explore the beaches and upland areas of islands, blithely unaware that residents are keeping a flinty eye on them. While visitors are normally within their rights to be on the beach, I recall how strange it was when a group settled in for a picnic immediately in front of our house. And on an island near Victoria the owner uses a motion-activated camera on the side of her tool shed for research on island wildlife. She has an interesting clip that shows a stranger breaking the lock on the shed and removing a bucket. She also has one that shows a different stranger breaking in to put away tools that they had accidentally left on their job site.

Islanders find themselves offering help to recreational boaters who run afoul of rocks or deadheads, whose engines have failed, or who are lost. We used to hear stories (maritime myths?) of people who used the chart images on the old BC Ferries placemats for navigating. While this still seems improbable, there are certainly people on the water who are just learning how to find their way. Roger has many tales of coming to the aid of people on Thrasher Rock, Brant Reef, or the unnamed rock just north of Bath Island that surprises a lot of boaters. And Linda and her family on Valdes have pulled many boats out of the unexpectedly shallow waters alongside parts of Gabriola Pass. She confesses that she no longer rushes to their aid. "They still hit rocks, but there are lots of others who can rescue them. It's a terrible thing to say, but we'd go out and help people and most of the time they never said thank you."

Another common concern is danger trees. On Snowberry, Chic is conscious that their beautiful forest poses a threat. "When you walk through the woods, everything that is up is going to come down. A branch doesn't look like much hanging from the tree. But when it hits you, you can become quadriplegic. You learn to be aware of your environment and to think of risks with every step that you take, everything that you do." He and Kathy have taken special care to reinforce their workshop/cabin against falling trees. "It's an interesting aspect of design in this environment. Some islands don't have many trees. But in our spot, we're sleeping in a tiny loft in the top of a tiny workshop in the midst of a forest. We're surrounded by trees that are 100 to 130 feet tall. When those fall, they hit with force." He laughs when he adds, "If you're sleeping, you don't want to wake up dead in the bottom of the shop, being terribly embarrassed that your cabin didn't hold up to the forces of falling trees." He describes the chaos of blowdowns. "Last year, even though it wasn't a big year for downed trees, there was this kerfuffle where one tree took down one and then another. There was a huge pile of pickup sticks, and it took me all day with a chainsaw to dismember it." Impacts of falling trees are anticipated in the design of his cabin and house. "The design is not only for static and active loads. You add all the possible loads from all angles—you beef up the angle braces and the size of the beams to take horizontal blows. That's what island design is all about."

Islanders also need to be cautious about the impacts of tree removal when they want to improve views, access, and building sites. Disrupting the ways trees relate to one another increases vulnerability to wind among the remaining trees, branches, and root systems.

Blowdowns, also known as windthrow or windfalls, such as the one that Chic describes, may result when too much of the buffering layer is removed.

The prospect of earthquakes and tsunamis concerns everyone in the Pacific Northwest. Shaking and liquefaction are every bit as frightening—and damaging—on island as they are in the city. But islanders may be better off than urban friends and relatives in the days following such an event since they tend to have self-sufficient systems for power and water, along with stocks of food. On the other hand, islanders may be more vulnerable to tsunamis in certain locations. Many islanders live near the shore. They may not be part of a communication network that will alert them to a threat. And some may not have access to high enough ground to get above devastating waves. Islanders on the exposed west and north coasts or in other vulnerable areas are cautioned by Caroline Woodward, who is equally at risk on Lennard Island. "Always have an escape plan, or several such plans, with first aid kits and goods and water caches in the mix."[3]

Staying healthy

WITH ALL THE physical activity of island life, islanders comment that they have never been healthier. On Snowberry Island where the building site is thirty-seven metres above the dock and some distance away, Chic and Kathy laugh about the exercise they get. "I'll go down to the boat—down the equivalent of ten storeys—and then back up. And then down again to get the things I forgot. You don't think about it as exercise. It's not like going going to the gym to do ten reps. It's just what you do. You leave the island feeling really good, but if you're not here for just a few weeks, you lose your tone, your core. It's a lifestyle."

You rarely meet an islander who is out of shape, overweight, or incapable of scaling ladders, lifting heavy loads in and out of boats, or wielding a chainsaw. Propane bottles substitute for weights at the gym. And hours spent on construction, landscaping, and maintenance help to shape and tone far better than a treadmill. And you get the added satisfaction of accomplishing things, of engaging in physical work using tools, tractors, boats. As Geri comments, life on island has reminded her how important and rewarding it is to stretch your body and mind. And Yvonne Maximchuk says, "Besides an array of bruises decorating my flesh, I've noticed my body changing from the physical labour. My lower back feels much stronger from chainsawing and lying flat on my back in bed I feel a more substantial muscularity in my shoulders, biceps and pectoral muscles. I'm burned out at the end of each long day but refreshed in the morning and eager to get back at it."[4]

But even the most physically fit may experience illness, heart troubles, appendicitis, abscessed teeth, bad backs, and other maladies that are not necessarily caused by island living. These assume complex dimensions on an island. Doctors, dentists, and pharmacies are likely to be a long way away. And it may be complicated to arrange treatments that don't involve moving off island for extended periods. Ingenuity is once again tested. When Caroline Woodward's crown fell out a couple of weeks before Christmas on storm-washed Lennard Island, she recalls that

> there was nothing for it but to carry on for the coming months as the principal keeper was away on extended medical leave. Our wonderful dentist in Victoria couriered all the gear and instructions for taking dental impressions to the Tofino Lifeboat Station, which they promptly delivered to us along with our regular mail. We watched a YouTube demonstration several times as advised. Then we mixed up the goop and Dr. Jeff [her husband] and I maneuvered the first of two plates filled with it into my mouth. It made its way to Victoria and when back, fit perfectly.[5]

Residents in the Discovery group appreciate the willingness of a doctor and a nurse practitioner to visit Read Island every few weeks. It saves island residents time and travel. But they still need to get to a pharmacy for medications and to hospitals in Campbell River for tests and follow-up. And when Laurie was diagnosed with cancer, life on Maurelle had both advantages and challenges. Their close-knit community across the Discovery Islands rallied round them. And the clean air and distance from others minimized complicating infections. But it was not easy when things got tough. "Living where we do on a remote island, we could not simply call an ambulance or drive to the hospital. The doctors agreed that we were better off on our germ-free island so long as we could get in to town quickly if we had to. Normally, we could make it within a couple of hours, and even faster with an emergency helicopter evacuation, but now our anxiety was heightened by a raging storm preventing any prospect of getting to town quickly. Even helicopters can't fly at night in really bad weather."[6] After a number of long months, Laurie got through her cancer and is healthy today.

When emergency help is needed to deal with injury, health problems, security issues, or fire, life on islands gets even more complicated. Almost everyone I spoke with keeps emergency contact information and protocols for action near at hand for themselves—and for guests. VHF emergency call procedures, Coast Guard contact information, latitude and longitude details, names of doctors, and personal contacts are posted on fridges and doors, in guest rooms, and beside radio telephones. Instructions on what to do in case of fire are included. Islanders carry portable VHF radios or cell phones in case they find themselves in trouble while alone. And one islander says he hope that, if he does injure himself, it will be on the water since the Coast Guard has an impressive capability for quick response. The hovercraft, with its onboard operating facilities, is only minutes away from points in the Gulf Islands. And helicopters, normally deployed from Comox by BC's Joint Rescue Coordination Centre, are a reassuring sight in more remote areas, although as Rob notes, weather is a significant factor in any evacuation.

Sue Pickrell is a long-time Canadian Coast Guard (CCG) member who has worked as navigation officer on buoy tenders and icebreakers and served as skipper of the Vancouver-based hovercraft for over fourteen years. She emphasizes that it is wise to have contact information on hand for *both* the CCG and the Joint Rescue Coordination Centre in BC (JRCC, Telephone 911). Washington State residents also call VHF Channel 16 to reach the United States Coast Guard or dial 911 in emergency situations. As a general rule, the CCG responds to emergencies on the water, while the JRCC coordinates rescue activities (including water ambulance or helicopter evacuation) on land. And depending on circumstances, these agencies will work together to solve complex rescue problems, particularly in remote regions. When reporting an emergency, be clear about where you are, the nature of the problem, and the people involved. If you don't have cell coverage to reach the JRCC, the VHF radio operator will patch you through to the appropriate agency. The CCG also deals with marine pollution responses and marine mammals in distress. After hundreds of rescues along the West Coast, Sue reflects that islanders are a special breed—tough, resilient, and very appreciative when they do receive assistance.

Like Laurie, Rob had a severe health issue on Maurelle Island. But his required immediate attention and illustrates how quickly help can be coordinated across agencies in a remote area. He was on his sailboat at the dock, some distance from his house, when chest pain overwhelmed him.

The marine VHF radio was right above my head and for once I had the right piece of equipment, in working order, at the right place, at the right time. Without hesitation, I reached up and turned it on to Coast Guard Channel 16 and called a marine emergency distress signal, "Mayday, Mayday, Mayday!" I gave my name and location, told them I was having serious chest pains, and asked them to phone Laurie to coordinate further help. It turned out that a neighbour up channel heard the Mayday call and phoned Laurie before the Coast Guard did. In what seemed to me like no time at all, a bunch of people, including Laurie and Fern, the neighbour who had phoned, showed up, and very soon a big military helicopter that had trouble finding a place to land. Luckily for me, it was low tide at the time and the chopper was eventually able to land on the beach close by. I can remember seeing it maneuver backward into the beach and put down four hydraulic legs like a giant insect. The neighbours congregating at the dock lifted me into a small boat and took me over to the other side of the bay and then, as if in a scene from "M.A.S.H.," the military dudes bundled me into the chopper like a sack of spuds and off we went to town. Less than one hour from the initial incident we landed at Campbell River hospital.[7]

Rob's critical heart problem turned out to be a dissected aorta. It was remedied through a series of operations and he is back at home, grateful for BC's emergency and health care services.

Physical ailments are easy to talk about, even laugh about. But unhappiness and mental ailments, often lumped together as "island fever," are more difficult to analyze and discuss. As long as there have been islanders, people have probably experienced some form of island fever. Certainly the people I spoke with described moments of feeling blue on island. But I encountered real angst only in the pages of memoirs, perhaps because reflecting on difficult moments is part of the memoir process.

Sometimes melancholy is induced by weather, particularly in the short and gloomy days of winter. Michael Modzelewski writes about his first winter on island. "At first I enjoyed being stormbound. Because the house was on a rise so near the water, the land-boat gave me the feeling of being at sea but without actual concern about the waves. I sat warm and snug at the table, wood stove chugging at my back, coffee and rum close at hand. Through the tall windows I watched in comfort as the procession of storms blasted across Blackfish Sound." His sense of comfort didn't last.

> I thought I sat aloof, high and dry amidst the maelstrom, but one day I found myself clutching the table in a white-knuckled grasp. As the wind drove the high tide far up the beach, waves broke under the house, spattering spume hard against the windows . . . There was a malevolence in the air; I tasted it—like cold copper on the tongue. It was as if Nature was punishing the world, as if pent up anger found release, as if the throttle of rage was wide open and stuck there. Day after day the wind attacked. It tore anything weak from its moorings: trees, birds, kelp, seals were yanked like weeds.[8]

Celia Thaxter also writes about the power of wind-driven waves. "The waves blow up, and they get higher and higher, and there is nothing you can do. Set off in them, and they will shove at you. Wait them out and they will take their time in calming. You have one choice only and that is to accept them."[9]

On her northern lake, Elizabeth Arthur was intensely conscious of the impacts of wind and water.

> Life here is controlled by the wind and the waves it brings. The island is both hard to get to and hard to get away from. I would not mind so much if it were bigger, big enough to take a walk on, big enough so I could get away from the sound and the smell of the waves. It is small though, and there is no place on it where I can escape the presence of the lake below. It is so small that I can never forget that it's an island, isolated from the main mass of the earth by a tissue of moving water.[10]

She felt disabled by her inability to navigate. "I feel more and more helpless—at times bewildered. How can I accustom myself to this lake? Perhaps if I could run the boat, get away from the island by myself, it would make a difference to my life upon it. I pursue the thought, desperate and hopeful. It hardly seems possible that I am not strong enough to start the engine. Undoubtedly it is conviction that I lack, conviction that I can do it too—negotiate my own way around these dangerous waters."[11]

Gaining competence on the water took a while for Judith on Rendezvous, and growing confidence made a big difference in how she felt about being on island.

> For me, early on, it was very lonely and isolated because I was not a boater. I'd had little experience with boats. So I was kind of scared all the time. And the sailboat was inconvenient for getting into some people's places because their docks were funky. Or there was no dock—I'd have to anchor out and row in. It was a little discouraging. I was so nervous. I only went out in the boat on my own when I absolutely had to. It was okay when Jeff was around, but he wasn't there a lot of the time. Once the kids came, he carried on working in the Arctic, and I was alone for a month at a time. To get into the boat I needed some motivation, like going for groceries.

She worked to overcome her fears. "I was bound and determined I was going to do it. I just didn't know if I was doing it the way I should. Is this wind too strong? Should I be here? The kids were a concern—it's a lot easier to be out on your own in a boat than it is with a passenger."

It took Judith a while to realize that other women shared her initial discomfort with island living. "They're all spread out and they've all got funky boats—nobody's boat really works. We were all a little bit separated. But once we got a playschool started, we began to realize how much support was out there. Just getting together once a week and talking to other moms was really good. We didn't have the extended family out here. There were no grandmas or aunts or uncles to help. Not only did you have to build your house and set up your systems, you had to learn how to raise kids all on your own. That was difficult."

The wearing effects of isolation emerge in diverse ways. Philip Vannini offers an explanation. "Isolation is the other side of insulation; the reverse side of the process of de-synchronization from the mainland. Isolation is an affective experience marked by vulnerability, marginality, and inescapability. Whereas islanders feel pride and joy about being insulated, they often feel angry and resentful about being isolated. One of the manifestations of isolation is found in how quickly conflicts can escalate, how long they can persist, and how pervasive they become."[12] Both Elizabeth Arthur and Joy Orth talked about the ways in which their happy solitude transformed into overwhelming isolation. Arthur described tensions with her husband, a sense of being trapped. "Beyond us there were only walls, the rock and the ice. I and thou and nothing else. No distraction. No one else to talk with. No movies. No libraries. Not stereo with headphones. No products to buy."[13] And Orth, who was on her own with her children for many of her nine years on island, comments that "during long, low light winter days when the islander is cut off by weather or just the sheer difficulty of a long passage, it can be challenging to maintain good spirits. There have been lots of jokes and stories about cabin fever, but in Alaska, as in other northern climates, it can be a very real problem. It must be acknowledged."[14]

Focusing on routines and chores is an antidote to growing depression says Orth. "Keeping busy is a requirement. There's always daily work to do: cooking, washing, necessary cleaning, wood getting and generally maintenance. I've found that it's good to have some of these kinds of things that must be done—whether I like them or not. They make me feel I'm justified in spending the balance of my time in ways I enjoy. It also provides a safeguard against depression by forcing me to perform tasks that are necessary to others when I might be inclined to let it all go hang. Once the weather breaks, the problem diminishes."[15]

Almost 150 years earlier, Celia Thaxter made similar observations from her island home off the coast of New Hampshire. "The best balanced human mind is prone to lose its elasticity, and stagnate, in this isolation." She also offers thoughts on how to combat the malaise. "One learns immediately the value of work to keep one's wits clear, cheerful, and steady; just as much real work of the body as it can bear without weariness being always beneficent, but here indispensable. And in this matter women have the advantage of men, who are condemned to fold their hands when their tasks are done. No woman need ever have a vacant minute." Thaxter recommends the craft that kept my mom busy in her quiet moments. "Blessed be the man who invented knitting (I never heard that a woman invented this or any other art). It is the most charming and picturesque of the quiet occupations, leaving the knitter free to read aloud, or talk, or think, while steadily and surely beneath the flying fingers the comfortable stocking grows."[16]

Lack of money for necessities (and niceties) can also erode the pleasure of island life, even if your goal is simplicity, self-sufficiency. Joy Orth says, "I'd be less than candid if I failed to admit that lack of money has stopped us from doing many of the things we planned when we came here, as well as contributing to depression. Frustration is a powerful emotion and you must find ways to circumvent it."[17] But she recognizes that being rooted in a place, surrounded by things that define her, helps when times get tough. "Possessions, sometimes small ones, can do a lot to stay a flood of loneliness, bringing memories that allow you to feel...that there are people out there who love you...

these things, and many others that form the design on the fabric of life, are dear to me and precious beyond relation to value. They symbolize, to me, threads that time and distance cannot break and give me encouragement to carry on." Given her overall enthusiasm for life on island, Orth's comments about her moments of island fever are revealing. "I swear there have been times since coming here, when my spirits were falling faster than the rain pounding against the windows, that I'd have left on the next available ferry, had it not been for the huge old table that graces the main room of the cabin. I look at it, think of its ornate matching chairs stored in the attic, remember the agony of getting it here, think of the improbability of ever removing it, and decide to stay a little longer. Such is the power of the possession we love."[18]

And fatigue contributes to a moments of uncertainty. Over the years, Judith has played many roles in her family, on her island, and in support of the broader community. Recently she has stepped away from a range of tasks. She no longer produces the community newsletter or chairs the community association.

> I'd been doing these things for a long, long, long time and I think I monopolized the roles. That meant that other people weren't able to step in because I was already there. By stepping back, it's opened it up and other people are coming in to fill the breach. That's working really nicely. I think I was so tired, so exhausted from doing all of this stuff that I had a wee meltdown and decided that I had had enough. I almost immediately broke my leg, which meant that there was no way I could go back on my resolve. I dropped all of that stuff, so now I'm living the real island life. I'm really enjoying just being here. That's all I'm doing—I'm not trying to live other people's lives—I'm just doing my own life.

Being on island does not always mean that you've left mainland issues and worries behind, specially now that electronic and cellular communications are mostly unaffected by separating waters. And being on island may mean that those issues are more difficult to resolve, more wearing if solitude creates space to ponder problems and implications. As author Barry Smith points out, "A small island does not free us from the psychological baggage we ferry ashore; rather, island life provides only the briefest interlude before it starts to rummage about in our persona, seeking weaknesses to exploit. Bad history will surely muddy the waters of the future."[19]

Even though many islanders seem to experience times when they question the quality of their lives, most work through these periods. Problems are addressed, the sun comes out, the pleasures of place and accomplishments overcome doubts. Some islanders talk about emerging from the blues with greater self-awareness, a clearer sense of what they value and how to anticipate and deal with problems. This was Joy Orth's hard learning experience when bad weather swept their boat away. "That winter, for me, was one of discontent. As the wind blew and the snow piled to five feet I lay at night in our small attic, waking periodically as if from a nightmare, but the fear wasn't a dream. It was very real—the boats were gone. I brought up for question everything that we'd done, including coming here in the first place. The coming of the spring brought an ease of tensions, but a crack had opened in our container of faith and the healing left a weakness in the structure of the dream."[20] But she adds, "With all honesty, I can say that despite the painful lessons, it is great to live on an island."[21]

Stepping away

ANOTHER REMEDY FOR a touch of island fever is taking a break, although the initial adjustment to the mainland can be jarring. Caroline Woodward talks about her reaction to brief times away in the city. "I observe myself going through . . . a mild but definite transition similar to culture shock, every time I come off the light station." It takes a bit of getting used to. "What I do is stare at the new cars, at people, store windows, billboards, buildings under construction, everything. I look people right in the eye until I realize that makes a lot of strangers uncomfortable and then I quickly remind myself to dial it down, to settle into the casual, eyes-averted, diffident ways of the Western world. Going from a tiny island, population two or three, to any kind of human settlement brings out my own brand of personal intensity, but also my avid and ongoing curiosity about new things in the wider world."[22] At the same time the experience makes her appreciate how island life has shaped her perspectives and behaviours. "I also find myself increasingly impatient with pompous, unhelpful or rude people of all ages. I have to struggle mightily to curb my tongue. I'm just not exposed to nearly as many annoying people that I'm forced to be nice to anymore. I'm out of practice with social niceties, I guess."

Much farther away, author Ben Fogle reports that he found it very challenging to integrate back into the "real" world when he returned to London from remote Taransay in the Outer Hebrides. Fumes were noxious, the noises loud, the food overly rich, the air stale, and the lights too bright. For a long time after returning he struggled with the invisible hold of his "bewitching" island.[23]

And Elizabeth Arthur and her husband made a trek from their island to tiny Fort St. James once winter ice broke up. "After the first moments of excitement, the town seemed uneasy, frenzied. We had been too long away to adjust easily to the speed of life there, stimulating as a drug. Colours were overbright. Shop windows glared."[24] Nevertheless, they recognized the value of periodic breaks. "We try to go to town every two weeks now, to get the mail and visit friends and get in the truck and move. Sometimes the trips are tiring and hard, but they are necessary. In the absence of imaginative changes, making tracks keeps us sane ... we always return more contented. When we travel away from it, the house is a home to come back to."[25]

Other islanders adjust by rebalancing on- and off-island life in more permanent ways. Many islanders winter in Mexico, keep an apartment in town, or use winter months to visit family and friends in distant locations. Stepping away creates a healthy balance in their lives. But these people jealously guard their island time in spring, summer, and fall. Others become summer residents who often visit in the off-season to reconnect, to ensure that all is well. One islander, whose work makes it difficult to spend extended periods on island right now, knows that the future will bring more island time. He says that, in the meantime, "I have huge satisfaction in knowing it's here." In the end, making personal adjustments to keep the island reality a happy one makes good sense.

And there are islanders who find that they've made a lifestyle decision that doesn't work. Emily, on Protection Island, sees people come and go. "If they don't like living here, they leave pretty quick. They think it's going to be this wonderful paradise, and then they start living here and the reality sets in. And they don't like carrying their groceries from the ferry to the house. They don't like the separation from town. People buy a house and then a few months later it's back up on the market. You find out pretty quickly whether this lifestyle is going to work or not."

For others the reality of chores and challenges is not the problem; the difficulty lies in holding it all together with very little income. After almost two years on Nelson Island, Margaret McIntyre and her partner decided to leave their hardscrabble life, despite their love of the place and the pleasure they took as they learned new skills, new self-understanding. They were worn down by the work of trying to earn money on top of making a home on island. "You know, pioneering isn't nearly as romantic as I imagined. You need to be a philosopher...or a hardbitten hunk of toil...to be able to face the grimmer aspects of it."[26]

And for all, aging becomes a factor in the ongoing viability of island life. My mom and dad decided to sell Bath Island in the mid-1980s when they were in their mid-sixties. Clair and I had moved away ten years earlier, and Dad had retired from Vancouver work around the same time. He built a forty-two-foot "gentleman's fish-boat" and had a C licence that allowed him to fish for prawns and dogfish. Mom and Dad explored the coast and began to travel a bit. But buildings and systems constructed twenty years earlier needed significant maintenance, the dock needed replacing, and they had a sense that, in their late sixties, it was time for an easier life. I got a call one day saying that Roger had purchased the island and they were moving to a small upland property near Degnen Bay on Gabriola. From my perspective the decision to leave was as spontaneous as the decision to buy. But Roger tells me that they spent months arriving at a suitable price and negotiating the things that stayed on island and those that would go to Gabriola. The news that the island would no longer be in my life shocked and saddened me. But I also realized that it was their pension fund. There was no way that my husband and I could somehow purchase it from them, nor did our studies and jobs allow for a move from Victoria at the time.

As it turned out, their timing was good. Not only did they find a person who would love the island as they did (and welcome us whenever we visit), they encountered health issues shortly afterward that would have made it necessary to leave under more difficult circumstances. But once those issues were sorted out, Mom and Dad sold the fishboat, bought yet another sailboat, cruised the coast, travelled, made new friends, and enjoyed their new property. Life on an island served by ferries was, in many ways, simpler. The twenty-five years on Bath Island had been a very happy time in their lives, but not the only time.

Other islanders struggle with the notion of moving off island as they reach their seventies and beyond. Linda, who was living on Gabriola while her mom lived on her own on Valdes, visited almost daily until her mother's life on island became too challenging.

It was very hard for her. And it was hard to get her to move, but I basically gave her no alternative. She had got to the point where she couldn't start her boat engine anymore if she wanted to go to the store, and there was no cell coverage, although we had one of those early analog phones that truckers used. We'd get calls asking if we could come over to the island to start her engine. So that kept us close to home. We couldn't go anywhere, we couldn't travel. Finally my husband and I went to Portugal with another couple and my mom stayed with my aunt in Nanaimo while we were gone. Everybody said, "Linda, it's time." I knew it was time. She couldn't make the journey to the outhouse anymore. I knew it was time. I moved her to the retirement village on Gabriola. She wasn't there that long when she had hip surgery, which failed. She ended up in extended care. She'd always been very active and never wanted to go to a care facility. But she needed total care. It was hard. She was eighty-three.

Linda's mom spent a lifetime on Valdes. But many people seek an island property as a retirement project and confront aging issues within a matter of years, although some might argue that even a brief island interlude is worth it. Linda observes that island dreams get complicated fairly quickly. "People don't realize how much work it takes when they are thinking of leaving the city and moving to the Gulf Islands. And they're already older. After about ten years, they'll be in their seventies. All the work that they're going to need to do to sustain life will get much more difficult. I see that among the people who come here for the summer. My neighbours, who've been there for twenty years, are talking about how they can make it easier for themselves."

And Linda recognizes that she is getting older. This makes her time on island even more precious.

> I want to spend more time here. I resent the time that I spend away from here. I don't want to be growing a vegetable garden on Gabriola because it infringes on the time I could be spending on Valdes. Sometimes I just commune when I'm here, and sometimes I work on my flower garden. And there's always watering and housework. And in the winter, it's work time, getting the wood. Of course everything gets heavier as I get older, but I'm physically active. I'm in and out of boats and carrying things. I don't have to go to the gym. I do think about the long term, and I know that, as much as people think they're not going to get infirm, they do. It's just a fact of life. There will come a day when I can't come here anymore. That's just life.

On their small island shared with one other family, Jan reflects that they might have made different choices around design if they'd had a crystal ball. "Now that we're pushing seventy, it's not so great having a two-storey house. It's a lot harder to maintain, so that's one of the things I'd do differently. Getting up a thirty-foot ladder and painting the gable ends is hard. It's too scary, but you have to be prepared to do everything yourself. We do find occasional handymen, but it's not going to work every time."

Living with health conditions that grow more pressing with age heightens awareness of the distance the island is from care. Roger weighs the alternatives and opts for island living.

I'm not one of those people who is going to move away from here in order to be closer to the hospital. Not a chance. That's not how I've ever operated and I won't be starting that any time soon. I do have certain health issues, but I decided long ago when I heard about them that there was only one viable option. That's to carry on. The other day when I was in the channel pulling those heavy chains, I kind of underestimated how difficult it was going to be. I had my fins and snorkel. I'm thinking, "If my condition is ever going to blow up, it's going to be now." Because I'm not supposed to have sudden rushes of high blood pressure. And a sure bloody way of getting a sudden rush of high blood pressure is doing sudden big exertions like that. But nothing happened, and the chain is sitting there looking very nice.

Much as they would like to stay on island, other islanders anticipate more immediate difficulties. It was a sad moment when Rob and Laurie, who have already dealt with their share of illness, told me that they are confronting another problem. Rob says, "We started being idealistic, but have been seriously humbled by life, by serious illness, and how that effects our ability to continue. We'd love to be able to stay here, but the reality is that we're at a hard stage right now, especially me. I've just been diagnosed with Parkinson's disease. It can be held in abeyance, maybe for a while, but it will catch up with me."

And with aging comes a heightened awareness that there is finite time to tackle the bucket list of other adventures that the intrepid island people tend to have in the backs of their heads. The siren song of travel, mountains, oceans, even other islands can distract them, once all their major island projects are done. I talked with people who were making a move off island as they want to explore other dreams, lifestyles, places. Or want to be closer to grandchildren, friends, and aging parents. They regret the loss of their much-loved island. And they're grateful that they have had a remarkable experience that will contribute to how they approach the next stages of life. Leaving isn't a decision taken lightly. They devote time to figuring out if they can have both, but in the end, can't figure out how to do justice to either. And it's not easy to step away, heartstrings aside. Moving off an island home is almost as big a job as moving on.

Keeping perspective

THE VARIOUS CONCERNS expressed in this chapter aren't intended to discourage you. They are cautionary tales, realities that at least some people find themselves coping with, working around, responding to as they make a home on island. Life everywhere carries risk, uncertainty, shifting perspectives. Islands aren't bad places to confront such problems; in less lovely settings, those same risks and problems might be even harder to deal with. Chic on Snowberry has pondered such concerns and says, "I think a lot of people shy away from risk. They say, 'It's not worth it.' But if you don't take risk, you don't gain anything. Being cognizant and aware, assessing and evaluating, and responding to the risks is terribly important. You don't shy away. You take the risks, knowing what they are. And then you have all the benefits of living in a wonderful place."

Yvonne Maximchuk reached a philosophical balance as she struggled with both physical and emotional challenges when she settled on Gilford Island. She arrived at a point where she could say, "The double-edged sword, the half-full, half-empty glass, the paradox of everything is ever present. Living in the wilderness has taught me to stop complaining. It's a wonderful life: so what if my ambitions have exceeded my grasp? That's how it goes. Living here has taught me to pay attention to the messages, both external and internal, and to trust myself. In nature's solitude I've sought my own wisdom, my own voice and inspiration as one being among many, each with our own gifts to offer."[27]

In her description of nine years on an Alaskan island, Joy Orth captures the notion that meeting challenges is a big part of the experience. "The area deserves respect, not fear. Whatever a person's surroundings, there are things to be learned, skills that help ensure survival. If there is more knowledge necessary here than in some other places, that is as it should be. Any other way and it would no longer be wilderness."[28] And, as Margaret McIntyre reflects, if you end up returning to mainland life, "Once you have known beauty, the memory of it is always within you...it will stay with you wherever you are."[29]

Island studies scholar Laurie Brinklow, who is also an islander, observes that "after a while to live on an island becomes a badge of honour. You're proud that you're a little 'out there,' that maybe you have to work a little harder in order to survive. Islanders are a resilient lot, which can come from having to cope with and adapt to the harshest of the elements, the isolation, occasionally having the mainland cut off yet again."[30] But wherever they live, people change over time as they come to know themselves better. Needs change, interests shift, relationships strengthen or wane. Ultimately, a sense of comfort on island is a personal matter. There is no right or wrong approach.

(8)

THE PERFECT ISLANDER

Aside from its lack of a bay for secure moorage, Bath Island was pretty much perfect for us. It was large enough to offer variety and small enough that we knew it intimately. It was close enough to Gabriola that intervening waters were easily negotiated, and not so far from Vancouver that important social and work ties had to be severed. Views were beautiful, as were choices of building sites. It provided water, arable soil, and an endless source of firewood. Its climate was mild and fairly protected, at least compared with that of other West Coast islands, and we could swim in the summer. Oysters, clams, and fish were just outside the door. And life was always engaging as the seasons rolled by. The island was good for our souls.

And we were well suited to Bath Island. As Mom said in her log, "We fell in love as soon as we set foot on shore." Dad had many of the skills as well as the energy needed to plan and build houses, moorage, systems. And what he didn't know, Mom and Dad were happy to learn, discuss, try out. Mom had the tenacity needed to manage everything from the house and garden to kids and projects. And she enjoyed her own company on the many days she spent on her own. Both Mom and Dad were drawn to the simplicity of island life and embraced its complexity. And Clair and I grew into islandness, happy to be caught up in this grand adventure.

ISLANDS AND ISLANDERS come together in intriguing, rewarding, occasionally difficult relationships. And, as in any relationship, they have to meet one another's needs and put up with idiosyncrasies to create a lasting bond. The key is a good match.

Islands have much to offer in this partnership. Each is unique in its location, size, and charms. Yet, for all their wonderful diversity, islands have common qualities. The interplay of beaches, bluffs, forests, and meadows gives them special character. Hidden interiors are intriguing. Surrounding waters add appeal and create the separation that shapes a special lifestyle characterized by solitude, challenge, independence, learning. These special places offer connections with nature, opportunities for reflection, fluid concepts of time, and distance from the grids of mainland life.

Some particular combination of these qualities attracts islanders, arouses desire, and inspires romantic dreams: always a good start to a relationship. But an island's distinctive features just set the stage for a long-term relationship. The islander must also bring special qualities if the relationship is to work. Richard Nelson recognizes the reciprocity of a growing love for an island. "Although the island has great significance for me, it's no more inherently beautiful or meaningful than any other place on earth. What makes a place special is the way it buries itself inside the heart, not whether it's flat or rugged, rich or austere, wet or arid, gentle or harsh, warm or cold, wild or tame. Every place, like every person, is elevated by the love and respect shown toward it, and by the way in which its bounty is received."[1]

So what qualities can an islander bring to this unusual match? What makes a relationship sustainable? There is, of course, no single profile of a perfect islander, just as there is no single perfect island or relationship. But there are characteristics that seem to predispose people to a rewarding life on island.

I'll begin the list by suggesting that a deep love of both the place and the experiences it offers is a prerequisite. This love affair may start with an immediate visceral reaction as you step ashore. Or it may take you some time to appreciate the mix of beauty and character that makes an island a match for your needs, an intimate part of your life. But one way or another, coming to love an island and its features is a critical foundation for a lasting relationship. This love will sustain you when things get complicated. It will make the effort worthwhile and ensure that you treat the island with the respect that it deserves.

Love of place is a constant refrain among islanders. David fell in love with his remote island years ago and bought his property knowing that it would be a long time before he could spend significant time there. "I love the physical setting, I love the beauty, and I love the self-reliance that it requires. I treasure the solitude. It's just such a wonderful, wonderful place to be." Jan and Sy fell in love with the area at the mouth of Jervis Inlet when their friends Bob and Sue first took them there, and knew that their small island was perfect for them. That bond continues today. Jan looks across her lovely garden to the sparkling bay below and says, "There is nothing I regret about moving here. I love living here." And David Cox writes about the essence of his experience on island. "The present moment is often so enchanting, so totally occupying, you are ravished by it. It is a momentous love affair with life."[2]

The notion of a heartfelt relationship is captured by John Fowles as he describes his engagement with an island. "Eventually it let me feel it was mine: which is the other great siren charm of islands—that they will not belong to any legal owner, but offer to become a part of all who tread and love them."[3] In the harsher waters off the west coast of Scotland, Adam Nicolson also understands that love is not about ownership. He received the deeds to the Shiants as a birthday present and loves them more than any other place on earth. But he recognizes that he does not have an exclusive right to them. They are part of many peoples' lives.[4]

And Richard Nelson observes that his love for an island has both magical and ordinary qualities. "Sometimes I feel burdened by the shapeless desire that brings me here ... while the island can be a lonely place, it also gives an elemental comfort much like shared human love. As with any love, it can seem almost imaginary, like wandering through a far paradise, savouring pleasures too rich and sweet to exist beyond fantasy. But at other times it seems entirely commonplace, filled with the ordinary but indispensable satisfactions."[5]

Seductive as it is, love of place is only a starting point for a good relationship. You also need a realistic sense of what is involved in living on island and a range of characteristics and abilities that ensure the reality becomes even better than the romantic vision. Joy Orth says, "We discovered there's a lot more involved in a move such as ours than simply finding a place you love and moving in. It takes real organization to live on the bounty of the wilderness around you."[6]

Islanders themselves list qualities that are necessary for happy island living. There is no single prescription, but common characteristics emerge. Outstanding among these are tenacity and resilience.

Roger, for example, says that successful islanders should be "resourceful; willing and able to deal with adversity; independent. They should be opinionated, handy around boats in particular, committed to preserving a sort of authentic natural environment, and have an affinity with other islanders." He recognizes that, like many other things in life, living on island involves distinctive knowledge, skills, and attitudes. Of these, he says, "Attitudes are probably the most important, although we know the three things are all embedded in each other. There has to be a pretty high level of enthusiasm and tenacity, a get-up-and-go attitude. Get out of bed and get something done." Being positive and proactive is also important. "You've got to see things through a lens of possibility: you'd better not function in a world where 'I can't' keeps coming up. Because out on an island there's going to be a lot of things you haven't done before, but you'll have to tackle them. And these may happen when you're there by yourself and have to depend on your own judgement."

Caroline emphasizes the value of good health, combined with outlook. "What matters most is fitness, both mental and physical, plus a sense of humour and an optimistic attitude."[7] Misty calls for stubborn determination. And David and Suromitra emphasize the value of strong planning skills along with willingness to roll up your sleeves and get on with the work. This is echoed by David Conover, who wrote, "Study and planning ... were the keys to this life."[8] He spoke from experience in adding that money is also important.

Chic and Kathy see themselves as stewards and emphasize the duty of care that goes with an island relationship. As well, Chic calls for "lots of practical skills, self-discipline, and stick-to-it-iveness." He reflects that a willingness to do the work is a big part of enjoying the accomplishments. "If you're just going to be a gentleman islander and say, 'We have plenty of money, I'll just pay for this and that,' you may not make it. It might not even be as satisfying as you'd like." Both Kathy and Chic have happily tackled tasks that never cropped up in their urban lives. As Kathy says, "I've learned to try anything. Get in there and do stuff. I don't worry about it. I'm not wearing clothes that I can't get dirty and not worried about makeup—none of that matters. You're just living and you're out here." And Emily and Tom emphasize the importance of flexibility. "It has to be built into everything that you do. If you can't get to your workplace in the morning or are late, that can't be a problem."

A researcher who studied life on the Discovery Islands also observed common qualities of people who live on islands. "Islanders tend to be very independent thinkers, to trust themselves and their own thoughts before accepting what other people tell them, and it's not that they don't have respect for authority but they don't necessarily feel that they are less equal than somebody with more money or a position of authority or power."[9] According to other researchers who study off-the-grid living, the key to success is a positive outlook. While skills help, they can be learned. "It requires someone who is not easily intimidated. Someone with a great deal of self-efficacy and confidence. And someone with a strong interest in that lifestyle. You have to be handy, you have to be someone who knows how to fend for themselves."[10]

From these reflections (and at the risk of generalizing islandness) it seems safe to say that the perfect islander will be, among other things, resilient, confident, enthusiastic, tenacious, quick-witted, optimistic, proactive, fit, self-reliant, independent, adaptable, self-disciplined, flexible, and handy. He or she will also bring creativity, ingenuity, a strong environmental ethic, and a get-up-and-go attitude to the island relationship. Good organizational skills, a ready sense of humour, and engaging social skills are also desirable. And some observers rank inventiveness and resourcefulness as most important of all.[11] Not surprisingly, these qualities effectively describe the people that I had such a good time talking with.

For the right people, there's a powerful sense of satisfaction and accomplishment in nurturing an island relationship. Part of the charm of making a life on island, according to the *Private Islands* newsletter, is "the way it requires you to stretch your boundaries; it requires a special kind of independent, entrepreneurial personality to follow through and thrive in the island world. As the saying goes, 'things worth having in life are rarely simple to obtain,' and such things are all the more significant and meaningful for the effort they require. Private islands bring a rare kind of pleasure to their owners; not just of possessing something truly beautiful and unique, but of knowing that you're the kind of person capable of attaining it."[12]

Islanders also offer advice on how to live successfully on island. There is a call for minimalism, although the term means different things to different people. Tom and Emily have embraced a mindset of deliberate simplicity. "It's conscious elimination of things that might potentially stress us." A big part of that is not being a slave to possessions. Judith thinks along the same lines.

Transposing your city lifestyle to the island is just creating more problems over the long term. You just can't do that and stay here for any length of time. And then, of course, you age and you keep expecting those systems to keep on working, but they all age too. So you're looking at either a huge expense or a lot of labour to replace them. The less you can make do with, the more you can actually enjoy the life. Just pare it right down to absolute bare minimum. Just what you need and that's all. That's based on all my experience. I built too big a house, I've got too large a garden.

Of course, simplicity is complicated and not always achievable. The choice of amenities is personal. For some islanders, developing systems to support island living is a creative process that also enables them to tackle the full range of activities required for satisfying lives on island. As Roger says, the perfect island is one that allows you to do everything you need to do without leaving. Other islanders prefer simplicity at every turn, although some find the process of paring things down quite challenging. David Cox, for example, sought a simple lifestyle but writes that "minimalism is not for the lazy or the budget conscious."[13] He goes on to say, "I was initially attracted to minimalism. I like the idea of simple. City living was getting me down and, quite frankly, I understood less and less of what was going on. I aspire to little, want for nothing and desire even less. Minimalism sounded like my cup of tea. But I have reluctantly concluded I don't have the money or the brains required to be simple. I guess that I am destined to remain a complicated man. It's easier."[14]

Other advice on island living ranges from practical to philosophical. Linda emphasizes that "you have to know how to use a power saw. You have to know how to use a boat, be able to run an engine." She adds that newcomers need to think carefully about whether they can sustain the lifestyle, particularly if they're embarking on a retirement project.

Geri comments that you will quickly learn that you are quite capable of doing many things you've never tried before and adds that you don't need to be an expert to be successful. "As long as you have a sense of adventure and are fit, you should go for it. It's a glorious experience. The island will teach you what you need to know." David Conover makes a similar observation. "The island is a great teacher . . . Every day we learned something new, often without knowing it and most often about ourselves." He goes on to say that "we learned too that in every step there must be a compromise—between what we wanted to do and what we could do within our means and strength."[15]

Making mistakes is part of learning to live on island time and nothing to be embarrassed about. Chic reflects that "you learn through experience. So make lots of mistakes—that's the name of the game. It's all about coming up with wisdom." And both Judith and Laurie recommend also learning from others who live close by. Judith says, "Talk a lot to the locals who've lived here for a long time. And avoid all the mistakes that they made. And maybe get a more realistic view of what the life is like." Joe emphasizes the importance of being attentive to all that is around you, particularly on the water. "You have to be aware of tides, winds, distractions." Roger echoes this, saying "you've got to be on full alert most of the time."

Like Joe and Roger, Rob encourages prospective islanders to be "mindful, particularly when you're out on the water." He also sees opportunities to be more in the moment, "more connected with the world around you. Abandon belief systems that suggest you're separate and superior. They're a threat. We're all in the same boat, everything is related. You should just relax and breathe in the situation...stuff is going on around us all the time, all we have to do is pay attention."

Despite the varied experiences that make stories of islands and islanders so fascinating, there is a shared passion for a life in these special places, a sense of privilege, and a quiet pride in being successful in a challenging environment. Many aspects of this life are, indeed, simple. You have greater autonomy, fewer external demands. The immediacy of nature places you in a more holistic, more authentic context. Solitude creates space for greater self-awareness. And you are more in tune with needs rather than wants. At the same time, many aspects of this life are complicated. You replace generic mainland systems with specialized island systems that you, alone, are responsible for. You need a much larger toolbox and the skills to go with it. And you need to figure out how to negotiate surrounding waters, day-to-day tasks, and personal relationships in new ways. Sustaining the match between islander and island, balancing solitude and social activities, and harmonizing simplicity and complication are daily challenges. These shifting dualities make island life endlessly interesting. This is something that wise islanders understand. Finding your optimal balance among all the wonderful choices that islands present is the key to a satisfying life on island time.

ACKNOWLEDGEMENTS

TALKING WITH ISLANDERS in the San Juans and along the BC coast has been a privilege and pleasure—thank you all for welcoming me and for sharing your thoughts, your joys, your occasional troubles, and your passion for island living. I hope that *Complicated Simplicity* honours your remarkable experiences and captures your wisdom. I am also grateful to the many people who introduced me to islanders, talked with me about their experiences providing island services, or shared island perspectives through their writing. It's fascinating how many people have island connections and insights.

And thank you to all the people whose support and interest kept me focused throughout the research and writing. Rod, it was great to have your company as we sailed to diverse islands. Thank you for negotiating rocky beaches and for joining in on endless conversations about islands and islanders. And the constant enthusiasm of my friends Naomi Chard, Donna Livingstone, Cheryl Alexander, and Roger Boshier has been a great support. I appreciate your enduring interest in this project, value your thoughtful critiques of various drafts, and always enjoy your reflections on island experiences.

I am particularly grateful to Lara Kordic at Heritage House Publishing for her initial interest in *Complicated Simplicity* and for all her advice and guidance. Lara and her colleagues Sarah Weber, Lenore Hietkamp, Leslie Kenny, Marial Shea, Jacqui Thomas, and Nandini Thaker have been a pleasure to work with and have brought their own special magic to the book creation process.

NOTES

Chapter 1—**The Draw of Islands**

1. Godfrey Baldacchino, "Studying Islands: On Whose Terms? Some Epistemological and Methodological Challenges to the Pursuit of Island Studies," *Island Studies Journal* 3, no. 1 (2008). All extracts from *Island Studies Journal* reprinted with permission of the publisher.

2. D.H. Lawrence, "The Man Who Loved Islands." In D.H. Lawrence, *The Woman Who Rode Away and Other Stories*, ed. Dieter Mehl and Christa Jahnson (Cambridge: Cambridge University Press, 2002), 39–71.

3. United Nations, "UN Convention on the Law of the Sea" (New York: United Nations, 1982).

4. Stephen A. Royle, Islands: *Nature and Culture* (London: Reaktion Books, 2014), 8.

5. Christian Depraetere and Arthur L. Dahl, "Island Locations and Concentrations," in *A World of Islands*, ed. Godfrey Baldacchino (Charlottetown: Island Studies Press, 2007).

6. "Island," in *Oxford Living Dictionary* (Oxford University Press, 2016), accessed March 28, 2017, https://en.oxforddictionaries.com.

7. John Fowles, *Islands* (London: Jonathan Cape, 1978), 56. This excerpt, and others from *Islands*, reproduced in the print version by permission of The Random House Group Ltd. ©1978, and in the e-book version by kind permission of the Estate of John Fowles.

8. Gillian Beer, "Island Bounds," in *Islands in History and Representation*, ed. Rod Edmond and Vanessa Smith (London: Routledge, 2003), 42.

9. Ian Kinane, *Theorising Literary Islands: The Island Trope in Contemporary Robinsonade Narratives* (London and New York: Rowman & Littlefield International, 2016).

10. Ella Wheeler Wilcox, *The Beautiful Land of Nod* (Chicago: Morrill, Higgins & Company, 1892).

11. Pete Hay, "What the Sea Portends: A Reconsideration of Contested Island Tropes," *Island Studies Journal* 8, no. 2 (2013).

12. Godfrey Baldacchino, "Islands, Island Studies, Island Studies Journal," *Island Studies Journal* 1, no. 1 (2006).

13. David Platt, "Islandness," in *Holding Ground: The Best of Island Journal 1984–2004*, ed. Philip Conkling and David Platt (Rockland, ME: Island

Institute, 2004), 1. All extracts from *Holding Ground* reprinted with permission of the Island Institute.

14. K.R. Olwig, "Are Islanders Insular? A Personal View," *Geographical Review* 97, no. 2 (2007): 178. Reprinted with permission of the author. Note that this article is also available in the forthcoming anthology of Kenneth Olwig's work, *The Meanings of Landscape: Essays on Place, Space, Nature and Justice* (London: Routledge).

15. Ian Townsend, *The Myth of Island Living*, podcast, Background Briefing, December 12, 2010, accessed March 3, 2016, http://www.abc.net.au/radionational/programs/backgroundbriefing/the-myth-of-island-living/2983150#transcript.

16. Samuel A. McReynolds, "Community Sustainability in the Year-round Islands of Maine," *Island Studies Journal* 9, no. 1 (2014): 84.

17. J. Edward Chamberlin, *Island: How Islands Transform the World* (Kathonah, NY: Bluebridge, 2013), 182. All extracts from *Island* reprinted with permission of the author.

18. Margaret McIntyre, *Place of Quiet Waters* (Don Mills, ON: Longmans Canada Limited, 1965), 2.

19. Naomi A. Bosch, "Discovery Islands, Earth Islands: The Theory and Practice of Island Imagery in Environmental Thought" (Claremont, CA: Pomona College, 2015), 44. All extracts from this thesis reprinted with permission of the author.

20. Jean Howarth, *Secrets the Island Is Keeping* (Toronto: Summerhill Press, 1988).

21. Barbara Fernald, "Island Home Helps Me Grieve Great Loss," *The Working Waterfront* (October 26, 2015), accessed November 19, 2015, http://www.islandinstitute.org/working-waterfront/island-home-helps-me-grieve-great-loss. All extracts from *The Working Waterfront* reprinted with the permission of the Island Institute.

22. Grant Lawrence, *Adventures in Solitude: What Not to Wear to a Nude Potluck and Other Stories from Desolation Sound* (Pender Harbour, BC: Harbour Publishing, 2010), 68. All extracts from Harbour Publishing reproduced with permission of the publisher.

23. Philip Vannini, *Ferry Tales: Mobility, Place, and Time on Canada's West Coast* (New York: Routledge, 2011), 78.

24. Royal Canadian Mounted Police Island District website, accessed March 2016, http://bc.rcmp-grc.gc.ca/ViewPage.action?siteNodeId=195&languageId=1.

25. Pete Hay, "A Phenomenology of Islands," *Island Studies Journal* 1, no. 1 (2006): 31.

26. Yvonne Maximchuk, *Drawn to Sea: Paintbrush to Chainsaw—Carving Out a Life on BC's Rugged Raincoast* (Halfmoon Bay, BC: Caitlin Press, 2013), 36–37. All extracts from *Drawn to Sea* reproduced with permission.

27. Elizabeth Arthur, *Island Sojourn* (New York: Harper and Row, 1980), 165–66. All extracts from *Island Sojourn* reprinted with permission of the author.

28. Union of British Columbia Indian Chiefs, "Certainty: Canada's Struggle to Extinguish Aboriginal Title" (Vancouver: UBCIC, 1998), accessed April 26, 2016, https://www.ubcic.bc.ca/certainty_canada_s_struggle_to_extinguish_aboriginal_title.

29. Tourism Tofino, accessed March 2016, https://tourismtofino.com/news/2014/03/08/getonthewater-with-misty-and-oren-lawson-of-ocean-outfitters/.

30. Celia Thaxter, *Among the Isles of Shoals* (Boston: James R. Osgood and Company, 1873). Kindle edition.

31. Rob Wood, *At Home in Nature: A Life of Unknown Mountains and Deep Wilderness* (Victoria: Rocky Mountain Books, 2017), 57. All extracts from *At Home in Nature* reprinted with permission of the publisher.

32. Joy Orth, *Island: Our Alaskan Dream and Reality* (Edmonds, WA: Alaska Northwest Publishing Company, 1987). All extracts from *Island: Our Alaskan Dream and Reality* reprinted with permission of Joy Orth Estate.

33. Michael Modzelewski, *Inside Passage* (New York: HarperCollins, 1991), xviii. All extracts from *Inside Passage* reprinted with permission of the author.

34. Richard Nelson, *The Island Within* (New York: Vintage Books, 1991), 172. All extracts from *The Island Within* reprinted with permission of the author.

35. Godfrey Baldacchino, "The Lure of Islands: A Spatial Analysis of Power Relations," *Journal of Marine and Island Cultures* 1, no. 2 (2012): 10.

36. David Conover, *Once Upon an Island* (Don Mills, ON: PaperJacks, 1972), 118. All extracts from *Once Upon an Island* reprinted with permission of Barbara Conover.

37. Ibid., 120.

38. J. David Cox in blog post "Off-the-Grid-Living," April 27, 2016, http://offthegridhomes.org (site discontinued).

39. Vannini, *Ferry Tales*, 109.

40. June Burn, *Living High*, 6th ed. (Woodinville, WA: San Juan Publishing, 2011 [1st ed. 1941]), vii. All extracts from *Living High* reprinted with permission of June Burn's Estate.

41. David VanderZwaag, "We Bought Our Own Private Island," *Mother Earth News*, March/April (1978). All extracts from "We Bought Our Own Private Island" reprinted with permission of the publisher.

42. Private Islands Inc., "Private Islands Buyer's Guide" (Private Islands Inc., 2014), 5. All extracts from Private Islands Inc. reprinted with permission.

43. Adam Nicolson, *Sea Room: An Island Life in the Hebrides* (London: HarperCollins, 2002).

44. Fowles, *Islands*, 11.

45. Philip Conkling, "On Islanders and Islandness," *Geographical Review* XCVII (2007): 199–200.

46. Lasqueti Island website, accessed February 2017, http://lasqueti.ca/island-info/lasqueti-life.

47. Vannini, *Ferry Tales*, 78.

48 Laurie Brinklow, "Stepping-Stones to the Edge: Artistic Expressions of Islandness in an Ocean of Islands," *Island Studies Journal* 8, no. 1 (2013): 49.

49. George Putz, "On Islanders," in *Holding Ground: The Best of Island Journal 1984–2004*, ed. Philip Conkling and David Platt (Rockland, ME: Island Institute, 2004), 28.

50. Laurie Brinklow, "How Small an Island Do You Need?," *Island* 124 (Autumn 2011): 20. Reprinted with permission of the author.

51. Nelson, *The Island Within*, xiii.

Chapter 2—The Perfect Island

1. Private Islands Inc., 5.

2. Lawrence Durrell, *Reflections on a Marine Venus: A Companion to the Landscape of Rhodes* (London: Faber, 1960), 16.

3. Jonathan Raban, *Passage to Juneau: A Sea and Its Meanings* (New York: Vintage Books, 1999), 53. Reprinted with permission of the publisher.

4. Steven Roger Fischer, *Islands: From Atlantis to Zanzibar* (London: Reaktion Books, 2012), 12.

5. Raban, *Passage to Juneau*, 54.

6. Law Reform Commission of British Columbia, *Report on Limitations, Part II General* (Vancouver: Law Reform Commission of British Columbia, 1974), 56, accessed April 26, 2018, http://www.bcli.org/sites/default/files/report15.pdf.

7. Andree Brooks, "The Magic of an Island Home," *New York Times*, June 20, 1982.

8. Hilary Stewart, *On Island Time* (Vancouver: Douglas & McIntyre, 1998), 1. All extracts from Douglas & MacIntyre publications reprinted with permission.

9. Wallace J. Nichols, *Blue Mind: The Surprising Science That Shows How Being Near, In, On, or Under Water Can Make You Happier, Healthier, More Connected, and Better at What You Do* (New York: Little, Brown and Company, 2014).

10. Herman Melville, *Moby-Dick*; or, *The Whale* (New York: Harper & Brothers, 1851) Chapter 1, http://mel.hofstra.edu/moby-dick-the-whale-proofs.html

11. Modzelewski, *Inside Passage, 129.*

12. *World Sea Temperature*s website, accessed February 24, 2017, https://www.seatemperature.org.

13. Environment and Climate Change Canada, *British Columbia Regional Marine Weather Guide*, accessed February 18, 2016, https://www.ec.gc.ca/meteo-weather/default.asp?lang=En&n=7C8C8223–1.

14. Ibid., *National Marine Weather Guide*, accessed February 18, 2016, https://www.canada.ca/en/environment-climate-change/services/general-marine-weather-information/regional-guides/national.html.

15. Ibid., *British Columbia Regional Marine Weather Guide.*

16. F.W. Jarrad, *The British Columbia Pilot: Including the Coast of British Columbia, from Juan De Fuca Strait to Portland Canal, Together with Vancouver and Queen Charlotte Islands* (London: The Hydrographic Office, Admiralty, 1888.), 11.

17. Modzelewski, *Inside Passage*, xvii.

18. Jarrad, *British Columbia Pilot*, 11.

19. David Lowenthal, "Islands, Lovers, and Others," *The Geographical Review* 97, no. 2 (2007): 212.

20. Alison Watt, *The Last Island: A Naturalist's Sojourn on Triangle Island* (Madeira Park, BC: Harbour Publishing, 2002), 78.

21. Nicholas J. Gotelli, *A Primer of Ecology* (Sunderland, MA: Sinauer Associates, 2001).

22. John R. Gillis, "Not Continents in Miniature: Islands as Ecotones," *Island Studies Journal* 9, no. 1 (2014): 155.

23. Nelson, *The Island Within*, 101.

24. Hugh Aldersey-Williams, *The Tide* (New York: W.W. Norton & Company, 2016), 97.

25. Christina Viviani, Maureen Welton, and Kenneth Torrance, *Tafoni: Natural Design of Weathered Stone* (Langley, BC: 18Karat, 2008).

26. Les Peterson, "British Columbia's Depopulated Coast," in *Raincoast Chronicles First Five*, ed. Howard White (Madeira Park, BC: Harbour Publishing, 1973).

27. Robert Morales and Eric McLay, "The Ongoing Search for Respect at Grace Islet," *Times Colonist*, August 1, 2014.

28. Stewardship Centre for British Columbia Green Shores Technical Working Group, *Coastal Shore Jurisdiction in British Columbia* (North Vancouver: Stewardship Centre for British Columbia, 2009), accessed April 11, 2016, http://www.salishsea.ca/resources/Riparianrights/Greenshores%20 JurisdictionIssueSheet_finalVer4.pdf.

29. Nicolson, *Sea Room*.

30. Islands Trust and the San Juan Preservation Trust, *A Place in the Islands*, 2nd ed. (Victoria: Islands Trust and the San Juan Preservation Trust, 2007), 33.

Chapter 3—Sea Room

1. Thaxter, *Among the Isles of Shoals*.

2. Roger Boshier, "Wet and Boisterous: The Lumpy Romance of Commuting by Boat," in *The Cultures of Alternative Mobilities: Routes Less Travelled*, ed. Philip Vannini (Farnham: Ashgate Publishing, 2009).

3. Tom Groening, "The Sea Continues to Lure Linda Greenlaw," *The Working Waterfront* (November 23, 2015), accessed November 30, 2015, http://www.islandinstitute.org/working-waterfront/sea-continues-lure-linda-greenlaw.

4. Maximchuk, *Drawn to Sea*, 37.

5. Orth, *Island*, 74.

6. Conover, *Once Upon an Island*, 148.

7. VanderZwaag, "We Bought Our Own Private Island."

8. Wood, *At Home in Nature*, 231.

9. Modzelewski, *Inside Passage*, xviii.

10. Charity Robey, "Dr. Frank Adipietro: Commuting Floats His Boat," *Northforker Health and Fitness* (2014).

Chapter 4—Settling In

1. Orth, *Island*, 16, 18.

2. Private Islands Inc.

3. Witold Rybczynski, *The Most Beautiful House in the World* (New York: Penguin, 1989).

4. Jean Howarth, *Island Time* (Toronto: Summerhill Press, 1988), 187.

5. Islands Trust and the San Juan Preservation Trust, 7.

6. Modzelewski, *Inside Passage*, 2.

7. Maximchuk, *Drawn to Sea*, 44.

8. Arthur, *Island Sojourn*, 12, 24–25.

9. Private Islands Inc.

10. VanderZwaag, "We Bought Our Own Private Island."

11. McIntyre, *Place of Quiet Waters*, 71.

12. Environment and Natural Resources Canada, *Residential Water Use*, accessed May 2017, https://www.canada.ca/en/environment-climate-change/services/environmental-indicators/residential-water-use.html.

13. Eric Nicol, *When Nature Calls: Life at a Gulf Islands Cottage* (Madeira Park, BC: Harbour Publishing, 1999), 105–6.

14. Islands Trust and the San Juan Preservation Trust, 23.

15. Helen Piddington, *The Inlet: Memoir of a Modern Pioneer* (Madeira Park, BC: Harbour Publishing, 2001), 137.

16. Rob Wood, "Wind against the Tide: Challenges and Rewards of Living Close to Nature" (Unpublished manuscript, 2016), 25, 59.

17. Private Islands Inc.

18. Piddington, *The Inlet*, 138.

19. McIntyre, *Place of Quiet Waters*, 62.

20. Ibid., 126.

21. Conover, *Once Upon an Island*, 83.

22. Orth, *Island*, 55.

23. Maximchuk, *Drawn to Sea*, 45, 47.

24. Nicol, *When Nature Calls*, 58–59.

25. Orth, *Island*, 14–15.

26. Nicol, *When Nature Calls*, 55.

27. Arthur, *Island Sojourn*, 42–44.

28. Wood, *At Home in Nature*, 72–73.

Chapter 5—**On Island Time**

1. McIntyre, *Place of Quiet Waters*, 41.

2. J. David Cox, *Our Life Off the Grid: An Urban Couple Goes Feral* (Surge Narrows, BC: OTG Publishing, 2015). All extracts from *Our Life Off the Grid* reprinted with permission of the author.

3. British Columbia Forest Service, *Marine Log Salvage Procedures and Guidelines* (Victoria: Province of British Columbia, 2010).

4. VanderZwaag, "We Bought Our Own Private Island."

5. Orth, *Island*, 78.

6. Conover, *Once Upon an Island*, 68.

7. Wood, *At Home in Nature*, 215.

8. Bill Proctor and Yvonne Maximchuk, *Tide Rips and Back Eddies: Bill Proctor's Tales of Blackfish Sound* (Madeira Park, BC: Harbour Publishing, 2015), 209.

9. Nelson, *The Island Within*, 268.

10. Proctor and Maximchuk, *Tide Rips*, 211.

11. Orth, *Island*, 29.

12. Nicol, *When Nature Calls*, 104.

13. Cox, *Our Life Off the Grid*, "Burping the Fridge."

14. McIntyre, *Place of Quiet Waters*, 182.

15. Ibid., 178.

16. Caroline Woodward, *Light Years: Memoir of a Modern Lighthouse Keeper* (Madeira Park, BC: Harbour Publishing, 2015), 129.

17. Sandy Oliver, "Yes, It Is 'So Much Work,'" *The Working Waterfront* (2015), accessed November 4, 2015, http://www.islandinstitute.org/working-waterfront/yes-it-so-much-work.

18. Philip Vannini and Jaigis Hodson, "Island Time: The Media Logic and Ritual of Ferry Commuting on Gabriola Island, BC," *Canadian Journal of Communication* 32 (2007): 273.

19. Boshier, "Wet and Boisterous."

20. Materfamilias blog, "Commuting, Island Style," *Materfamilias Writes*, November 16, 2011, accessed January 18, 2018. http://materfamiliasknits. blogspot.com/2011/11/commuting-island-style.html?m=0.

21. Cox, *Our Life Off the Grid*.

22. Conover, *Once Upon an Island*, 26.

23. Paul Freathy and Eric Calderwood, "The Impact of Internet Adoption upon the Shopping Behaviour of Island Residents," *Journal of Retailing and Consumer Services* 20, no. 1 (2013): 115.

24. Cox, *Our Life Off the Grid*.

25. Orth, *Island*, 31.

26. VanderZwaag, "We Bought Our Own Private Island."

27. Vannini, *Ferry Tales*, 87.

28. Arthur, *Island Sojourn*, 24.

29. Woodward, *Light Years*, 92.

30. Philip Vannini and Jonathan Taggart, *Off the Grid: Re-assembling Domestic Life* (London: Routledge, 2014), 25.

31. McIntyre, *Place of Quiet Waters*, 141.

32. Piddington, *The Inlet*, 163.

33. Townsend, *The Myth of Island Living*.

34. Modzelewski, *Inside Passage*, 121.

35. Michael Poole, *Ragged Islands* (Vancouver: Douglas & McIntyre, 1991), 239.

36. Conover, *Once Upon an Island*, 153.

37. Maximchuk, *Drawn to Sea*, 231.

38. Thaxter, *Among the Isles of Shoals*, 94.

39. Conover, *Once Upon an Island*, 152.

40. Proctor and Maximchuk, *Tide Rips*, 22–23.

41. McIntyre, *Place of Quiet Waters*, 167.

42. Modzelewski, *Inside Passage*, 10.

43. Wood, *At Home in Nature*, 77.

44. Rick Gustavson website, accessed February 2017, http://www.rickgustavson. com/q-a-with-fircom-owners-gambier-island/.

45. Piddington, *The Inlet*, 145.

46. Vannini, *Ferry Tales*, 109.

47. Ibid., 108.

48. Wood, *At Home in Nature*, 197.

49. Cox, *Our Life Off the Grid*.

Chapter 6—**Connections**

1. Fowles, *Islands*, 105.

2. Woodward, *Light Years*, 197.

3. Arthur, *Island Sojourn*, 45.

4. Ibid., 167–68.

5. Ibid., 220.

6. Wood, *At Home in Nature*, 92.

7. Ibid., 89–90.

8. Ibid., 101.

9. Conkling, "On Islanders and Islandness," 199.
10. Bosch, "Discovery Islands," 37.
11. Ibid., 52–53.
12. Woodward, *Light Years*, 51.
13. Townsend, *The Myth of Island Living*.
14. Freathy and Calderwood, "The Impact of Internet Adoption."
15. Woodward, *Light Years*, 91.
16. Conover, *Once Upon an Island*, 27.
17. Wood, *At Home in Nature*, 207–8.
18. Woodward, *Light Years*, 197.

Chapter 7—**Not Quite Paradise**
1. Piddington, *The Inlet*, 137.
2. Modzelewski, *Inside Passage*, 16.
3. Woodward, *Light Years*, 43.
4. Maximchuk, *Drawn to Sea*, 42.
5. Woodward, *Light Years*, 108.
6. Wood, *At Home in Nature*, 172–3.
7. Ibid., 182–3.
8. Modzelewski, *Inside Passage*, 8–9.
9. Thaxter, *Among the Isles of Shoals*.
10. Arthur, *Island Sojourn*, 115.
11. Ibid., 119.
12. Vannini, *Ferry Tales*, 89.
13. Arthur, *Island Sojourn*, 167–8.
14. Orth, *Island*, 101.
15. Ibid.
16. Thaxter, *Among the Isles of Shoals*.
17. Orth, *Island*, 103–4.
18. Ibid., 105.
19. Barry Smith, *The Island in Imagination and Experience* (Salford, UK: Saraband, 2017).
20. Orth, *Island*, 73.
21. Ibid., 74.
22. Woodward, *Light Years*, 179.
23. Ben Fogle, *The Teatime Islands* (London: Penguin Books, 2003), xv.
24. Arthur, *Island Sojourn*, 91.
25. Ibid., 179.
26. McIntyre, *Place of Quiet Waters*, 175.
27. Maximchuk, *Drawn to Sea*, 271.
28. Orth, *Island*, 74.
29. McIntyre, *Place of Quiet Waters*, 280.
30. Brinklow, "How Small an Island Do You Need?" 21.

Chapter 8—**The Perfect Islander**
1. Nelson, *The Island Within*, xii.
2. Cox, *Our Life Off the Grid*.

3. Fowles, *Islands*, 11.

4. Nicolson, *Sea Room*.

5. Nelson, *The Island Within*, 46.

6. Orth, *Island*, 15.

7. Woodward, *Light Years*, 195.

8. Conover, *Once Upon an Island*, 142.

9. Bosch, "Discovery Islands," 42.

10. Philip Vannini and Jonathan Taggart, *Off the Grid: Re-assembling Domestic Life* (New York: Routledge, 2015), 209.

11. Ibid.

12. Private Islands Inc., 5.

13. Cox, *Our Life Off the Grid*.

14. Ibid.

15. Conover, *Once Upon an Island*, 77.

BIBLIOGRAPHY

Aldersey-Williams, Hugh. *The Tide*. New York: W.W. Norton & Company, 2016.

Arthur, Elizabeth. *Island Sojourn*. New York: Harper & Row, 1980.

Baldacchino, Godfrey. "Islands, Island Studies, Island Studies Journal." *Island Studies Journal* 1, no. 1 (2006): 3–18.

———. "The Lure of Islands: A Spatial Analysis of Power Relations." *Journal of Marine and Island Cultures* 1, no. 2 (2012): 55–62.

———. "Studying Islands: On Whose Terms? Some Epistemological and Methodological Challenges to the Pursuit of Island Studies." *Island Studies Journal* 3, no. 1 (2008): 37–56.

Beer, Gillian. "Island Bounds." In *Islands in History and Representation*, edited by Rod Edmond and Vanessa Smith, 32–42. London: Routledge, 2003.

Bosch, Naomi A. "Discovery Islands, Earth Islands: The Theory and Practice of Island Imagery in Environmental Thought." Pomona College senior thesis, 127. Claremont, CA: Pomona College, 2015.

Boshier, Roger. "Wet and Boisterous: The Lumpy Romance of Commuting by Boat." In *The Cultures of Alternative Mobilities: Routes Less Travelled*, edited by Philip Vannini, 300. Farnham, UK: Ashgate Publishing, 2009.

Brinklow, Laurie. "How Small an Island Do You Need?" *Island* 124 (Autumn 2011): 18–22.

———. "Stepping-Stones to the Edge: Artistic Expressions of Islandness in an Ocean of Islands." *Island Studies Journal* 8, no. 1 (2013): 39–54.

British Columbia Forest Service. *Marine Log Salvage Procedures and Guidelines*. Victoria: Province of British Columbia, 2010.

Brooks, Andree. "The Magic of an Island Home." *New York Times*, June 20, 1982.

Burn, June. *Living High*. 6th ed. Woodinville, WA: San Juan Publishing, 2011 (1st ed. 1941).

Chamberlin, J. Edward. *Island: How Islands Transform the World*. Kathonah, NY: Bluebridge, 2013.

Conkling, Philip. "On Islanders and Islandness." *Geographical Review* XCVII (2007): 191–201.

Conover, David. *Once Upon an Island*. Don Mills, ON: PaperJacks, 1972.

Cox, J. David. *Our Life Off the Grid: An Urban Couple Goes Feral.* Surge Narrows, BC: OTG Publishing, 2015. Kindle edition.

Depledge, M.H., and W.J. Bird. "The Blue Gym: Health and Wellbeing from Our Coasts." *Marine Pollution* 58, no. 7 (July 2009): 947–8.

Depraetere, Christian, and Arthur L. Dahl. "Island Locations and Concentrations." In *A World of Islands*, edited by Godfrey Baldacchino, 57–103. Charlottetown: Island Studies Press, 2007.

Durrell, Lawrence. *Reflections on a Marine Venus: A Companion to the Landscape of Rhodes.* London: Faber, 1960.

Environment and Climate Change Canada. *British Columbia Regional Marine Weather Guide.* Accessed February 18, 2016. https://www.canada.ca/en/environment-climate-change/services/general-marine-weather-information/regional-guides/british-columbia.html.

———. *National Marine Weather Guide.* Accessed February 18, 2016. https://www.canada.ca/en/environment-climate-change/services/general-marine-weather-information/regional-guides/national.html.

Environment and Natural Resources Canada. *Residential Water Use.* Accessed February 2017. https://www.canada.ca/en/environment-climate-change/services/environmental-indicators/residential-water-use.html.

Fernald, Barbara. "Island Home Helps Me Grieve Great Loss." *The Working Waterfront* (October 26, 2015). Accessed November 19, 2015. http://www.islandinstitute.org/working-waterfront/island-home-helps-me-grieve-great-loss.

Fischer, Steven Roger. *Islands: From Atlantis to Zanzibar.* London: Reaktion Books, 2012.

Fogle, Ben. *The Teatime Islands.* London: Penguin Books, 2003.

Fowles, John. *Islands.* London: Jonathan Cape, 1978.

Freathy, Paul, and Eric Calderwood. "The Impact of Internet Adoption upon the Shopping Behaviour of Island Residents." *Journal of Retailing and Consumer Services* 20, no. 1 (January 2013): 111–19.

Gillis, John R. "Not Continents in Miniature: Islands as Ecotones." *Island Studies Journal* 9, no. 1 (2014): 155–66.

Gotelli, Nicholas J. *A Primer of Ecology.* Sunderland, MA: Sinauer Associates, 2001.

Groening, Tom. "The Sea Continues to Lure Linda Greenlaw." *The Working Waterfront*, November 23, 2015. Accessed November 30, 2015. http://www.islandinstitute.org/working-waterfront/sea-continues-lure-linda-greenlaw.

Hay, Pete. "A Phenomenology of Islands." *Island Studies Journal* 1, no. 1 (2006): 19–42.

———. "What the Sea Portends: A Reconsideration of Contested Island Tropes." *Island Studies Journal* 8, no. 2 (2013): 209–32.

Howarth, Jean. *Island Time.* Toronto: Summerhill Press, 1988.

———. *Secrets the Island Is Keeping.* Toronto: Summerhill Press, 1988.

Islands Trust and the San Juan Preservation Trust. *A Place in the Islands*, 2nd ed. Victoria: Islands Trust and the San Juan Preservation Trust, 2007.

Jarrad, F.W., and William Sharp. *The British Columbia Pilot: Including the Coast of British Columbia, from Juan de Fuca Strait to Portland Canal, together with Vancouver and Queen Charlotte Islands.* London: The Hydrographic Office, Admiralty, 1888.

Kinane, Ian. *Theorising Literary Islands: The Island Trope in Contemporary Robinsonade Narratives.* London and New York: Rowman & Littlefield International, 2016.

Law Reform Commission of British Columbia. *Report on Limitations, Part II General.* Vancouver: Law Reform Commission of British Columbia, 1974. Accessed April 26, 2018. http://www.bcli.org/sites/default/files/report15.pdf.

Lawrence, D.H. "The Man Who Loved Islands." In D.H. Lawrence, *The Woman Who Rode Away and Other Stories.* Edited by Dieter Mehl and Christa Jahnson. Cambridge: Cambridge University Press, 2002, 39–71.

Lawrence, Grant. *Adventures in Solitude: What Not to Wear to a Nude Potluck and Other Stories from Desolation Sound.* Pender Harbour, BC: Harbour Publishing, 2010.

Lowenthal, David. "Islands, Lovers, and Others." *The Geographical Review* 97, no. 2 (2007).

Materfamilias. "Commuting, Island Style." *Materfamilias Writes.* Materfamilias blog entry, November 16, 2011. Accessed January 18, 2018. http://materfamiliasknits.blogspot.com/2011/11/commuting-island-style.html?m=0.

Maximchuk, Yvonne. *Drawn to Sea: Paintbrush to Chainsaw—Carving Out a Life on BC's Rugged Raincoast.* Halfmoon Bay, BC: Caitlin Press, 2013.

McIntyre, Margaret. *Place of Quiet Waters.* Don Mills, ON: Longmans Canada, 1965.

McReynolds, Samuel A. "Community Sustainability in the Year-round Islands of Maine." *Island Studies Journal* 9, no. 1 (2014): 79–102.

Melville, Herman. *Moby-Dick; or, The Whale.* New York: Harper & Brothers, 1851. http://mel.hofstra.edu/moby-dick-the-whale-proofs.html.

Modzelewski, Michael. *Inside Passage.* New York: HarperCollins, 1991.

Morales, Robert, and Eric McLay. "The Ongoing Search for Respect at Grace Islet." *Times Colonist*, August 1, 2014.

Nelson, Richard. *The Island Within.* New York: Vintage Books, 1991.

Nichols, Wallace J. *Blue Mind: The Surprising Science That Shows How Being Near, In, On, or Under Water Can Make You Happier, Healthier, More Connected, and Better at What You Do.* New York: Little, Brown and Company, 2014.

Nicol, Eric. *When Nature Calls: Life at a Gulf Islands Cottage.* Madeira Park, BC: Harbour Publishing, 1999.

Nicolson, Adam. *Sea Room: An Island Life in the Hebrides.* London: HarperCollins, 2002. Kindle edition.

Oliver, Sandy. "Yes, It Is 'So Much Work.'" *The Working Waterfront*, October 26, 2015. Accessed November 4, 2015. http://www.islandinstitute.org/working-waterfront/yes-it-so-much-work.

Olwig, K.R. "Are Islanders Insular? A Personal View." *Geographical Review* 97, no. 2 (2007): 175–90.

Orth, Joy. *Island: Our Alaskan Dream and Reality.* Edmonds, WA: Alaska Northwest Publishing Company, 1987.

Oxford Living Dictionary. Oxford University Press, 2016. https://en.oxford dictionaries.com.

Peterson, Les. "British Columbia's Depopulated Coast." In *Raincoast Chronicles First Five,* edited by Howard White, 156–63. Madeira Park, BC: Harbour Publishing. 1973.

Piddington, Helen. *The Inlet: Memoir of a Modern Pioneer.* Madeira Park, BC: Harbour Publishing, 2001.

Platt, David. "Islandness." In *Holding Ground: The Best of Island Journal 1984–2004,* edited by Philip Conkling and David Platt, 1. Rockland, ME: Island Institute, 2004.

Poole, Michael. *Ragged Islands.* Vancouver: Douglas & McIntyre, 1991.

Private Islands Inc. "Private Islands Buyer's Guide." Private Islands Inc., 2014.

Proctor, Bill, and Yvonne Maximchuk. *Tide Rips and Back Eddies: Bill Proctor's Tales of Blackfish Sound.* Madeira Park, BC: Harbour Publishing, 2015.

Putz, George. "On Islanders." In *Holding Ground: The Best of Island Journal 1984–2004,* edited by Philip Conkling and David Platt, 28–31. Rockland, ME: Island Institute, 2004.

Raban, Jonathan. *Passage to Juneau: A Sea and Its Meanings.* New York: Vintage Books, 1999.

Robey, Charity. "Dr. Frank Adipietro: Commuting Floats His Boat." *Northforker Health and Fitness* (September, 2014).

Royle, Stephen A. *Islands: Nature and Culture.* London: Reaktion Books, 2014.

Rybczynski, Witold. *The Most Beautiful House in the World.* New York: Penguin, 1989.

Smith, Barry. *The Island in Imagination and Experience.* Salford, UK: Saraband, 2017. Kindle edition.

Stewardship Centre for British Columbia Green Shores Technical Working Group. *Coastal Shore Jurisdiction in British Columbia.* Green Shores Issue Sheet (October 2009). North Vancouver: Stewardship Centre for British Columbia, 2009. Accessed April 11, 2016. http://www.salishsea.ca/resources/Riparianrights/Greenshores%20JurisdictionIssueSheet_finalVer4.pdf.

Stewart, Hilary. *On Island Time.* Vancouver: Douglas & McIntyre, 1998.

Thaxter, Celia. *Among the Isles of Shoals.* Boston: James R. Osgood and Company, 1873. Kindle edition.

Townsend, Ian. *The Myth of Island Living.* Podcast audio. Background Briefing, December 12, 2010. Accessed March 3, 2016. http://www.abc.net.au/radionational/programs/backgroundbriefing/the-myth-of-island-living/2983150 -transcript.

Union of British Columbia Indian Chiefs. "Certainty: Canada's Struggle to Extinguish Aboriginal Title." Vancouver: UBCIC, 1998. Accessed April 26, 2016. https://www.ubcic.bc.ca/certainty_canada_s_struggle_to_extinguish_aboriginal_title.

United Nations. "UN Convention on the Law of the Sea." New York: United Nations, 1982.

VanderZwaag, David. "We Bought Our Own Private Island." *Mother Earth News* (March/April 1978). Accessed April 6, 2016. https://www.motherearthnews.com/nature-and-environment/private-island-zmaz78mazjma.

Vannini, Philip. *Ferry Tales: Mobility, Place, and Time on Canada's West Coast.* New York: Routledge, 2011.

Vannini, Philip, and Jaigis Hodson. "Island Time: The Media Logic and Ritual of Ferry Commuting on Gabriola Island, BC." *Canadian Journal of Communication* 32 (2007): 261–75.

Vannini, Philip, and Jonathan Taggart. *Off the Grid: Re-assembling Domestic Life.* New York: Routledge, 2015.

Viviani, Christina, Maureen Welton, and Kenneth Torrance. *Tafoni: Natural Design of Weathered Stone.* Langley, BC: 18Karat, 2008.

Watt, Alison. *The Last Island: A Naturalist's Sojourn on Triangle Island.* Madeira Park, BC: Harbour Publishing, 2002.

Wilcox, Ella Wheeler. *The Beautiful Land of Nod.* Chicago: Morrill, Higgins & Company, 1892.

Wood, Rob. *At Home in Nature: A Life of Unknown Mountains and Deep Wilderness.* Victoria: Rocky Mountain Books, 2017.

———. "Wind against the Tide: Challenges and Rewards of Living Close to Nature." Unpublished manuscript, 2016.

Woodward, Caroline. *Light Years: Memoir of a Modern Lighthouse Keeper.* Madeira Park, BC: Harbour Publishing, 2015.

World Sea Temperatures.Org. Global Sea Temperatures website. Accessed February 24, 2017. https://www.seatemperature.org.

INDEX

ABOUT THE AUTHOR

JOY DAVIS combines deep coastal roots and a love for island living with an established career in cultural heritage. She spent much of her youth living with her family on Bath Island (near Gabriola Island, off the south coast of British Columbia) and exploring the coastal waters aboard her grandfather's sailboat. Davis holds an MA in museum studies and a PhD in educational studies, and she directed the University of Victoria's museum and heritage programs for twenty-five years. Since retiring from UVic, she has worked as a consultant and associate editor for the journal *Museum Management and Curatorship*, is a member of the Advisory Group for the Coalition of Museums for Climate Justice, and serves as a Trustee on the Greater Victoria Library Board. In 2015, she won the Canadian Museums Association Distinguished Service Award. She lives in Victoria, BC, balancing family, sailing, writing, and community engagement.